Editor
Kim Fields

Editorial Project Manager
Mara Ellen Guckian

Cover Artist
Brenda DiAntonis

Illustrators
Danlyn Iantorno
Renée Christine Yates

Managing Editor
Ina Massler Levin, M.A.

Creative Director
Karen J. Goldfluss, M.S. Ed.

Art Production Manager
Kevin Barnes

Art Coordinator
Renée Christine Yates

Imaging
Rosa C. See

Publisher
Mary D. Smith, M.S. Ed.

Authors

Jimmie Aydelott and Dianna Buck

Teacher Created Resources, Inc.
6421 Industry Way
Westminster, CA 92683
www.teachercreated.com

ISBN-13-978-1-4206-8238-0

© *2007 Teacher Created Resources, Inc.*
Made in U.S.A.

Teacher Created Resources

Table of Contents

Summary of Standards for Language Arts

Writing

- Uses the general skills and strategies of the writing process
- Uses stylistic and rhetorical techniques in written compositions
- Uses grammatical and mechanical conventions in written compositions
- Gathers and uses information for research purposes

Reading

- Uses the general skills and strategies of the reading process
- Uses reading skills and strategies to understand and interpret a variety of literary works
- Uses reading skills and strategies to understand and interpret a variety of informational texts

Listening and Speaking

- Uses listening and speaking skills and strategies for a variety of purposes
- Uses viewing skills and strategies to understand and interpret visual media
- Understands the characteristics and components of the media

*Used with permission by McRel (Mid-continent Research for Education and Learning) www.mcrel.org

Introduction

Celebrate the day with a page from the past! Each daily page in this publication contains a high-interest, short account of a historical event, fun celebration, festival, or birthday of some important person (some of whom you may never have heard). A response designed around Bloom's Taxonomy actively engages the reader's attention. In addition, each daily page includes:

- A story-related **independent Activity**
- A **Word Play** exercise related to the featured story
- **Other Events** occurring on that same day in history
- A **Fascinating Factoid** not covered in the story

The dates and facts of the events covered are as authentic as possible. In cases where discrepancies were noted during research, the most frequently used date and data for the event were used in this publication.

There are endless possibilities for ways to use the daily pages. Some ideas are:

- Incorporate the pages into your opening exercise. (Have the page duplicated and ready for students when they arrive. You may choose to read and discuss the story, and then complete the other activities throughout the day as time permits.)

- Use the pages as a source of information if you start your day with a morning message for your students. (Your message might be, "Good morning, students! Did you know that today is the day that the largest banana split was made? We're going to read about it later in the day.")

- Assign the daily page as an alternative to regular homework.

- Conduct a reading mini-lesson in the history/social studies content area with the daily pages.

- Offer the daily pages for extra credit work.

- Provide enrichment with the daily pages.

You will surely find even more ways to use these pages to enhance learning opportunities for your students. Whether you use every page or just pick and choose, this publication can help you make learning in your classroom an awesome experience!

July

July 1
First U.S. Zoo Opened
• • • • • • • • • • • • • • • •

Other Events This Day
- Teddy Roosevelt and the Rough Riders charge up San Juan Hill (1898)
- First Tour de France bicycle race began (1903)

Like many other Philadelphia landmarks, the Philadelphia Zoo is an American first. It is still in the same location today as it was when it opened on this day in 1874. Although the charter was approved in 1859, it was another 15 years before it was ready to open due to the Civil War. On opening day, over 3,000 people came by foot, streetcars, carriages, and even steamboats! The sky was clear, a brass band played, and flags waved. Admission was 25 cents for adults and 10 cents for children. (That rate stayed the same for more than 50 years!)

The zoo is home to many exotic animals. The first year of operation, the zoo had 813 animals and over 228,000 visitors. Today, there are more than 1,600 rare and endangered animals, and more than a million visitors pass through the gates each year. The zoo has been the home of many unusual animals such as the naked mole rat, the langur, capybaras, a leaf-eating monkey, and two white lions (of which there are probably no more than a dozen in the wild). Most of the exhibits resemble the animals' natural habitats. If you want to get up close, you can have colorful lorikeets eat from your hand or "take a ride through the African plains" on a camel's back. The Philadelphia Zoo is a thrilling place to visit!

Response

It is one thing to see animals' pictures in a book. It is quite different to see them in person. Explain how seeing an animal in person is better than in a picture.

Fascinating Factoid: *Solitude,* the neoclassical style home of John Penn (grandson of the founder of Pennsylvania, William Penn), is an attraction at the zoo.

Word Play

Many sounds can be heard at a zoo. Match each animal to its method of communication.

_____ 1. hen   a. laugh
_____ 2. dog   b. cluck
_____ 3. donkey   c. roar
_____ 4. peacock   d. bray
_____ 5. elephant   e. whinny
_____ 6. ferret   f. trumpet
_____ 7. dove   g. scream
_____ 8. blue jay   h. honk
_____ 9. ape   i. coo
_____ 10. crow   j. caw
_____ 11. pig   k. gibber
_____ 12. grasshopper   l. chirp
_____ 13. bear   m. chatter
_____ 14. goose   n. bleat
_____ 15. goat   o. dook
_____ 16. horse   p. bark
_____ 17. hyena   q. growl
_____ 18. lion   r. oink

Activities

- Select your favorite animal and make a shoebox diorama of it in its natural habitat. Make a plaque to be placed near the diorama, giving information about the animal and its habitat.

- Brainstorm and explain a special exhibit to attract visitors to your local zoo (e.g., a camel ride, birds eating out of your hand).

July 2
Sam's the Man

• •

Other Events This Day

• First U.S. elevated railroad began service in New York City (1867)

• Hitler ordered invasion of England (1940)

Sam Walton built a business empire that made him the world's number one retailer and, at the time of his death, he was second richest man in the world. Mr. Walton was an optimist. In his autobiography, he wrote, "If you believe in your dreams, there's no limit to what you can do."

Mr. Walton was a child of the Depression. He worked hard to survive. As a child, he milked cows, and by age eight, he sold magazine subscriptions. At age 12, he had a paper route, which he continued through college to support himself. Sam was smart and a natural-born leader. When he was faced with major setbacks, he persevered.

Mr. Walton opened his first Wal-Mart® on this day in 1962 in Rogers, Arkansas, after having begun his retail career at a Ben Franklin® store. Mr. Walton was innovative; he sold things cheaper than his competitors, which increased the volume of what he sold. He praised his employees, offered paid vacations and holidays, and gave employees stock options and store discounts. Mr. Walton believed that happy employees meant happy customers and that "individuals don't win, teams do."

Sam Walton once said, "I would like to be remembered as a good friend to most everyone whose life I've touched; as someone who has maybe meant something to them and helped them in some way." Mr. Walton was a friend to society. He gave to charities, including his church. Each of his stores honors a graduating high school senior with a college scholarship.

Response

In your opinion, what three characteristics of Sam Walton contributed to his success?

Fascinating Factoid: In 1984, Sam Walton did the hula on Wall Street. He promised to do so if the company had a pre-tax profit of eight percent the preceding year.

Word Play

Mrs. Jones took her four children food shopping at the local Wal-Mart Supercenter. They all wanted something different for dinner, so she told them they could each pick out their own food for dinner that night. Using the clues below, figure out which child (James, Jenny, Joanie, or Jerry) is eating what food (fried chicken, hot dog, pizza, cheeseburger) for dinner.

• *James* needed chili and mustard to eat with his choice.
• *Jenny* reminded her mom that she is allergic to cheese.
• *Joanie* reminded her mom that she needed buns for her dinner.
• *Jerry* wanted his selection to be the foot-long kind.

The Jones Children	Fried Chicken	Sandwich	Hot Dog	Cheese-burger
James				
Jenny				
Joanie				
Jerry				

I would like to be remembered as...

Activities

• Complete the following statement: "I would like to be remembered as . . . ."

• Imagine that you have inherited a business from Uncle Mo. What is its name? What do you sell? Create a newspaper advertisement for your business.

July 3
Battle of Gettysburg Ended

• • • • • • • • • • • • • • • • • • •

Other Events This Day

• First U.S. savings bank opened its doors (1819)

• Idaho became 43rd U.S. state (1890)

The Tenth Amendment of the U.S. Constitution gave states the power to resolve issues not determined by the federal government. The southern states felt this covered issues such as slavery. The northern states opposed slavery; the southern states—who depended on it—wanted to continue slavery. The southern states seceded from the union and became the Confederate States of America. Jefferson Davis was the president and commander-in-chief of the Confederate Army. A horrendous war ensued between the northern and southern states. With General Robert E. Lee in command of the Confederate armies, the South won many battles over the North.

At 1:00 P.M. on July 1, 1863, the largest cannonade that ever occurred on North American soil began on the battlefield at Gettysburg, Pennsylvania. The Confederate cannons overshot their enemy. As the Confederates formed a long line across an open field and began to advance, the smoke cleared and the Union army was able to attack them with their artillery fire. Two out of every three soldiers were killed. The battle ended with the Confederates retreating to Virginia. On July 3, 1863, this battle, considered to be the most famous and important battle of the Civil War, ended with victory for the Union army.

This battlefield site of 5,733 acres remains today as a national park open to Civil War buffs and tourists.

Response

Do you think the outcome of the war might have been different had the South won the Battle of Gettysburg? Explain.

Fascinating Factoid: There was one Gettysburg citizen killed in the famous battle. A bullet pierced the door of Mrs. McClellan's home and struck her, killing her instantly.

Word Play

Civil War soldiers had a wide variety of nicknames for their different army items and experiences. Match each nickname to its meaning.

_____ 1. housewife

_____ 2. bones

_____ 3. haversack

_____ 4. johnny

_____ 5. sawbones

_____ 6. accoutrements

_____ 7. yank

_____ 8. hardtack

_____ 9. vittles

_____ 10. muster

_____ 11. picket

a. dice

b. cloth bag for carrying rations and utensils

c. Union soldier's term for Confederate soldier

d. guard or guard duty

e. surgeon

f. food or rations

g. Confederate soldier's term for Union soldier

h. flour, salt, and water biscuit

i. to assemble and be counted for military service

j. sewing kit

k. soldier's fighting equipment, made of leather

Activities

• Locate pictures of the flags of the Union and Confederacy. Research the symbolism of the flags. Create your own flag for the Union or Confederacy.

• Read *Pink and Say* by Patricia Polacco, a story of friendship between two boys during the Civil War.

July 4
A Day to Celebrate!

July 4 is the day that the United States celebrates its birthday. It is the day that the Thirteen Colonies declared they would no longer be ruled by England's King George III. The colonists had been paying taxes to England, but had no say in what went on in the government. The Colonies tried to work out their differences but they were unsuccessful.

In June 1776, the Continental Congress met and Thomas Jefferson was chosen to write the first draft of a declaration of independence from England. He presented it to fellow Congress members on June 28. Changes were made and copies of the declaration were distributed. Although people proclaimed liberty with the writing of this declaration, the signing was not complete until August of that year.

The first July Fourth celebration took place the next year in 1777. Bells rang, ships fired guns, and candles and firecrackers were lit. In 1783, Independence Day became an official national holiday.

One can find some sort of celebration in just about every city and town in America. In Philadelphia, there is a re-enactment of historical scenes and the reading of the Declaration of Independence where it was first read at Independence Hall. Native Americans hold a three-day powwow in Flagstaff, Arizona. Hundreds of candles are lit and floated in the water in Lititz, Pennsylvania. In Boston the USS *John F. Kennedy* comes into Boston Harbor in full sail, and the Boston Pops Orchestra plays a musical concert of patriotic songs as more than 150,000 people watch an incredible display of fireworks over the water.

Response

What part do celebrations play in honoring our past?

Fascinating Factoid: The 56 signers of the Declaration of Independence included two future presidents, three vice presidents, and 10 members of the U.S. Congress.

Word Play

Unscramble the words to discover some respected U.S. symbols.

1. __ __   __ __ __ __ __ __ __ S. U. APCIOTL
2. __ __ __ __ __   __ __ __ __ __ HWTIE OSEUH
3. __ __ __ __ __ __ __ __   __ __ __ __ AENRCAIM GALF
4. __ __ __ __   __ __ __ __ __ ADLB GALEE
5. __ __ __ __ __ __   __ __ __ __ LEYIRBT LELB
6. __ __ __ __ __   __ __ __ CUNLE MAS
7. __ __ __ __ __ __ __   __ __ __ __ __ __ __ CINLOLN MIRALEOM
8. __ __ __ __ __ __ __ __   __ __ __ __ __ __ __ __ TARNIGLON NAILAONT __ __ __ __ __ __ __ MECETREY
9. __ __ __ __ __   __ __ __ __ RETGA ELAS
10. __ __ __ __ __ __   __ __   __ __ __ __ __ __ TSAUET FO BLIRETY

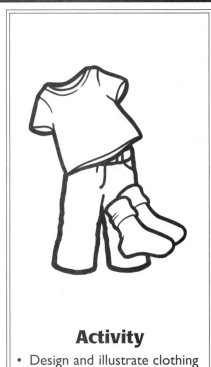

Activity

- Design and illustrate clothing especially for a Fourth of July celebration.

July 5
Elvis Made His First Recording

● ● ● ● ● ● ● ● ● ● ● ● ● ● ● ● ● ●

Other Events This Day

• First recorded U.S. tornado (1643)
• Statue of Liberty reopened after its refurbishing (1986)

Elvis Aaron Presley was known as the "King of Rock 'n' Roll." As of 2006, almost three decades after his death, he still holds the all-time record for best-selling artist in popular music history. Sales of Elvis's records have passed one billion worldwide.

Elvis was born in Tupelo, Mississippi, in 1935. Although his family was poor, he was surrounded by music, especially gospel, at the Pentecostal church where he sang in the choir. By listening to blues and spirituals, Elvis taught himself to play the chords on an acoustic guitar.

After graduating from high school, Elvis visited the Memphis Recording Service—home of Sun Records. There Elvis's amazing career began with the making of his first recording—*That's All Right, Mama* and *Blue Moon of Kentucky.* It was 1954. When the up-tempo record hit the market, it sold 6,000 copies in one week. Elvis recorded several songs with Sun Records, and then switched to RCA records. He began a string of TV performances, which ignited the "Elvis Craze." His gyrating hips and energetic singing kept him number one on the pop charts and the box office for seven years.

At the height of his career, Elvis was drafted into the Army and spent two years in Germany where he met his future wife, Priscilla. After his tour of duty, he focused on making movies and soundtrack albums. In the 1960s, Elvis began touring heavily, performing to capacity crowds around the country. His career was cut short when he died at the early age of 42, but he remains alive in the minds and hearts of all those who loved his music.

Response

Rumors exist that Elvis is alive. What do you think?

Fascinating Factoid: Elvis often rented the Zippin Pippin roller coaster at Libertyland in Memphis, Tennessee, for himself so he could ride it nonstop.

Word Play

Elvis Presley had over 100 Top 40 recordings during his lifetime. Choose a word from the word box to complete each Top 40 recording below.

1. "Hound _____"
2. "_____ Christmas"
3. "Love Me _____"
4. "Return to _____"
5. "_____ Hotel"
6. "_____ Rock"
7. "All _____ Up"
8. "It's Now or _____"
9. "Are You _____ Tonight?"
10. "Don't Be _____"
11. "Good Luck _____"
12. "Viva _____"
13. "_____ Minds"

Never	Blue	Dog
Sender	Tender	Jailhouse
Las Vegas	Shook	Heartbreak
Lonesome	Cruel	Charm
Suspicious		

Activities

• Make your own list of outlandish kings. Be creative (e.g., king of burping, king of bubble gum bubbles).

• Brainstorm, research, and list people or animals who are often referred to as kings (e.g., king of the jungle, king of the hill, king of the wild frontier).

July 6

Mr. President

• • • • • • • • • • • • • • • • • •

President George W. Bush was born on this day in 1946. He is the 43rd U.S. president. He was 54 years old when he was first elected. That puts him about in the middle of the age range of all presidents. Do you know the oldest and youngest men to be elected to the U.S. presidency? Do you know that the youngest man elected wasn't really the youngest man to hold office? Our oldest president was Ronald Reagan, who was 69 years of age when he was elected, and the youngest was John F. Kennedy who was 43. However, it was Theodore Roosevelt who was the youngest to ever become president. At age 42, he took office upon the death of President McKinley, and he became the youngest man to ever hold the presidential office.

George W. Bush is 5' 11" (1.8 m) tall. How does he measure up to the other presidents? Well, he is about 7 inches (17.8 cm) taller than the shortest president and about 5 inches (12.7 cm) shorter than the tallest. James Madison was the shortest at 5' 4" (1.6 m), and Abraham Lincoln was the tallest, measuring in at 6' 4" (1.9 m).

President Bush graduated from Yale University with a bachelor's degree in history and then from Harvard Business School with a Master's in Business Administration (MBA). There were nine presidents who never attended college. There is only one who earned a doctoral degree—Woodrow Wilson. Harvard University has the distinction of having produced the most presidents, with a total of six. Yale is second with five presidential alumni.

President Bush and wife, Laura Welch Bush, have two children—twin daughters. Did all the presidents have children? Six presidents had no children. Did you know that James Buchanan is the only U.S. president who never married?

Response

Why do you think people are so interested in presidential trivia?

Fascinating Factoid: Although George W. Bush is the 43rd president, he is only the 42nd man to have served. President Cleveland was elected to two nonconsecutive terms.

Word Play

George and Laura Bush are a well-known couple. Choose a name from the word box to complete each set of famous couples.

1. George & _____

2. Adam & _____

3. Romeo & _____

4. Fred & _____

5. Mickey & _____

6. Donald & _____

7. Barney & _____

8. Anthony & _____

9. Superman & _____

10. John Smith & _____

11. Robin Hood & _____

| Maid Marion |
| Martha |
| Pocahontas |
| Eve |
| Juliet |
| Lois Lane |
| Wilma |
| Minnie |
| Cleopatra |
| Daisy |
| Betty |

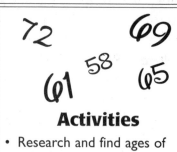

Activities

• Research and find ages of several men when they became president. Figure the average age of those men. What was the median age? Which presidents were close to the average age when they were elected?

• Create a trivia list of questions and answers about pets in the White House.

July 7
Chocolate Introduced in Europe

● ● ● ● ● ● ● ● ● ● ● ● ● ● ● ● ● ●

Other Events This Day

- First U.S. Military Draft (1863)
- First time women were hired as FBI agents (1972)

Some sources say that chocolate was first introduced in Europe on this day in 1550. The National Confectioners Association has even set aside July 7 as Chocolate Day!

What comes to mind when you think of chocolate? Is it the smooth, sweet taste of a chocolate candy bar? Believe it or not, for the first 90 percent of its existence, chocolate was not something to eat, but it was a drink! It wasn't sweet either. The drink was frothy and bitter.

The seed of the cacao (*kah-kow*) tree was discovered many centuries ago in South American rain forests. The pods of the cacao tree contain seeds that can be processed into chocolate. The Mayans and Aztecs, ancient peoples of Mexico and Central America, were the first to make chocolate. They ground the seeds and added water or wine and seasonings, such as pimento, cinnamon, and chili peppers, to make a spicy drink.

It is believed that Columbus was the first European to see and taste chocolate, but the Spanish conquistadors (Cortez, in particular) were credited with being the ones who brought it back to Europe. It was first introduced in Spain, and the Spaniards wanted to keep it secret; only monks were allowed to make chocolate. It would be roughly 200 years before chocolate was available to the masses. It finally spread throughout Europe, and during the 1700s, chocolate houses became as popular as coffee houses.

An English chocolate company introduced the first chocolate that was made to eat in 1847. In 1879, a Swiss chemist invented milk chocolate by adding powdered milk.

Response

Do you think you would have acquired a taste for chocolate had you been around in the 1500s?

Fascinating Factoid: The Aztecs used cacao beans as money. Ten beans reportedly would buy a turkey or rabbit!

Word Play

There are many different kinds of candy made using chocolate. Determine which chocolate bar each person below likes. Use the clues in the following sentences and the grid to help you. Put an X in the columns that do not apply to the person and a check mark to show the candy bar that person likes.

- *Amy* doesn't like Big Bar, and one person can't stand Baby Bar.
- *James* and *Michael* like either Big Bar or Mammoth Bar.
- *Robyn* likes Baby Bar better than Mammoth Bar.
- *Michael* likes Big Bar less than Baby Bar.

	Mammoth Bar	Big Bar	Baby Bar	Amazing Bar
Amy				
James				
Michael				
Robyn				

Activities

- There are chocolate-covered cherries, nuts, raisins, ice cream, pretzels, and much more. Make a two-column chart. In one column, list foods that classmates have eaten with chocolate. In the other column, list what other foods they think would taste better with chocolate.

- Design a food sculpture that includes chocolate (e.g., a spider body could be made from a chocolate sandwich cookie, with legs made of chocolate-covered pretzels).

July 8
A Big Problem Solved

Other Events This Day
- First American passport issued (1796)
- *The Wall Street Journal* began publication (1889)

In the past, smallpox was a dreaded killer disease—one out of every three people who were infected died. An estimated 300 million people died of smallpox in the 20th century alone. It was called the "speckled monster."

When infected, a person came down with a terrible fever; then pustules (small inflamed swellings filled with pus) formed all over the body. If a person survived a bout with smallpox, the scabs from the sores could cause scarring; the disease could also lead to blindness.

Smallpox was believed to have begun in Africa and spread to India and then to China. The earliest evidence of the disease was found on the mummy of an Egyptian pharaoh who died in 1157 BCE. The first recorded smallpox epidemic was in 1350 BCE. Smallpox spread throughout Europe in the 11th and 12th centuries CE and in American colonies in the 17th and 18th centuries CE.

Thanks to the experiments and studies of Edward Jenner, a vaccine was developed to give immunity to the disease. Dr. Jenner was an English physician who noticed that milkmaids who developed cowpox, a less serious disease, did not get smallpox. He experimented by taking fluid from a cowpox pustule and injecting an eight-year-old with it. Six weeks later, the boy was exposed to smallpox but did not catch the disease.

Benjamin Waterhouse, one of the best-educated American physicians of his time, heard of Dr. Jenner's work and corresponded with him. He got some cowpox vaccine from Dr. Jenner; Dr. Waterhouse was so confident of its safety that he vaccinated his own five-year-old son and a household servant on this day in 1800. This was the first successful vaccination performed in the United States using a cowpox serum to prevent smallpox.

Response

Why do you think Dr. Waterhouse chose his son to be part of the first trial with the new vaccine?

Fascinating Factoid: During a time when Dr. Waterhouse was in Europe studying medicine, he lived with future U.S. President John Adams (who had been sent there on government business).

Word Play

Smallpox was a big problem for society in the past. *Small* and *big* are *antonyms*—words that have opposite meanings. *Synonyms* are words that mean the same. If you can write the following synonyms for *small* and *big*, you are no "small fry" when it comes to vocabulary!

Synonyms for Small

1. l __ __ __ l __
2. __ __ __ y
3. m __ c __ __ __ __ __ __ __
4. m __ __ __ __ c __ __ __
5. p __ t __ __ __ e
6. s __ __ __ __ __
7. __ l __ __ d __ __
8. m __ __ __ t __

Synonyms for Large

9. h __ __ __
10. g __ __ __ t
11. g __ __ __ __ t __ __
12. t __ __ __ __ __ __ __ o __ __
13. i __ m __ __ __ __
14. v __ __ __ m __ __ __ __ __
15. b __ __ k __
16. e __ __ __ __ __ __ s

Activities

- Find and list vaccinations all children must receive before entering school.
- Although smallpox was no laughing matter, you can create a humorous poem about a fictional disease and its cure (e.g., chocolate fever).

July 9
Tennis, Anyone?

Other Events This Day
- U.S. President Zachary Taylor died (1850)
- Doughnut cutter patented (1872)

Wimbledon is the most well-known and prestigious tennis event in the world. It now boasts of crowds of half a million people and prize money for the winners of around $1 million.

The tournament was first played on this date in 1877 in London at the All England Lawn Tennis and Croquet Club. As the name suggests, the matches were played on real grass. There were 22 players for the only tournament that year—a men's singles championship. There was a three-plank stand, which held about 30 of the 200 spectators at the finals. The rackets were the shape and weight of snowshoes. The balls were covered in hand-sewn flannel. There was a strict dress code: "Gentlemen are kindly requested not to play in shirt sleeves when ladies are present."

Today Wimbledon is one of four tournaments known as the Grand Slam. The main events are gentlemen's singles, gentlemen's doubles, ladies' singles, ladies' doubles, and mixed doubles. It always begins six weeks before the first Monday in August and spreads over a two-week period. The players must wear predominately white clothing. Rackets today are made of a composite graphite, titanium, or hyper-carbon. In addition to the monetary prize, winners receive a silver cup or dish presented by the Duke of Kent and his wife, the Duchess.

Response

If you could, would you rather have seen the first tournament or attend the current event? Explain.

Fascinating Factoid: The British are proud of Wimbledon, but no British man has won the singles there since 1936, and no British woman has won since 1977.

Word Play

How good are you at "talking" tennis? Fill in the missing blanks with letters to identify each word commonly associated with tennis.

1. LI __ E __ __ A __
2. FA __ __ T
3. S __ N __ L __ S
4. __ D __ AN __ A __ E
5. P __ I __ T
6. __ E U __ E
7. L __ __ E
8. B __ __ L
9. __ I __ E __ I __ E
10. B __ S __ L __ N __
11. __ O U __ __ E S
12. U __ P __ __ E
13. M __ T C H
14. R __ C K __ T
15. N __ T
16. __ E __ V E

Activities

- Brainstorm and list recycling possibilities for antique tennis rackets.
- Survey schoolmates to see how many like to play tennis, how many have attended a live tennis match, and how many have watched Wimbledon on TV. Display your results on a graph.

July 10
The Nine-Day Queen

Other Events This Day
- Wyoming became 44th U.S. state (1890)
- First police radio system operated (1933)

Most of us dream about what it would be like to rule over others and to have power, money, and devoted subjects. In nondemocratic countries, the person in charge obtains the position through force, public pressure, or by birthright.

In 1553 in England, Lady Jane Grey was only 15 when her father-in-law, the Duke of Northumberland, masterminded a scheme to have her crowned as queen. Her grandmother was Princess Mary Tudor. But Jane was not in line to assume the throne unless her cousins Edward, Mary, and Elizabeth died of natural causes. When Edward VI died, much to her surprise and horror, Jane found out that her uncle's will had been changed. Her father-in-law had convinced Edward VI to write a new will in which he named Jane Grey as his successor. Upon hearing that Edward VI had died, Jane fell down and cried bitterly. At first she refused to be queen. But faced with pages of signatures verifying the will had been changed, and having to deal with tremendous pressure from her parents and father-in-law, she reluctantly proceeded to the Tower of London and was proclaimed queen on July 10, 1553.

Unfortunately, Jane's father-in-law had underestimated the power of the masses. The people of England loved Mary and were determined to have her rule. It took only nine days for Jane's reign to fall apart. Mary was crowned, and Jane was taken as a prisoner to the Tower of London. Mary didn't really want to see harm come to Jane but felt forced politically to condemn her to death. Jane showed great dignity and courage at her execution on February 9, 1554.

Response

What do you think would be the biggest advantage and disadvantage of being the ruler of your own country?

Fascinating Factoid: Jane was so short she wore chopines—shoes with special cork soles designed to make her appear taller.

Word Play

Solve the following word and number brainteasers.

Example: 9DQ = Nine Day Queen

a. 1W on a U = _____

b. 2H in a W = _____

c. 2N in a D = _____

d. 3BM = _____

e. 4Q in a G = _____

f. 5F on a H = _____

g. 5P in a N = _____

h. 6S on a H = _____

i. 7C in a R = _____

j. 8L on a S = _____

Activities

- It seems unfair that Jane begged not to be queen and then ended up being executed for doing what was asked of her. Write an account about something in your life that you consider unfair.

- Write a five senses poem about injustice or unfairness (i.e., what does injustice sound like, feel like, etc.).

July 11
E. B. White's Birthday

Other Events This Day
- U.S. Marine Corps created by Congress (1789)
- Martin Luther King Jr. posthumously awarded Presidential Medal of Freedom (1977)

E. B. White is well known for his children's books such as *Charlotte's Web* and *Stuart Little*. However, E. B. White, nicknamed Andy, spent most of his life writing for adults. He wrote essays, magazine articles and columns, books, and even a manual for writing that was popular as a textbook for high schools and colleges.

Mr. White was born on this day in 1899 in Mount Vernon, New York. Elwyn Brooks White was the youngest child born to loving parents. His father was a piano manufacturer.

While in college, Mr. White worked on the college newspaper and became a reporter upon graduation. In 1927, he worked for *The New Yorker* magazine where he became well known. From 1938–1943, he worked for *Harper's* magazine as a columnist.

In 1945, Mr. White wrote his first children's book, *Stuart Little*, which is considered a classic. This title, along with Mr. White's other books, *Charlotte's Web* and *The Trumpet of the Swan*, include the theme of friendship. Children would always ask him if the stories were true. He always answered, "No, they are imaginary tales . . . but real life is only one kind of life—there is also a life of the imagination."

Mr. White died of Alzheimer's disease on October 1, 1985. His awards included a gold medal for essays and criticism, a Pulitzer Prize special citation, and honorary degrees from seven American colleges and universities.

Response

Explain what Mr. White meant when he wrote ". . . real life is one kind of life—there is also the life of the imagination."

Fascinating Factoid: Mr. White once claimed that although there were some unclaimed books on his shelf, he only owned one book, *Walden,* and that he kept it in much the same way as one carries a handkerchief.

Word Play

Mr. White used the theme of friendship for some of his children's books. If the word *friendship* is divided, you see the words *friend* and *ship*. When we think of a ship, we usually think of a big boat. However, *ship* is also a suffix that means a quality or condition. Write as many words as you can by using *ship* as a suffix.

Example: penmanship

_____
_____
_____
_____
_____
_____
_____

Activities

- Mr. White wrote about a beautiful spider named Charlotte and her incredible web. Research spider webs. Make a detailed chalk drawing on black construction paper of one type of web.

- Mr. White's books were about friendship. Create your own story about friendship. It could be about the meaning of friendship or about one of your friends.

July 12
Itchin' to Etch?

• • • • • • • • • • • • • • • • •

Other Events This Day
- Paper bag manufacturing machine patented (1859)
- U.S. Congress authorized Medal of Honor (1862)

What has a bright red frame, gray screen, two white knobs, and looks a little like a TV screen? Give up? It's none other than an Etch-a-Sketch®.

The idea for this toy is attributed to Arthur Granjean. In the late 1950s, he created the *L'Ecran Magique* (magic screen) in his garage. He took it to the International Toy Fair in Nuremburg, Germany. Representatives for the Ohio Art Company saw the toy but they weren't initially impressed by it. However, when they took a second look, they decided to buy the toy and market it. Before releasing it to the public, they changed the name to Etch-a-Sketch.

The first Etch-a-Sketch was produced on this day in 1960. Little did the producers know that it would become the best-selling drawing toy in the business.

The underside of the screen is coated with a mixture of aluminum powder and plastic beads. The knobs control horizontal and vertical rods that meet and move a stylus. The stylus scrapes the screen, leaving a visible line. To erase and start over, one has to turn the Etch-a-Sketch over and shake it to recoat the surface.

The Ohio Art Company has tried using different colors, but people seem to prefer the standard. For its 25th anniversary, they made an Etch-a-Sketch in silver with sapphires and blue topaz. Etch-a-Sketch is now available in miniature, travel-sized, and glow-in-the-dark versions. Over 100 million models have been sold. There is even an Etch-a-Sketch Club, with an average of 2,000 members who range in age from 2 to 82!

Response
Why do you think the Etch-a-Sketch Club would have senior citizen members?

> **Fascinating Factoid:** If you were to scrape the entire screen with the stylus, it would become virtually transparent.

Word Play
Part of the following story words have been accidentally wiped from the Etch-a-Sketch screens below. Finish each word.

1. A ___ R ___ ___ ___ ___ ___ ___
(classified or designated)

2. H ___ ___ ___ ___ ___ ___ ___ ___ L
(parallel to the horizon)

3. V ___ ___ T ___ ___ ___ ___ ___
(parallel to the horizon)

4. S T ___ ___ ___ ___ ___
(writing instrument)

5. M ___ N ___ ___ ___ ___ ___ ___
(something on a small scale)

6. A ___ ___ ___ ___ ___ ___ ___ ___ ___ Y
(recurrence of the date of notable event)

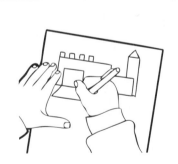

Activity
- The Ohio Art Company has created a calendar of Etch-a-Sketch art for their 30th anniversary. Using an Etch-a-Sketch or pencil and paper, draw a page (in Etch-a-Sketch style) for the month of July.

First World Cup Soccer Game Played

• • • • • • • • • • • • • • • •

When people in the United States think of football, they think of a brown pigskin ball and a field marked off in 10-yard increments. When the rest of the world thinks of football, they see 22 people kicking a black and white pentagon-patterned ball on a field divided into halves.

FIFA (Fédération Internationale de Football Association) began World Cup Soccer on this date in 1930. There were 13 teams, including the United States, competing in the country of Uruguay. In the final game of that World Cup, Uruguay defeated Argentina and became the first country to win the World Cup. The teams battled in front of a crowd of 93,000. Today there are 32 teams involved in World Cup Soccer with approximately 30 billion spectators. It is the most watched event in the world.

The first World Cup was called the Jules Rimet Trophy after the first president of FIFA. To date, only South American and European countries have won the tournament. Six out of 17 World Cups have been won by the host country.

Since the beginning of the championship, the popularity of the event has continued to grow. The fans are as passionate about the game as the players. Whether you call it soccer or football, it is a thrilling game of continuous action from start to finish.

Response

Why do you think only South American and European countries have won a World Cup in the past?

Fascinating Factoid: The first World Cup mascot was a lion-like boy called Willie. Willie was used during the 1966 World Cup in England.

Word Play

Kick around some vowels and place them in the blank spaces to complete each soccer word.

1. C __ R N __ R K __ C K
2. K __ C K __ F F
3. M __ T C H
4. S H __ N G __ __ R D
5. S C __ R __
6. S __ C C __ R
7. S P __ R T
8. G __ __ L
9. F __ __ __ T B __ L L
10. M __ D F __ __ __ L D __ R
11. G __ __ L __ __
12. B __ L L
13. P __ N __ L T Y
14. S T __ D __ __ __ M
15. __ F F S __ D __
16. P __ T C H
17. H __ __ D __ R
18. R __ F __ R __ __
19. __ B S T R __ C T __ __ N
20. R __ D C __ R D

Activities

• Research famous soccer players. Choose your favorite and make a trading card for him or her (much like baseball trading cards).

• On a large sheet of poster paper, draw a Venn diagram using the shape of a football and a soccer ball (rather than circles). Compare and contrast the two games.

July 14

Woody Guthrie's Birthday

• • • • • • • • • • • • • • • •

Other Events This Day
• 38th U.S. president Gerald Ford's birthday (1913)
• All political parties, except the Nazi party, were outlawed in Germany (1933)

Think about the songs you like to listen to. Chances are those songs connect with your own experiences. They reflect your thoughts, feelings, and life situations. The same can be said about the songs written by Woody Guthrie.

Today is the birthday of Woodrow Wilson Guthrie. He was born in the small town of Okemah, Oklahoma, in 1912. Mr. Guthrie lived through some of the most significant events in history and captured those days in "tell it like it is" ballads and folk songs.

Although Mr. Guthrie's life was full of hardships and heartache, he was a keen observer of life and he felt especially bonded to those who shared his experience of being poor and oppressed. People were struggling with mortgages, debts, bills, sickness, and worries; however, Woody Guthrie found things to write songs about. At first he wrote funny songs and then wrote about what he thought was wrong and how to make it right. He wrote songs about what everyone else was thinking about.

Mr. Guthrie wrote hundreds of songs, including his most famous "This Land is Your Land." He was recognized numerous times for his music. He was inducted into the Songwriters Hall of Fame, the Rock and Roll Hall of Fame and Museum. He was awarded the Folk Alliance Lifetime Achievement Award. He was also awarded a Grammy®. The Smithsonian Institution worked with the Woody Guthrie Foundation on a major traveling exhibition of his life and legacy.

Response

If you were to write a song about current times and what is right and wrong with the world, what would you write about?

Fascinating Factoid: Woody Guthrie was named after President Woodrow Wilson, who was elected president the same year that he was born.

Word Play

"This Land is Your Land" has become a popular patriotic song. Match each set of lyrics to its patriotic song.

____ 1. "Let freedom ring"

____ 2. "O'er the ramparts we watched"

____ 3. "The men will cheer and the boys will shout"

____ 4. "Forever in peace may you wave"

____ 5. "We saw the men and boys as thick as hasty pudding"

____ 6. "I saw below me that golden valley"

____ 7. "'Cause the flag still stands for freedom"

____ 8. "Stand beside her and guide her through the night"

____ 9. "For amber waves of grain"

a. "America"

b. "America, the Beautiful"

c. "God Bless America"

d. "God Bless the U.S.A."

e. "The Star-Spangled Banner"

f. "This Land Is Your Land"

g. "When Johnny Comes Marching Home Again"

h. "Yankee Doodle"

i. "You're a Grand Old Flag"

Activities

• Think about your favorite song. Describe how it is similar to the type of music Woody Guthrie wrote. Write about how the song makes you feel and why you think the artist wrote it. Also, explain why it is your favorite.

• Think about all the songs you like. Write a letter nominating its writer to the Songwriters Hall of Fame. Be sure to explain why you believe that songwriter is deserving of the honor.

July 15

I Can't Believe It's Not Butter®!

Other Events This Day

- Georgia became last Confederate state to be readmitted to the Union (1870)
- World's tallest man (almost 9 feet [2.7 m]), Robert Wadlow, died (1940)

On this day in 1869, Hoppolyte Mege-Mouriez of Provence, France, patented the forerunner of one of the products that today has people exclaiming, "I can't believe it's not butter®!" This butter substitute was called oleomargarine. Of course, many improvements have been made since that time. Today, it is called it margarine.

Mr. Mege-Mouriez invented a butter substitute for Napoleon, who needed it for his army and navy because butter spoiled too rapidly. Little did Mr. Mege-Mouriez realize what a controversy his product would spawn. When it came to America in about 1874, the dairy industry did not like the competition with the real thing. The Federal Margarine Act put heavy taxes on making yellow margarine and required expensive licenses for manufacturers, wholesalers, and retailers of margarine. Without yellow coloring, margarine was not very appetizing. It looked like shortening. The margarine folks got around the law of coloring margarine by including little packets of food coloring capsules in the containers. Consumers simply added the color themselves.

Other attempts were made to discourage the margarine industry. At one time in history, the armed forces and other federal agencies were not allowed to use margarine for anything other than cooking. Finally, in 1951, the tax system came to an end and the other regulations began to fall away.

The first tub margarine and vegetable oil spreads were introduced to Americans in the 1960s. Today's market offers reduced-fat and fat-free margarine products.

Response

Why do you think the federal government passed legislation against margarine makers?

Fascinating Factoid: Margarine is a major source of Vitamin E.

Word Play

Is the statement "I can't believe it's not butter" a double negative? *Double negatives* happen when you put two negative words (like *no* and *not*) together in the same sentence, talking about the same thing.
Example: Tommy <u>doesn't</u> listen to <u>no</u> one.

The words *doesn't* and *no* are both negative and both talking about the same thing.

Circle the negative words in each sentence. On another sheet of paper, rewrite each sentence to eliminate the double negatives.

1. They will never sell none of those things.

2. It isn't no big deal that you get to go to the party.

3. Mary shouldn't have nothing to do with making cookies.

4. That old car won't get you nowhere now.

5. Letycia hasn't met nobody with a name like hers.

6. It don't make no difference anyhow.

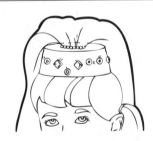

Activities

- Margarine tubs are often used in craft projects. Design and make a margarine tub craft. If tubs aren't available, illustrate and describe your project, giving directions on how to make it.

- Research and copy a recipe using margarine. Select one that sounds delicious. If possible, try it out.

July 16

Meter Matters

• •

Other Events This Day

- Joan of Arc led French Army in Battle of Orleans (1429)
- Kissing banned in England to stop germs from spreading (1439)

Parking space is sometimes limited around businesses and shopping areas, especially in downtown areas. This situation led to the first parking meter. Mr. Carl C. Magee was on the traffic committee of the Oklahoma City Chamber of Commerce. He was given the task of solving the parking-space problem. People who worked in the downtown area were parking in spaces for the entire day and leaving few, if any, spots open for customers or clients. Mr. Magee came up with a solution. Whether it is a good or a bad solution depends on whether you have enough quarters when you need to park!

On this day in 1935, the world's first parking meter was installed in downtown Oklahoma City, Oklahoma. It was hoped that the parking meters would discourage long-term parking, as well as make money for the city. It was such a success that cities everywhere now "cash in" on the idea.

At first the devices were mechanical. Coins were deposited and a knob was turned to activate a timer. A fully electronic meter became available in 1992. Electronic parking meters can do different things like adjust rates for different times of the day and collect information about coin counts and violation statistics.

Currently it is estimated that there are about five million U.S. parking meters in use. That sounds like some serious cash by the end of each day!

Response

Name at least one other way you think downtown-parking problems could be solved. Explain.

Fascinating Factoid: One of the earliest documented parking regulations was in Rome, Italy. Romans did not allow vehicles to enter the business district between certain hours due to traffic congestion.

Word Play

A parking meter measures time you have paid to park in a particular parking space. There are many other kinds of meters. Write the name of each meter using the clue given.

1. _ _ _ _ meter (measures altitude)
2. _ _ _ _ _ _ meter (measures wind speed)
3. _ _ _ _ _ (measures air pressure)
4. _ _ _ meter (measures distance)
5. _ _ _ meter (measures electrical resistance)
6. _ _ _ _ meter (measures steps)
7. _ _ _ _ _ _ _ _ meter (measures properties of light)
8. _ _ _ _ _ _ meter (measures speed, velocity)

Figure out what each measure means.

9. sphygmomanometer _____
10. dosimeter _____
11. accelerometer _____
12. colorimeter _____

Activities

- Imagine that your town or city has 500 parking meters. If the meter collected just 25 cents an hour, estimate how much money the city could collect in one business week (Monday–Friday) of parking from 7:00 A.M. to 5:00 P.M.

- Make a list of projects the parking-meter income from your area could be spent on. Select your first, second, and third choices.

July 17
Disneyland® Opened

Other Events This Day
- First military hospital approved (1775)
- First U.S. dental school (Harvard School of Dental Medicine) established (1857)

The year was 1955. Play-Doh®, Crest® toothpaste, and instant oatmeal were first introduced. Rosa Parks was arrested for refusing to give up her seat on the bus to a white man. The polio vaccine was given to millions of school kids, and the first corporate MacDonald's® opened.

The day was July 17. The place was Anaheim, California. Eleven thousand lucky people were invited to the grand opening, and 20,000 others made counterfeit tickets or paid $5 to climb a ladder over a fence. A 15-day heat wave caused women's heels to stick in the not-quite-set asphalt. Plumbers were on strike. There were no water fountains! Regardless of that disastrous opening day, Disneyland® was, and still is, an amazing success. This theme park was built in one year with 18 major attractions. Admission was $1 and the cost of rides was 10 to 35 cents.

Today, visitors can still enjoy many of the same attractions. Disneyland now has over 60 attractions. More than 13 million people visit yearly, surpassed only by Disney World® in Florida. Since that first day, Disney managers have become experts at handling masses of people and their needs and wishes. Walt Disney had a vision to build a "magical park" where children and parents could have fun together. Not only was his vision realized in his lifetime, it has now mushroomed into global enterprises.

Response
What qualities do you think Walt Disney possessed to make him so successful?

Fascinating Factoid: Each year over four million hamburgers, 1.6 million hot dogs, and 3.2 million servings of ice cream are served at Disneyland.

Word Play
You'll be the star of Disneyland if you can make 50 words using only the letters in the word Disneyland. Write words on the lines below. Continue on the back of this sheet.

_____

_____

_____

_____

_____

_____

_____

_____

_____

_____

Activities
- Write a diary entry about a trip to Disneyland (real or imaginary). Be sure to include observations and discoveries made using your five senses (e.g., saw, heard, smelled, touched, tasted).

- Research and list the theme lands at Disneyland. Create a new theme land. Be sure to include several attractions that you think would draw a huge crowd. Describe the setting.

July 18
Crayola® Introduced Scented Crayons

Other Events This Day
- Great fire destroyed most of Rome (64 CE)
- Nadia Comaneci scored first perfect score (10) in gymnastics at the Olympics (1976)

The first box of Crayola® crayons had only eight colors: yellow, green, brown, red, blue, orange, purple, and black. It was sold in 1903 for five cents. The scent of regular crayons is reported to be among the 20 most recognizable scents to American adults.

Today is the anniversary of the first special scented crayon set, which hit the market in 1994. Those innovative crayons were food-scented. It seems they smelled too much like the real thing because small children were eating them, so Crayola took them off the market. They tried again with the scented crayons in 1997 using nonfood scents. These were called Color 'N Smell. These, however, were not successful. After some informal surveys, Crayola found that children said the names of the crayons didn't match the scents. They thought that the Cedar Chest scent smelled like fire, or even worse. They said that the Daffodil smelled more like a leather jacket or dead worms.

Today, Crayola markets specialty sets of glitter, pearl brite, and techno-brite crayons. They produce boxes of 120 colors. Some color names are plain like blue, and some are exotic like Caribbean green. At times, the company has asked the public to name a color or vote colors *in* or *out.* Crayola makes about three billion crayons daily. The crayons are sold in more than 80 countries. Just about every American recognizes the Crayola brand. You might say we are crazy about our crayons!

Response

Predict what you think the next specialty set from Crayola might be. Then tell how you would feel about such an innovation.

Fascinating Factoid: According to the *Christian Science Monitor,* enough crayons are bought in a year to make a giant crayon 36 feet (11 m) in diameter and 251 feet (76.5m) long.

Word Play

Can you identify some of the colors in a Crayola 64 Box? Unscramble and write each color name.

1. critopa _____
2. arauiqeamn _____
3. sbteteirewt _____
4. htliste _____
5. getamna _____
6. ziame _____
7. dredonolg _____
8. lonem _____
9. seflh _____
10. ripenelkwi _____
11. dihroc _____
12. nevaldre _____
13. rubreylm _____
14. mloasn _____
15. peais _____
16. fonorcwrel _____

Activities

- If possible, visit the Crayola.com website. Explore the many fun facts, activities, and games.
- Create a contemporary abstract work of art by using a black marker and making big swirls/scribbles all over a large sheet of white paper. After you have an interesting design on your paper, fill in the spaces with your favorite crayon colors.

July 19
Is a Foot Really a Foot?

Other Events This Day
- Dr. Roy Scholz became first surgeon to use fiberglass sutures (1939)
- Geraldine Ferraro became first woman nominated for vice presidency by a major political party (1984)

Long, long ago, people measured in units called cubits. A *cubit* was the length from a man's elbow to the end of his middle finger. The good news was that it was "handy." The bad news was that not all arms were created in equal length. While the cubit is no longer used as a standard of measurement, the *foot* unit started out as the length of a man's foot. An *inch* was the width of a man's thumb, and the distance from the tip of a man's nose to the end of his outstretched fingertips was a *yard*. This system had the same problems as the cubit system.

In the 13th century CE, King Edward I of England ordered a permanent measuring stick be made and used throughout the kingdom. It was similar to what we know today as a yardstick. He called it the *iron ulna* after the name of the bone in the forearm. He also decreed that the *foot* unit of measure would be one-third of a yard and the *inch* one thirty-sixth of a yard.

In modern times, the iron ulna was replaced with the ruler and tape measure. It was on this day in 1868 that the spring tape measure (which rolls into a coil) was patented. The patent was given to Alvin J. Fellows although he was really improving on earlier versions. Tape measures come in metal, plastic, and fabric. Cloth and plastic tape measures are usually used in sewing while the metal ones are better suited for carpentry. For many reasons (and measurements), tape measures are just about indispensable.

Response

Think of an example of how using the cubit system of measurement might be a disadvantage and an advantage.

Fascinating Factoid: Today there is a method of using a ray of light to measure distances to within a millionth of an inch.

Word Play

Write the best unit of measurement to measure each of the following (inches, feet, yard, miles).

1. length of highway
_____

2. width of table
_____

3. length of football field
_____

4. length of river
_____

5. length of your pencil
_____

6. width of your math book
_____

7. height of door
_____

8. height of basketball goal
_____

On the back of this sheet, make four columns. In the first column, list several things for which the **inch** would be the best unit of measurement. In the next column, list things for which the **foot** would be the best unit of measurement. In the third column, list things for which the **yard** would be the best unit of measurement. In the last column, list things for which the **mile** would be the best unit of measurement.

Activity

- Trace around your foot. Use it to estimate how many of your feet it would take to go from one side of your classroom to the other. Check your answer to determine if you made a good estimate. Measure the length of your foot and compare it to the standard foot unit of measure.

July 20
A Legendary Life

· · · · · · · · · · · · · · · · ·

Other Events This Day
- Women's Army Auxiliary Corps began basic training (1942)
- U.S. *Viking I* landed on Mars (1976)

Have you ever had someone break a promise to you? If you answered yes, then you will understand part of the reason for the fighting between Native Americans and white Americans in the 1800s. Treaties were repeatedly broken. The Native Americans were forced to move and give up their lands and hunting grounds. Sometimes the Native Americans refused to give in without a fight, resulting in fierce and bloody battles.

Probably the best-known Native American chief was Sitting Bull, chief of the Dakota Sioux Tribe. He was a man of vision who was religious and deeply loved his land. He was fearless in protecting it and his people's way of life. When gold was discovered in the Black Hills of South Dakota in the area of the Sioux sacred land, prospectors began to rush into the area. In spite of promises by the U.S. government that the land would forever belong to the Native Americans, they now wanted the Native Americans to leave the area for white settlers. Sitting Bull and his people refused.

The Battle of Little Big Horn is one of the best-known encounters where the Native Americans, led by Sitting Bull, completely wiped out the Seventh Cavalry under General George Custer. After the battle, the Sioux disbanded. They thought it was the end of the fighting, and they would be left alone to live in peace on their lands. But the Americans did not give up, and the Native Americans eventually lost their sacred grounds. It was on this day in 1881, five years after Custer's defeat, that Sitting Bull finally surrendered to the U.S. Army.

Response

What do you think was on Sitting Bull's mind the day he surrendered?

Fascinating Factoid: Sitting Bull traveled for a short time with Buffalo Bill Cody's Wild West Show.

Word Play

Through the ages, there have been many notable chiefs of Native American tribes. Identify each chief's tribe by unscrambling the word.

1. Sequoyah (HECORKEE) _____

2. Pushmataha (THCOWAC) _____

3. William Colbert (ASWCAHICK) _____

4. Opothleyaholo (ERECK) _____

5. Osceola (ONELMESI) _____

6. Cochise (CAPHAE) _____

7. Geronimo (PACEAH) _____

8. Chief Joseph (ZEN RECEP) _____

9. Quanah Parker (MENHCCOA) _____

10. Crazy Horse (KALTOA) _____

Activities

- If possible, read *A Boy Called Slow*, a picture book about Sitting Bull. Native Americans were named for personal attributes (e.g., Sitting Bull was named for a bull sitting intractably on its haunches). Sitting Bull was determined and unmovable when it came to his convictions. Give yourself a descriptive name and tell why you chose it to represent who you are.

- Native Americans drew stories on their teepees using symbols and pictures. Research some of the symbols or make up your own and draw a story.

July 21

National Women's Hall of Fame Founded

• • • • • • • • • • • • • • •

> **Other Events This Day**
> • Confederate forces won victory at Bull Run in first major battle of the Civil War (1861)
> • First train robbery west of the Mississippi performed by the James Gang (1873)

There are Halls of Fame all over this country. The Baseball Hall of Fame is in Cooperstown, New York. The Country Music Hall of Fame is in Nashville, Tennessee. The National Cowboy Hall of Fame is located in Oklahoma City, Oklahoma. Michigan is home to the Automotive Hall of Fame. The National Toy Hall of Fame moved from Oregon to Rochester, New York. Halls of Fame help us remember important people who have made our lives richer by their contributions to society.

On this day in 1969, the National Women's Hall of Fame was founded. The Hall is located in Seneca Falls, New York, which is the site of the first Women's Rights Convention held in 1848. As stated in its mission statement, The National Women's Hall of Fame was established to "Honor in perpetuity these women, citizens of the United States of America whose contributions to the arts, athletics, business, education, government, the humanities, philanthropy, and science, have been the greatest value for the development of their country." So far over 200 women have been inducted into the Women's Hall of Fame. With a historic bank as its home, the Hall offers educational activities, special exhibits, and events.

Response

Name one woman that you think should be in the Women's Hall of Fame and explain your selection.

Fascinating Factoid: There is also a National Women's Baseball Hall of Fame and a National Women's Basketball Hall of Fame. Plus, several states have Halls of Fame to honor women from their states.

Word Play

Over 200 women have been inducted into the Women's Hall of Fame. Unscramble the word next to each name to determine the occupation of some women in the Hall of Fame.

1. Lucille Ball — NIEDMCONEE
2. Clara Barton — SURNE
3. Elizabeth Blackwell — COTORD
4. Nellie Bly — OJUNILRATS
5. Pearl S. Buck — RITWER
6. Mary Cassatt — TISRAT
7. Amelia Earhart — TIXRVAIA
8. Mae Jemison — TASNORTAU
9. Wilma Mankiller — TVINEA MERNACIA HIFCE
10. Annie Oakley — SRATOSOREPHH
11. Billie Jean King — NISTEN LAYPER
12. Beverly Sills — PEORA NISREG
13. Oprah Winfrey — LTAK HWSO TEHOSSS
14. Maria Tallchief — LABRLENIA

Activities

• Plan a Hall of Fame for your school. Consider such things as criteria for selecting inductees, type of induction ceremony, panel of judges, etc.

• Write a letter of recommendation for your grandmother (or another female relative) to be considered for induction in the Women's Hall of Fame next year. Be sure to tell how she has contributed to benefit society.

July 22
Going Solo

• • • • • • • • • • • • • • • • • • •

Going solo can be fun but also scary. What interesting solo experiences have you had? Perhaps you have ridden a bus, plane, or train by yourself. *The Guinness Book of World Records* has numerous listings for people accomplishing new, and sometimes dangerous, solo feats.

Today is the anniversary of such an event—the completion of a solo flight around the world. Famous aviator Wiley Post made his daring flight in 1933. He took off from Floyd Bennett Field in New York and ended his famous flight there. He devised and installed an autopilot system and radio-direction finder on his airplane, the Winnie Mae.

Mr. Post loved mechanical things. When he was 11, he saw his first air show. He was fascinated. Years later, he lost his left eye in an oil field accident. He used the settlement money from that accident to buy his first airplane. He became the personal pilot of a wealthy oilman. A dirigible—not an airplane—held the current around-the-world flight record. Mr. Post decided it was time for an airplane to take that record. The first time, he and another pilot set the new record in 8 days, 15 hours, and 51 minutes. That wasn't enough. Mr. Post wanted to do it alone. Two years later, making only 11 stops, Wiley Post completed the first solo around-the-world flight in 7 days and 19 hours!

Response

Think about the characteristics that Wiley Post must have had to accomplish such a great feat. Name two or three of your own personal characteristics.

Fascinating Factoid: The Winnie Mae was not pressurized, so Wiley Post wore a pressurized suit, allowing him to fly high enough that he discovered the jet stream.

Word Play

Our language has many gender-specific words (words that refer to female only or male only). For example, Wiley Post was an aviator; however, Amelia Earhart was an aviatrix. Supply each missing word.

1. waiter _____
2. _____ actress
3. _____ usherette
4. comedian _____
5. sculptor _____
6. poet _____
7. duke _____
8. _____ heroine
9. _____ stewardess
10. landlord _____
11. author _____
12. executor _____

When? Who? Why? Where? What?

Activities

- Create a **Five Ws** poem. Look in a newspaper. Find an article and underline each word or phrase that tells who, what, when, where, why, and how. Turn the words and phrases into a poem. Each line should tell one of the Ws. Add a last line that ties it all together.

- Make a Rewards/Risks Chart. In one column, list all the positive things about doing something solo. In the second column, list all the negative things about doing something alone.

July 23
Typographer Patented

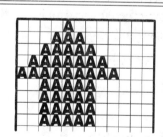

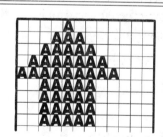

Other Events This Day

- Ulysses S. Grant, 18th U.S. president, died (1885)
- The Hale-Bopp comet discovered by Alan Hale and Thomas Bopp (1995)

Did you write your last report by hand or computer? Chances are if it was long, you did it on the computer. It is so easy to type, move, cut and paste, and correct mistakes with just a touch of the keyboard. It hasn't always been that easy to produce written documents!

It is believed that the first attempt to make a machine that put letters on paper was in the early 1700s. There was a patent awarded to Henry Mill for "an artificial machine or method for the impressing or transcribing of letters singly or progressively one after another, as in writing . . . ." No model, illustration or other information about this machine exists.

On this day in 1829, an American named Austin Burt received a patent for a typographer. It looked a lot like a butcher's block and used type bars. It took a long time to type words. A person could actually write faster than he or she could type!

In 1873, Remington & Sons built a typewriter designed by Samuel Sholes. It looked much like the modern-day typewriter. Mistakes could not be seen because the type bars struck on the underside of the paper. It only typed uppercase letters. By 1909, however, there were 89 typewriter manufacturers, and the typewriter was on its way to becoming a necessity. Improvements continued throughout the history of the typewriter, including an electric typewriter. Today we use the computer to produce most documents, but typewriters are still used to fill out forms and applications.

Response

Name some times when people prefer to write by hand—not with a typewriter or computer.

Fascinating Factoid: The first novel ever produced on a typewriter was *The Adventures of Tom Sawyer.*

Word Play

A *pangram* is a sentence that contains all letters of the alphabet. Often when learning to type or taking a typing test, you are asked to type this pangram, "The quick brown fox jumps over a lazy dog." Write some pangrams of your own.

_____

_____

_____

_____

_____

_____

_____

Activities

- Use one repeating letter, to make a design. If you do not have a keyboard available, draw your design on graph paper.

- If you have access to a keyboard, use the symbols to make drawings. For example, an armadillo can be made with ~()))">.

July 24
Machu Picchu Discovered

Other Events This Day
- Brigham Young and other Mormons arrive at Salt Lake City, Utah (1847)
- Instant coffee invented (1938)

Hiram Bingham discovered Machu Picchu, the lost city of the Incas, in the country of Peru on this day in 1911. Its great snow peaks, looming above the clouds, and the beauty of the luxurious vegetation awed him.

Machu Picchu is located on a tropical jungle/forest mountain 7,000 feet (2.1 km) above sea level. It is about 0.4 sq. miles (1 sq. km) in area and located in the Andes Mountains. There are streets and stairways (3,000 steps) as well as water canals and courtyards. The rooms are rectangular, except for one with curved walls. Many of the rooms have only three walls. Doors and windows have niches where idols and other objects were placed. The walls were built without cement. There is a sundial of polished stone and a shrine made of a large block of granite. It is thought that the shrine was used for astrological purposes.

The story of Machu Picchu is unclear. It could have been the advanced settlement of the Incas or a royal estate. With its high altitude, it could have been used for commercial or military purposes. However, because of the number of women's bodies found among the ruins, the most likely theory is that it was a sanctuary or temple of Inca priests where young girls were taught to serve the Incas and the high priest. Whatever its purpose, Machu Picchu is the most important tourist attraction in Peru.

Response
What is your theory about Machu Picchu?

Fascinating Factoid: A jail with underground dungeons was found in one section of the buildings.

Word Play
Machu and Picchu both end with the letter combination of -chu. List words below in which this same combination can be found at the beginning of words, inside words, and at the end of words.

Beginning
_____   _____
_____   _____
_____   _____

Middle
_____   _____
_____   _____
_____   _____

End
_____   _____
_____   _____

Activities
- Research Peru and create a travel poster. Remember Machu Picchu is its most important tourist attraction.
- Imagine that you are taking a trip to Peru in August. Make a list of clothing and other items you will need for your trip.

July 25
Lance's Legacy

Other Events This Day
- George Stephenson introduced first steam locomotive (1814)
- First bikini shown at Paris fashion show (1946)

Lance Armstrong is a hero not only for his athletic abilities, but also for his strength of spirit. Mr. Armstrong has triumphed over the greatest cyclists in the world to win the Tour de France a record seven times. With the same dogged determination, he triumphed over life-threatening cancer.

Mr. Armstrong was born in 1971 in Texas. He began competing in triathlons at age 13. He won the U.S. amateur championship in 1991 in cycling. He finished last in his first professional cycle race in 1992. The following year he won the World Road Championships. In 1996, the bottom fell out of his career. Mr. Armstrong was diagnosed with stage three cancer. He had a 40 percent chance of survival. After surgery and extensive treatment, Mr. Armstrong recovered. He looks upon his battle with cancer as his greatest achievement.

Capping off an incredible comeback, Lance Armstrong won his first Tour de France on this day in 1999. That was only the beginning. His fame and the popularity of cycling grew rapidly as he continued to win the Tour de France year after year. After riding 2,232.7 miles (3,593.2 km) in three weeks, Mr. Armstrong won his world-record-setting seventh Tour de France in 2005. As he stood on the podium after this win, he stated that it was time for him to retire from the competition. When asked about his legacy, he said that only time would tell; however, for millions of people, his legacy is the promise of hope.

Response

Why might "hope" be considered Lance Armstrong's legacy?

Fascinating Factoid: Together with Nike, Mr. Armstrong created a clothing collection—10//2—referring to the day he was diagnosed with cancer. A portion of the sales goes to the Lance Armstrong Foundation charity.

Word Play

How many wheels does a bicycle have? Two, right! *Bi-* means two. *Uni-* means one, *tri-* means three, and *quad-* means four. Identify each cycle.

a. cycle with one wheel _____

b. cycle with three wheels _____

c. cycle with four wheels _____

Using one of the number prefixes above, fill in each blank below.

1. An imaginary horse that has one horn is a _____ corn.

2. Four babies born at the same time to the same mother are called _____ ruplets.

3. _____ lingual means speaking two languages.

4. _____ annual means occurring twice a year.

5. _____ ogy means a group of three dramatic or literary works related in subject or theme.

6. An animal with four legs is a _____ ped.

7. A group of four is called a _____ tet.

On the back of this sheet, list other words using each of the number prefixes mentioned above.

Activities

- Research the 10//2 clothing line and create a sales brochure for your favorite item.

- Research the Tour de France. Report your findings in a creative way (e.g., make a map of the race route, list the rules and regulations of the race, create flags of the countries that the contestants in the last race represented).

July 26
Federal Bureau of Investigation Created

• • • • • • • • • • • • • • • •

Other Events This Day
• Benjamin Franklin became first postmaster (Philadelphia) (1739)
• New York became 11th U.S. state to ratify U.S. Constitution (1788)

On this day in 1908, Attorney General Charles Bonaparte, serving during the presidency of Theodore Roosevelt, hired 9 detectives, 13 civil rights investigators, and 12 accountants as permanent employees of the Department of Justice. These people were assigned in areas such as antitrust, unlawful servitude, and land fraud under the supervision of a chief examiner. This is considered to be the beginning of the Federal Bureau of Investigation (FBI), although it was not officially named until 1909 when it was named by Mr. Bonaparte's successor. He also changed the title of Chief Examiner to Chief of the Bureau of Investigation.

The mission of the FBI is "To protect and defend the United States against terrorist and foreign intelligence threats, to uphold and enforce the criminal laws of the United States, and to provide leadership and criminal justice services to federal, state, municipal, and international agencies and partners."

The FBI is the main investigative branch of the U.S. Department of Justice. This agency investigates crimes and assists other law enforcement agencies with services such as fingerprint identification, laboratory examinations (forensics), and police training. The FBI maintains field offices in major U.S. cities and has more than 50 international offices. Today the FBI has over 30,000 employees, including over 12,000 special agents and over 17,000 support staff working as intelligence analysts, language specialists, scientists, and information technology specialists.

Response

What do you consider to be the most important task of the FBI? Explain.

Fascinating Factoid: The FBI's budget for 2005 alone was over $5 billion.

Word Play

The FBI has many special agents—some language experts. Be a language expert and investigate the relationship between each group of words (e.g., part of speech).

1. lighthouse, birdhouse, doorstep   __compound words__

2. deer, moose, sheep _____

3. beautiful, enormous, wonderful _____

4. sleuth, snoop, spy _____

5. Tom, Joe, Mary _____

6. on, over, around _____

7. and, but, therefore _____

8. retire, untie, preschool _____

9. talking, worker, goodness _____

10. happily, rapidly, loudly _____

11. buzz, thump, pop _____

Activities

• Research the field of fingerprinting. Learn how to lift prints. Make a chart of your own fingerprints and classify them according to information you found during research.

• The FBI publishes a list of its top 10 most wanted criminals. Create your own top 10 list of your most wanted gifts, friends, etc.

July 27
Bugs Bunny's Birthday

● ● ● ● ● ● ● ● ● ● ● ● ● ● ● ● ● ● ● ●

Other Events This Day
- *Billboard* magazine published its first singles bestseller chart (1940)
- Armistice signed ending the Korean Conflict (1953)

"Eh, what's up, Doc?" It was on this day in 1940 that Bugs Bunny came out of his hole and asked Elmer Fudd that famous question. The cartoon was called *A Wild Hare*. The story line of this first cartoon served as a pattern for future Bugs cartoons. Bugs always tried to drive a hunter named Elmer Fudd insane. The methods he used changed with each cartoon, but there was the common "winners against losers" theme. Many common phrases, such as "Of course, you ree-lize, dis means war" and "I knew I should have taken that left turn at Albuquerque," popped up in Bugs cartoons.

Bugs didn't have a name until 1941 when Mr. Turner, one of the animators, wrote *Bugs Bunny* on his model sheet, meaning it was the character created by Ben "Bugs" Hardaway. Following that cartoon, the rabbit was named *Bugs* after his creator. The name fit because it was a popular term for indicating craziness.

In fall 1960, *The Bugs Bunny Show* aired for the first time on ABC and remained on TV for 40 years. Bugs served as the mascot for Warner Brothers. He was one of the first cartoon characters, along with Mickey Mouse, to have a star on the Hollywood Walk of Fame. He was the first cartoon character to be honored on a U.S. postage stamp, which is number seven on the top 10 most popular U.S. stamps. He has appeared in video games and movies. Memorabilia and fans of this "kwazy wabbit" are everywhere!

Response

Why do you think *The Bugs Bunny Show* was able to stay on TV for 40 years?

Fascinating Factoid: When the movie *Who Framed Roger Rabbit?* was made by Disney, Warner Brothers allowed Bugs to be in the movie only if he got equal screen time as the Disney star Mickey Mouse. Therefore, both characters are always together on the screen.

Word Play

Bugs Bunny's nemesis is a character named Elmer Fudd. Elmer had a few speech problems. Can you interpret the following Elmer Fudd dialect?

1. I'm going to get dat cwazy wabbit if its de wast ding I ever do.

2. Dat wascalway wabbit has bodered me for de wast time.

3. Bugs Bunny is a fictionaw cawtoon wabbit that appeaws in *Wooney Tunes* and *Mewwie Mewodies* and is one of the most wecognizabwe chawactews, weaw ow imaginawy, in the wowwd.

4. No one weawwy knows who actuawy cweated Bugs Bunny. Dewe awe many peopwe who hewped cweat him, but no one knows who de one pewson was.

Activities

- There are two dogs and five animated characters on the Hollywood Walk of Fame. Make a list of your guesses as to the nonhuman stars on the walk. Check your answers. Predict the next cartoon character star and give supporting reasons for your choice.

- Choose an animal that you think would make a good cartoon character. Make a drawing of the animal in cartoon form. Give it a name, personality, dialect (the way he speaks), etc.

July 28
Hamburger Invented

• • • • • • • • • • • • • • • • • • • •

Other Events This Day

- Fingerprints first used as means of identification (1858)
- First singing telegram delivered (New York City) (1933)

How do you define *hamburger*? Is a bun necessary or could it be meat between two slices of bread? Is it made from ground beef or sliced meat? Is it in patty form or could it be more like meatballs? Your answers to the questions may determine whom you think created the first hamburger. As with other products, several people claim to have invented it.

The word *hamburger* is thought to come from Hamburg, Germany. It started with their tradition of putting roast pork in a roll. The German sandwiches were different from our American definition of *hamburger*. According to whatscookingamerica.net, a restaurant owner in Tulsa, Oklahoma, served the first hamburger on a bun in 1891.

Charlie Nagreen of Seymour, Wisconsin, created a sandwich he called a hamburger at a county fair, but he used a flattened, fried meatball between two slices of bread. On this day in 1900, Louis Lassen, the original owner of Louis' Lunch in New Haven, Connecticut, put a beef patty between two pieces of bread for the lunch bunch. He added tomatoes, onions, and cheese. Then there are two men at the 1904 St. Louis World's Fair who say they were the inventors of the hamburger. The claim for the patty to be placed on a bun has two contenders—a cook in Wichita, Kansas, who in 1916 flattened a hamburger steak to a thinner patty and created individual buns to take the place of the bread slices. It may not be possible to determine who invented the hamburger as several have contributed to the evolvement of the hamburger that we know and love today.

Response

Describe your favorite hamburger.

Fascinating Factoid: The Hamburger Hall of Fame has the world's largest hamburger, weighing in at 8,266 pounds (3,749.4 kg).

Word Play

Things are not always what their names indicate. Take the hamburger, for example. The name would indicate that it would be made of ham; but it's not—the hamburger is made of beef. Find a word in the Word Box to complete the table below to learn of other things that are not really as the names indicate.

Name	What It Is Not	What It Really Is
1. firefly	fly	_____
2. prairie dog	dog	_____
3. horned toad	toad	_____
4. silkworm	worm	_____
5. peanut	nut	_____
6. shooting star	star	_____
7. banana tree	tree	_____
8. koala bear	bear	_____
9. lead pencil	lead	_____
10. bald eagle	bald	_____

feathered	caterpillar	graphite	beetle
rodent	marsupial	lizard	meteorite
		legume	herb

Activity

- Imagine you are opening a new hamburger restaurant. Give it a name. Plan and illustrate a menu for your restaurant.

July 29
Belle Boyd Was "Busted"!

Other Events This Day
- "Dennis the Menace" comic strip first appeared (1938)
- President Eisenhower signed congressional act that created NASA (1958)

Marie Isabella "Belle" Boyd was one of the most famous and beloved of all Confederate spies during the Civil War. Her nickname, Siren of the South, was most fitting. She was beautiful, captivating, poised, and confident, charming the enemy at every turn. Ms. Boyd was born to a typical Southern family. Her father was a store merchant and tobacco plantation owner. They were a prominent slaveholding family in the Shenandoah Valley of Virginia.

Ms. Boyd's first encounter with the enemy was during an altercation between her mother and a Union soldier at their home. She shot and killed the officer, but was not imprisoned because the officers who investigated said that it was justified. Ms. Boyd did, however, end up in prison three times in her life for spying. One of her arrests happened on this day in 1862, when she was imprisoned in the Old Capitol Prison in Washington DC.

Ms. Boyd began her work as a Confederate spy when she was 17. She used her charms on the Union soldiers to pick up bits and pieces of military information for the Confederates. She was not only clever, but she was also incredibly brave. She was an excellent horseback rider and made heroic crossings through heavy Union gunfire to get secret messages to the Confederate generals.

Ironically, Ms. Boyd fell in love with a Union soldier, Samuel Harding, who was her captor. They got married and he helped her escape to Canada and ultimately England. Upon his return to America, Mr. Harding was imprisoned for treason and died in prison. Ms. Boyd returned as a member of a theatrical tour in 1869.

Response

Belle Boyd was sometimes called "Le Belle Rebelle." How do you think she earned this nickname?

Fascinating Factoid: Belle Boyd was awarded the Southern Cross of Honor for her bravery.

Word Play

See how good you are at "spying" the misspelled words below. Circle each misspelled word. Rewrite those words correctly.

1. wierd
2. vacuum
3. twelfth
4. relevent
5. liesure
6. concensus
7. existance
8. firey
9. gauge
10. calendar
11. collectable
12. column
13. immediate
14. innoculate
15. indispensible
16. millennium

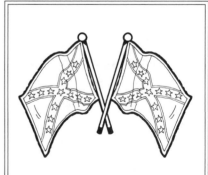

Activity

- Belle Boyd regularly sent written messages to the Confederate generals. She did not use a cipher. Discover the meaning of the word *cipher*. Create a cipher that Ms. Boyd might have used to create a message for General Stonewall Jackson, a famous Confederate general.

July 30
That's a Gr-r-r-r-reat Breakfast!

Other Events This Day

• First Penguin book published, starting paperback revolution (1935)

• President Johnson signed Medicare bill (1965)

• • • • • • • • • • • • • • • • • • •

In 1894, Dr. John Harvey Kellogg and his brother Will Keith (W. K.) Kellogg unintentionally invented a flaked cereal process using wheat. On this day in 1898, W. K. Kellogg developed the first flaked corn cereal, which is called cornflakes.

Dr. Kellogg and Will Keith ran the Battle Creek Sanitarium (a place of healing in western Michigan) for the rich and famous. The hospital stressed healthful eating with no meat, caffeine, alcohol, or tobacco. They were especially interested in a wholesome bread to go with their vegetarian diet. They had been working with cooked wheat, forcing it through rollers, which turned it into long sheets of dough. One day, they were called away during the process and the wheat dried. They decided to see what would happen when they put it through the rollers. Instead of long sheets of bread dough, the wheat flattened into small, thin flakes. When the flakes baked, they tasted crisp and light. They turned out to be a big hit at the hospital. In fact, patients wanted to take some home with them.

Seeing a big potential for the flakes, W. K. quit his job in 1906, bought commercial rights from his brother, and started his own company—the Battle Creek Toasted Corn Flake Company. W. K. came up with several successful advertising ideas and packaging improvements that led to the success of cornflakes. By 1914, cornflakes went international. Today, Kellogg's® produces cereals in more than 15 countries and markets its products in over 160 countries.

Response

Do you think cornflakes would be as popular without clever advertising ideas? Explain.

Fascinating Factoid: W. K. Kellogg established one of the world's largest foundations to fund projects in health, education, agriculture, leadership, and youth.

Word Play

Solve the cryptograms below to find favorite breakfast foods. Hint: The vowels are in place. Another hint: **F = 20**

After you have solved each puzzle, arrange the boxed letters to name a special breakfast food: ___ ___ ___ ___ ___   ___ ___ ___ ___ ___ ___

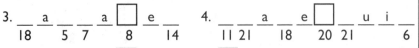

1. _ a _ _ □ e _
    9 20 20 22   14

2. □ o _ _ e e
    7   20 20

3. _ a _ _ a □ e _
    18 5 7   8   14

4. _ _ a _ e □ _ u i _
    11 21 18   20 21   6

5. _ u _ _ i □ _
    15 20 20 5 14

6. □e _ _ _
        11 11 14

7. □o _ e _ e _
       15 22 6

8. _ _ o u _ _ _ _ u _ □
    10   11 23 5   6 14

9. o a _ _ e □a □
        6 15   22

10. □ e _ _ _   _ o a _
    20 21 5 7 23   6 14 6

Activities

• Conduct a survey of your classmates to determine their favorite breakfast cereals. Use collected information to make a "Top 10 Cereals" list for your school.

• Design a new cereal box for Kellogg's Corn Flakes®. You might wish to cover an actual cereal box with paper. Draw and color your design on the paper. Include all the pertinent information found on a cereal box.

July 31
J. K. Rowling's Birthday

Other Events This Day
• First U.S. patent issued for a process of making fertilizer to Samuel Hopkins (1790)
• Mount Godwin-Austen, the world's second-highest peak, climbed for first time (1954)

Harry Potter and the Sorcerer's Stone is one of the most famous fantasy books ever written. The story of the author, J. K. Rowling, sounds a bit like a fantasy as well. Joanne "Jo" Rowling was born in England on this day in 1965. By the age of six, she knew she wanted to be a writer.

Ms. Rowling thinks that as a child, she was a little like three Harry Potter characters: Hermione, Harry, and Ron. During interviews, she has talked about how easily writing comes about the three friends because they are much like parts of her own personality. Some of the names and ideas for the other characters are from her life. She and her sister had playmates named Potter.

Ms. Rowling first thought of Harry Potter when she was riding on a train. She said the idea just popped into her head. When she started writing, Ms. Rowling was an unemployed, single mom. She would write in short time periods at a café while her daughter slept. Ms. Rowling never expected her books to be successful. In fact, she said that she "never really thought much past getting them published." The first 12 publishing houses turned her down. Finally, an editor from Bloomsbury, a small book publisher in the United Kingdom, agreed to publish her first book in 1997.

The following spring, an auction was held in the United States for publishing rights to Ms. Rowling's first book. Scholastic Books won and the title was changed to *Harry Potter and the Sorcerer's Stone*. Within five months, the awards started coming in. The series has since broken many sales records. Ms. Rowling's fortune has been estimated to be over $1 billion! The Queen of England honored Ms. Rowling by making her an Officer of the Order of the British Empire.

Response

Explain in what ways Ms. Rowling's life may be likened to a fantasy.

Fascinating Factoid: J. K. Rowling's full name is Joanne Rowling. Her first editor was afraid that boys might not buy a book written by a female author; therefore, she used two initials—**J** for *Joanne* and **K** for her grandmother's name, *Kathleen*.

Word Play

The Harry Potter books made J. K. Rowling rich and famous. Supply the missing letters in the words below to build a rich Harry Potter vocabulary.

1. m ____ ggl ____ s
2. H ____ g ____ a ____ t ____
3. ____ iza ____ ____
4. g ____ bl ____ t
5. H ____ rm ____ ____ ____ e
6. ____ pe ____ l ____
7. m ____ st ____ ____ y
8. w ____ ____ c ____
9. ca ____ ____ i ____ g
10. adv ____ n ____ u ____ ____

Activities

• Make an outline for your own fantasy story. Illustrate and describe the main characters.

• Create a new character for the next *Harry Potter* book. Describe him or her and explain how the character will fit into the story.

August

Date	Event	Page
1	First Cable Car Ride	37
2	First Lincoln Penny Issued	38
3	This Place Is the Pits!	39
4	Jazzin' It Up	40
5	Little Orphan Annie	41
6	Lucille Ball's Birthday	42
7	A Badge of Military Merit	43
8	President Richard Nixon Resigned	44
9	First Smokey Bear Poster Produced	45
10	Aspirin Formulated	46
11	Spork, Oh How I Adore Thee!	47
12	First Sewing Machine Patented	48
13	Annie Oakley's Birthday	49
14	Is It Over Yet?	50
15	The Wizard of Oz Premiered	51
16	First Issue of Sports Illustrated	52
17	Happy Birthday, Davy Crockett	53
18	First English Child Born in the New World	54
19	First Indianapolis 500 Speedway Race	55
20	Radio Station 8MK Is on the Air	56
21	Hawaii Became a State	57
22	First America's Cup Race	58
23	Blowing in the Wind	59
24	Potato Chips Invented	60
25	Can You Believe?	61
26	Nineteenth Amendment Passed	62
27	Guinness Book of World Records First Published	63
28	First Steam Locomotive Raced a Horse	64
29	Chop Suey Invented	65
30	Thurgood Marshall Became Supreme Court Justice	66
31	First Solar-Powered Vehicle	67

August 1
First Cable Car Ride

Other Events This Day
- First U.S. Census (1790)
- London Bridge opened to traffic (1831)

San Francisco has many tourist attractions, but one of the most famous is its cable car transportation system. On this day in 1873, at five o'clock in the morning, a few nervous men climbed aboard the first cable car for a test ride. The cable car, which looked like the modern day trolley, ultimately defined the city of San Francisco and become one of its icons.

Up until the time of the cable car, San Francisco had streetcars pulled by horses. It is said that the inventor was inspired to build the cable car because he saw a team of horses being whipped by the driver as they slipped on a steep street. This invention allowed a car to be pulled along tracks by a large metal rope (cable) forming a big loop that ran between the rails. The success of the San Francisco line led to the introduction of street railways in many other cities. However, the success of the cable car was short-lived. By the late 1880s, most cable cars were replaced by electrically powered streetcars (also known as trolleys).

The cable car system is still in limited use today as part of the San Francisco transport network (known as Muni), but because of its slow speed, small service area, and high fare, it has become mostly a tourist attraction.

Response

Name an attraction in your city or town and how it contributes to your community. If you do not have such an icon, what kind of attraction might be good for your area?

Fascinating Factoid: San Francisco was the first *and* last city in the world to have cable cars.

Word Play

San Francisco has long been famous for its tourist attractions. See if you can identify the ones given below.

1. _ _ _ _ _ _ _ _   _ _ _ _ _ _ _
   (former home of Al Capone)

2. _ _ _ _ _ _ _ _   _ _ _ _ _ _ _
   (most crooked street in America)

3. _ _ _ _ _ _   _ _ _ _   _ _ _ _ _ _ _
   (second longest single span bridge in the world)

4. _ _ _ _ _ _   _ _ _ _ _ _
   (largest island in the bay)

5. _ _ _ _ _ _ _ _ _ _
   (markets and stores which sell Chinese products)

6. _ _ _ _ _ _ _ _ _ _ _ _ _ ,_   _ _ _ _ _ _
   (attractions, food, shopping, and view of the bay)

7. _ _ _ _ _ _   _ _ _ _ _
   (historic transportation)

Activities

- Design a vehicle of the future that would address a concern of transportation today. Illustrate and label the features to show how it runs.

- The invention of the cable car was inspired by the problem of cruelty to animals. What have you seen that makes you believe we need to change or modify a current form of transportation? Write a short persuasive essay to a person or group that might be interested in your thoughts.

August 2
First Lincoln Penny Issued

• • • • • • • • • • • • • • • •

Other Events This Day
- *Alice's Adventures in Wonderland* published (1865)
- Lt. John Kennedy's PT boat #109 sank (1943)

The penny was first designed by Benjamin Franklin and minted in 1787. Over 300 billion one-cent coins, with 11 different designs, have been put in circulation since that time.

It was over 100 years before the penny had a picture of a U.S. president on its face. The Lincoln cent was first issued on this day in 1909 to commemorate the 100th anniversary of President Lincoln's birth in 1809. Controversy surrounded the issuance of the Lincoln-head penny. Some people felt that Lincoln was too important to be on such a common currency. Others didn't like the idea of abandoning the popular Indian-head cent, which had been in circulation since 1859.

Once the coin was released, another controversy arose over the initials of Victor David Brenner (the sculptor of the new design) being placed on the coin in a conspicuous spot. As a result, six different pennies were circulated in 1909 (two kinds of Indian pennies and four Lincolns).

The first penny was 100 percent copper. During World War II a penny was made of low-grade carbon steel with a zinc coating. The copper saved from the mint production was enough to meet the needs of 2 cruisers, 2 destroyers, 1,243 flying fortresses, 120 field guns, and 120 howitzers—enough for 1.25 million shells for large field guns! Coins produced today are 97.6 percent zinc and 2.4 percent copper. The change in metal saves the government $25 million every year.

Response

What might happen if the current penny design was changed?

Fascinating Factoid: Pennies made prior to 1982 make a distinctive ringing noise when dropped on a hard surface due to their composition, while post-1982 pennies make a dull thud.

Word Play

Money, or some form of the word, is used in many sayings. Complete each money saying.

1. "A penny saved is a penny e __ __ __ __ __." (Ben Franklin)

2. "Remember that __ __ m __ is money." (Ben Franklin)

3. "Lack of money is not an __ b __ __ __ __ __ __ ; lack of an idea is an obstacle!" (Ken Hakuta)

4. "A man is usually more careful about his money than his p__ __ __ c __ __ __ __ s." (Oliver Wendell Holmes)

5. "You can't get rid of poverty by giving __ __ o __ __ __ money." (P. J. O'Rourke)

6. "__ __ n __ __ made through dishonest practices will not last long." (Chinese proverb)

7. "Money talks, but all it ever says is __ __ __ __ b __ __." (Unknown author)

8. "Money is the root of all __ v __ __." (Bible)

9. "A __ __ __ l and his money are soon parted." (Unknown author)

10. "Some people think they are worth a lot of __ __ __ __ y just because they have it." (Fannie Hurst)

Activities

- Make a timeline of the penny. Draw the coin's front and back at the time of each change.

- Investigate/learn magic tricks that make coins disappear. Perform them for your classmates or family.

August 3
This Place Is the Pits!

The La Brea Tar Pits area, at the foot of the Santa Monica Mountains, was first known as a crime scene on this day in 1769. The victim was a woman, aged 18–25, about 4 feet 8 inches (1.4 m) tall. Her date of birth would have been some 9,000–11,000 years ago. Located in Los Angeles, California, the tar pits were described in a diary as "large marshes of a certain substance like pitch ... boiling and bubbling ... [coming] out mixed with an abundance of water."

William Black, a geologist, who visited the area in 1853, discovered the bones of the woman, affectionately known as "La Brea Woman." Her bones are the only human bones recovered among the bones of 1.5 million vertebrate and 2.5 million invertebrate fossils discovered in some of the hardened asphalt. In all, 140 species of plants and more than 420 species of animals have been uncovered. The animals included extinct species, as well as modern-day species: the American lion, saber-toothed cat, mastodons, and mammoths, as well as tapirs, ground sloths, weasels, and ground squirrels. The La Brea Tar Pit discovery is the largest find of bones from the Ice Ages (4,000–10,000 years ago).

Response
Give at least three reasons why you think remains of only one human have been found in the tar pits.

Fascinating Factoid: The description of the tar pits made by an expedition in 1769 was the first indication of oil in western America.

Word Play
Many species of animals have been excavated from the La Brea Tar Pits—some herbivores and some carnivores. Herbivores are plant eating, and carnivores are meat eating. Identify each animal as a herbivore (H) or carnivore (C).

Animals Excavated from the La Brea Tar Pits

_____ 1. dire wolf

_____ 2. American mastodon

_____ 3. African lion

_____ 4. saber-toothed cat

_____ 5. Colombian mammoth

_____ 6. ground sloth

_____ 7. ancient bison

_____ 8. dwarf pronghorn

_____ 9. short-faced bear

_____ 10. western horse

_____ 11. extinct camel

Other Animals

_____ 12. zebra

_____ 13. hyena

_____ 14. cheetah

_____ 15. giraffe

_____ 16. panther

_____ 17. hippopotamus

Activity
• Archaeologists piece together clues from what they know to make theories about what existed or took place in the past. Look through magazines or your social studies textbook for a picture of a place that is unfamiliar to you. Do not read the location's name. Make a list of items in the picture that give clues to different aspects of the environment and predict the location of the geographic area. If possible, compare your prediction to the actual location. Think about which items gave the best clues.

August 4
Jazzin' It Up

• •

Louis Daniel Armstrong, also known as "Satchmo," has been called the greatest jazz musician of the 20th century. His gravelly voice, daring trumpet innovations, and "irrepressible personality" made him unforgettable.

Mr. Armstrong was born to a poor family in New Orleans, Louisiana, on August 4, 1901. His father abandoned the family when he was a baby. Mr. Armstrong was often in trouble during his youth and at age 12, he was sent to reform school where he learned to play the cornet. After he got out of school, Mr. Armstrong worked selling papers, unloading boats, and selling coal from a cart. He didn't own an instrument at the time, but he constantly listened to bands and talked to older musicians every chance he got. Mr. Armstrong made his first recording when he was 22 while playing in a jazz band. He eventually switched from the cornet to the trumpet.

Mr. Armstrong is remembered for his singing and his incredible talent with the trumpet. In 1964, at age 63, his song, "Hello, Dolly," went to #1 on the pop chart which made him the oldest person to accomplish that feat. His recording of, "What a Wonderful World" became popular in the states when it was used in the movie, *Good Morning Vietnam*. During the latter part of his life, Mr. Armstrong toured the world with his band and he became known as "America's Ambassador." Poor health put a halt to his travels. He was hospitalized several times, but he continued playing and recording. Mr. Armstrong died in his sleep in 1971.

Response
What personal qualities or experiences do you think helped Mr. Armstrong achieve such success?

Fascinating Factoid: Louis Armstrong was extremely generous. It was said that he gave away almost as much money as he kept for himself. He also set up a nonprofit foundation for educating disadvantaged children in music.

Word Play
Match each notable African American with his or her accomplishment or contribution.

_____ 1. Jackie Robinson
_____ 2. Charles Drew
_____ 3. Rosa Parks
_____ 4. Martin Luther King Jr.
_____ 5. Thurgood Marshall
_____ 6. George Washington Carver
_____ 7. Elijah McCoy
_____ 8. Frederick Douglas
_____ 9. Matthew Henson
_____ 10. Mary Browser
_____ 11. Harriet Tubman

a. created the idea of blood banks
b. first African-American to play major league baseball
c. explorer and colleague of Robert Peary and in the first group to visit the North Pole
d. spy for the Union during the Civil War
e. associated with the Montgomery Bus Boycott
f. first African-American appointed to Supreme Court
g. Underground Railroad conductor
h. inventor who inspired the saying, "The Real McCoy"
i. scientist who revolutionized agriculture in the South
j. abolitionist, orator, and writer
k. leader of the U.S. Civil Rights Movement

Activities

• Louis Armstrong's music is available on several Web sites. Listen to "It's a Wonderful World." Write an additional stanza for the song.

• What is your favorite song? Describe a computer game, commercial, or TV series that could be created, based on that song.

August 5
Little Orphan Annie

Other Events This Day

- Henry Sullivan became first American to swim English Channel (1923)
- *Mariner 7* flies past Mars (1969)

Is the comic strip your favorite section of the newspaper? If so, you are not alone. Comics are one of the most read sections of the paper. Some comics are serious and thought-provoking, while others are funny or entertaining.

Today celebrates the first appearance of a famous comic strip called "Little Orphan Annie." Annie was a 12-year-old girl with a mop of curly red hair and empty circles for eyes. Although she was an orphan, she had an adoptive parent called Daddy Warbucks, who was caring and introduced her to a life of comfort. The comic strip storyline was one of Annie being separated from Daddy Warbucks time and again, having to endure hardship or peril—but somehow getting through using willpower, resourcefulness, hard work, or by the kindness of strangers. Annie typified the model American. She was clever, generous, self-sufficient, confident, and capable. In March 1943, *Coronet* magazine pronounced Annie "more of a heroine than Joan of Arc and more tragic and appealing than Helen of Troy."

The comic strip ran successfully for 44 years. It led to a popular Broadway musical and movie entitled *Annie*. The musical ran for more than 2,000 performances. In 1995, Annie was honored by having her likeness on a U.S. postage stamp.

Response

What would you add to Annie's character that would make her a modern American girl?

Fascinating Factoid: Little Orphan Annie was not an original name. It was the title of a poem written by James Whitcomb Riley.

Word Play

Little Orphan Annie was a character who frequently used the catchphrase, "Leapin' lizards!" Match each catchphrase with the character that frequently used it.

_____ 1. "Beam me up, Scotty!"
_____ 2. "Beep beep"
_____ 3. "Only you can prevent forest fires!"
_____ 4. "Good grief!"
_____ 5. "Hi ho, Silver, away!"
_____ 6. "Ho, ho, ho"
_____ 7. "I tawt I taw a putty tat"
_____ 8. "I'm smaaarter than the average bear!"
_____ 9. "Oh, bother!"
_____ 10. "Take a bite out of crime"
_____ 11. "That's all I can stands, I can't stands no more!"
_____ 12. "What's up, Doc?"
_____ 13. "Yabba-dabba-doo!"

a. Roadrunner
b. Fred Flintstone
c. Captain Kirk
d. Bugs Bunny
e. Popeye
f. Smokey Bear
g. McGruff
h. Charlie Brown
i. Winnie the Pooh
j. Lone Ranger
k. Tweety Bird
l. Yogi Bear
m. Santa Claus

Activities

- Find a copy of the poem, "Little Orphan Annie." Practice reading it to yourself and then, with your teacher's permission, read it to the class or to a classmate.

- Look at the comic section of the newspaper. What current comic would be most like "Little Orphan Annie"? Compare and contrast the two.

August 6
Lucille Ball's Birthday

Other Events This Day

• Alfred Lord Tennyson's birthday (1697)
• Gertrude Ederle became first U.S. woman to swim across the English Channel (1926)

Lucille Ball, born on this day in 1911, was a TV star during the 1950s. She is best known as the zany, accident-prone, lovable housewife in the *I Love Lucy Show*. That role jettisoned her into a career that gained her the titles "America's Favorite Redhead" and the "Queen of Comedy."

Ms. Ball has two stars on the Hollywood Walk of Fame—one for motion pictures and the other for TV. She was inducted into the National Women's Hall of Fame in 2002. She was nominated for a Golden Globe Award five times. *TV Guide* chose Lucille Ball as the greatest TV star of all time. She was the first woman inducted into the Television Hall of Fame. Interestingly, when Lucy was young (before her career in TV and movies) she enrolled in a school for dramatic arts. Her coach sent her home, telling her that she had no future as a performer.

Pages of trivia have been written about Lucille Ball. For example, she was fired from an ice cream parlor because she kept forgetting to put the bananas in the banana splits. Suffering from rheumatoid arthritis during her modeling career, she had to spend two years learning how to walk again. She only liked to see real birds, so she banned all pictures of birds from her house and any hotel room in which she stayed.

Ms. Ball was the first woman to be head of a production company. Her company pioneered the three-camera setup, the standard way of filming comedy series. Her company also produced the original series of *Star Trek*.

Response

How would you react if you were told (like Lucille Ball) that you had no future in an acting career and that was your dream? Explain.

Fascinating Factoid: Her husband, Desi Arnaz, had to give Lucy a ring from a drugstore because all the jewelry stores were closed. She continued to wear it for the rest of their marriage.

Word Play

A *hyperbole* is a figure of speech, which is an exaggeration that is not to be taken seriously, such as "I nearly died laughing." Lucille Ball was a comedienne who often used this type of figure of speech. Use a word from the Word Box to complete each hyperbole.

1. My teacher uses so much _____, that by the time she gets it on, it's already time to take it off!

2. My dog is so _____, fleas won't even live on him.

3. He is so _____, his head touches the ceiling.

4. My cat is as _____ as a barn.

5. I'm so _____, I could eat a horse!

6. I'm so _____, I'll be in bed a week!

Word Box

big	tall	makeup
ugly	hungry	tired

Activity

• Write your own comedy routine similar to the Word Play. You may use the starters below or think of your own.

He sleeps so much . . . .

He blows his nose so loud . . . .

She is so smart . . . .

August 7
A Badge of Military Merit

Other Events This Day
- U.S. War Department established (1789)
- *Kon-Tiki,* a raft which carried Thor Heyerdahl and five companions more than 4,000 miles, crashed into a reef in the Pacific (1947)

On this day in 1782, General George Washington wrote in his orders that an award/decoration be established to recognize anyone who "singularly performed deeds of valor or unusual merit." This award became the Badge of Military Merit. Nearly a year later, General Washington presented the badge to two soldiers from Connecticut. A third badge was awarded a year later.

After the Revolutionary War, the medal fell into disuse. General Douglas MacArthur reinstated it in 1932 to coincide with Washington's 200th birthday. The decoration was redesigned and given a new name—the Purple Heart. It was issued retroactively to those qualifying soldiers who served in World War I. The Purple Heart medal is the most expensive decoration to produce. The medal is bronze with an enamel purple heart on the front, surrounded by a gold border. It bears the profile of George Washington on its face. It is suspended from a purple ribbon with white edges. This medal is awarded to anyone wounded or killed as a result of injuries and wounds received while serving in any capacity with one of the U.S. armed forces.

The Purple Heart is different from other military decorations. The candidate is not recommended for the award. It is automatically received if a person meets the criteria. Five people share the distinction of having the most Purple Hearts—each having eight. The Purple Heart signifies sacrifice. Whenever you see it, remember that it represents blood that was shed—by wound or death—in defense of our freedom.

Response

What are some ways, besides the Purple Heart, our country recognizes its veterans?

Fascinating Factoid: Two of the original three awards presented by George Washington are still on display.

Word Play

Unscramble the name of each military medal.

1. DELAM FO OHRON __ __ __ __ __   __ __   __ __ __ __ __

   This is the highest honor the United States can bestow on members of the Armed Forces. It is awarded for "Conspicuous Gallantry and Intrepidity at the Risk of Life, Above and Beyond the Call of Duty, in Action Involving Actual Conflict with an Opposing Armed Force."

2. HITIENDSUGISD SRCOS

   __ __ __ __ __ __ __ __ __ __ __ __ __   __ __ __ __ __

   This medal is awarded for "Extraordinary Heroism in Connection with Military Operations Against an Opposing Armed Force."

3. EHT VELIRS RTAS __ __ __   __ __ __ __ __ __   __ __ __ __

   Awarded for "Gallantry in Action Against an Opposing Armed Force."

4. DGDEIISTSNUIH LNIYFG SOSRC

   __ __ __ __ __ __ __ __ __ __ __ __ __   __ __ __ __ __ __

   __ __ __ __ __

   Awarded for "Heroism or Extraordinary Achievement while Participating in Aerial Flight."

Activities

- If you know of a person who has received an award for military service, interview him or her and share the soldier's story with your class.

- Write a diary entry or a letter to your parents, pretending you have been awarded the Purple Heart (e.g., What happened that made you eligible? Where/how will you keep it? How do you feel about receiving such a prestigious award?).

August 8
President Richard Nixon Resigned

Other Events This Day
- Thomas Edison patented mimeograph (1876)
- Daughters of the American Revolution organized (1890)

When Richard Nixon announced he was stepping down as U.S. president on this date in 1974, he was the first and only president in American history to do so. The reason for his resignation was the eroding political support of his party, including some of the most loyal members. His family had urged him to stay in office and fight the charges against him.

President Nixon had been accused of "high crimes and misdemeanors." The charges came from a 1972 break-in at the offices of the Democratic National Committee in the building complex known as Watergate. The break-in was traced to President Nixon's committee to re-elect him as president. There were also tape recordings that showed the president trying to use the CIA to manipulate the investigation. President Nixon never admitted to any criminal wrongdoing, although he did acknowledge that some of his judgments were wrong. He said that "by taking this action, I hope that I will have hastened the start of the process of healing which is so desperately needed in America . . . I must put the interest of America first."

President Nixon still had two and a half years left in his term. Vice President Gerald Ford replaced him. After making his resignation speech, Richard Nixon climbed into the presidential helicopter and began the trip to his home in California. He stayed relatively secluded for some time but eventually became a visitor in Washington DC, even visiting President Clinton once in the Oval Office. President Nixon died in April 1994.

Response

How do you think President Nixon felt as he left his office and the White House? Explain.

Fascinating Factoid: As President Nixon, head bowed, walked slowly up the steps to the Executive Office before the speech, the crowd outside the gates waved U.S. flags and sang "America."

Word Play

Richard Milhous Nixon was the first (and only) U.S. president to resign from that office. There are many other notable firsts among U.S. presidents. Identify each president shown below.

1. _ _ _ _ _ _ _   _ _ _ _ _ _ _ _ _
   (first president to be inaugurated in Washington DC)

2. _ _ _ _ _ _   _ _ _ _ _ _ _ _   _ _ _ _ _ _ _ _
   (first president to wear contact lenses)

3. _ _ _ _   _ _ _ _ _
   (first president to live in the White House)

4. _ _ _ _ _ _ _   _ _ _ _ _ _ _ _
   (first president to be assassinated)

5. _ _ _ _ _   _ _ _ _ _ _ _ _ _
   (first unmarried man to be elected president)

6. _ _ _ _   _.   _ _ _ _ _ _ _ _
   (first Catholic president)

7. _ _ _ _ _   _ _ _ _ _ _ _
   (first president to be born in a hospital)

8. _ _ _ _   _ _ _ _ _ _ _
   (first president to be a Rhodes Scholar)

9. _ _ _ _ _ _ _ _   _ _ _ _ _ _ _ _ _
   (first president to receive a Nobel Peace Prize)

Activities

- Research and compile a list of other notable and/or interesting presidential firsts.

- Nixon wanted his presidency to be known for success in foreign affairs. He wanted to build peace among the United States and other nations and leave the world a safer place than when he took office. What would be the legacy you would choose to leave if you were to become president? Give examples of how you would accomplish your objectives.

First Smokey Bear Poster Produced

● ● ● ● ● ● ● ● ● ● ● ● ● ● ●

The first poster of Smokey Bear was produced on August 9, 1944. Smokey Bear became so popular that he was given his own zip code because he received so much mail.

To understand how Smokey Bear came about, we must go back to World War II. The spring following the bombing of Pearl Harbor, a Japanese submarine surfaced off the coast of Southern California and fired shells near Santa Barbara and the Los Padres National Forest. Luckily, the shells did not start a forest fire, but they made an impact. Wood from forests was needed for the war effort. Also, with so many firefighters in the armed forces, communities had to deal with forest fires the best they could. With this is mind, the Forest Service and the Wartime Advertising Counsel worked together to organize a nationwide forest fire prevention campaign.

First, there were posters and slogans with catchy phrases. The introduction of a bear came in 1944. They chose the name Smokey after "Smokey" Joe Martin, New York City Assistant Fire Chief. In 1950, there was a terrible forest fire in New Mexico and twenty-four fire fighters barely escaped. When the smoke cleared, they saw a little bear cub, burned and afraid, clinging onto a scorched tree. The cub was nicknamed "Hotfoot Teddy." The little bear gained nationwide attention and it was soon renamed Smokey, after the fire prevention symbol. Smokey eventually went to live at the National Zoo in Washington DC. He became the most popular exhibit at the zoo. The character of Smokey and his famous line, "Remember—only you can prevent forest fires," lives on!

Response

Why do you think Smokey was such a good choice for the campaign symbol? (Give several reasons and explain.)

Fascinating Factoid: Smokey was the first individual animal to be honored on a postage stamp. The stamp, issued in 1984, commemorated his 40th birthday.

Word Play

Smokey Bear has been a familiar character to people for over 50 years. Identify each of the following bears that are also well known.

1. _ _ _ _ _ _ _ _ _ _ _
   They had a surprise visitor.

2. _ _ _ _ _ _ _ _ _ _ _ _ _
   His friends were a tiger, a pig, and a donkey.

3. _ _ _ _ _
   He lived in a jungle.

4. _ _ _ _ _ _ _ _ _ _ _ _ _ _ _ _ _
   These bears are main characters in many books.

5. _ _ _ _ _ _ _ _ _
   These cuddly bears have pictures on their tummies.

6. _ _ _ _ _ _ _ _ _ _
   He coveted other people's picnic baskets.

7. _ _ _ _ _
   These are mascots for football and baseball teams in Chicago.

8. _ _ _ _ _ _ _ _ _ _
   These bears are good to eat!

Activities

- Brainstorm and list animals that are associated with advertisements or campaigns. Create your own zany animal and product associations (e.g., cat with milk on its lips for the "Got milk?" campaign).

- Research a fire safety issue (e.g., campfire safety, fire safety at home or school). Write a rap or catchy tune about fire safety for kids.

August 10
Aspirin Formulated

• • • • • • • • • • • • • • • • • •

Other Events This Day
• Missouri became the 24th U.S. state (1821)
• The Smithsonian Institute was established in Washington DC from funds left by British scientist James Smithson (1846)

It is estimated that one *trillion* _____ have been consumed worldwide in the last 100 years. *First clue:* Its history dates back to around 400 BCE. *Next clue:* Its basic ingredient comes from willow bark. *Final Clue:* It is used to relieve pain, reduce fevers, fight inflammation, and fight against heart disease and even some cancers.

If you said *aspirin*, you are right! The history of this drug goes back to Hippocrates—considered the father of modern medicine—who lived sometime between 460 and 377 BCE. Hippocrates left records of treatments for headaches, pains, and fevers, which included the use of powder made from the leaves and bark of willow trees. By 1829, scientists had figured out the powder was an ingredient called *salicin*. The problem with salicin was that it upset the stomach, so an ingredient was needed to "buffer" the salicin. The first person to create a product that would work, but not be so irritating to the stomach, was Charles Gerhardt.

Over 40 years later, Felix Hoffman stumbled across Mr. Gerhardt's work in his desperate search to relieve his father's arthritis pain. Mr. Hoffman conducted further experiments, and, on this day in 1897, he produced a pain reliever that didn't upset the stomach! Bayer marketed the drug, which was named Aspirin. The *A* came from acetyl chloride, the *spir* in spiraea ulmaria (the plant the salicylic acid comes from), and the *in* was a familiar ending for medicines. In 1900, Bayer introduced water-soluble tablets—the first ever medication to be sold in this form. Today, it is the most popular drug in the world.

Response
How do you think the old saying, "Take two aspirin and call me in the morning" came about?

> **Fascinating Factoid:** Mr. Hoffmann did not receive a patent or subsequent royalties for his discovery because his medicine was not original enough.

Word Play
Aspirin is a much-used treatment for all sorts of pains. What did people do before aspirin? A lot of people used home remedies. Unscramble each ailment suggested by the given remedy.

1. RESO TOTRAH __ O R __   __ __ __ __ O A __
   (a dirty sock worn around your neck at nighttime)

2. YBAB ETHNTIGE __ A __ __   __ E E __ __ I __ G
   (molasses)

3. OTHOCHAET __ O O __ __ A __ __ E
   (tooth of a dead horse rubbed over your jaw)

4. ADEHCHAE __ E A __ A __ __ E
   (buckwheat cakes on the forehead)

5. MOTCHASEHCA __ __ O __ A __ __ A __ __ E
   (root of rhubarb on a string worn around your neck)

6. OLDC __ O __ __
   (big red onion tied to the bedpost)

7. HSRMIEUTAM __ __ __ E U __ A __ I __ __
   (buckeye carried in the pocket)

Activities
• Research folk remedies such as those mentioned in the Word Play. Also locate a modern-day treatment for the ailment. Make a chart showing the folk remedy and the modern medicine remedy.

• Write you own remedy for the cure for the common cold or some other common childhood ailment.

August 11
Spork, Oh How I Adore Thee!

Other Events This Day

• First successful U.S. silver mine (Virginia City, Nevada) (1860)
• First federal prisoners arrive at Alcatraz (1934)

No other plastic utensil has come on the scene finding such devotion as the spork. The *spork* is an everything-in-one eating utensil (a combination of a fork and spoon). But it is not your ordinary, taken-for-granted utensil. The spork is adored and eulogized by followers everywhere.

Think about it. When you eat a meal with the standard metal knives, spoons, and forks, you may get utensil choices, but you also get to wash a lot more dishes! Think of the millions of dollars of silverware that those fast-food restaurants would have to purchase for their drive-through window service!

Some sources say that the spork was patented on this day in 1970, while other sources say that the trademark application for the spork was published on this day. Regardless of what took place on this day—whether it was the patent or the trademark—it was certainly a big day for sporks and spork lovers.

Sporks have not only had a valuable place in the world as an eating utensil, but they have also become popular playthings as well. One can push the flexible spork inside-out creating a "foon." Objects can be placed in the depression and then fired by pressing the spork back to its original shape. Foons offer a great new game for target practice. Believe it or not, the spork has spawned fan clubs. Several Web sites tell of spork lovers who illustrate their devotion by writing poems, songs, and rituals for the utensil.

Response

Explain why you think the spork has gained such popularity.

Fascinating Factoid: In Canada you can get a spam-like food called *Spork*. There are several bands with the name *Spork*. One of them uses sporks as their mascot and logo.

Word Play

A *spork* is a combination of a spoon and fork. Use two words from the Word Box to define each kitchen combination.

1. glup _____ & _____
2. placer _____ & _____
3. bower _____ & _____
4. ovenator _____ & _____
5. bloaster _____ & _____
6. knirk _____ & _____
7. skot _____ & _____
8. tontula _____ & _____
9. ketter _____ & _____
10. splade _____ & _____

Word Box

cup	blender	pot	saucer	plate
tongs	spatula	fork	oven	blade
kettle	spoon	toaster	knife	refrigerator
pitcher	skillet	glass	platter	bowl

Activities

• Create spork art. Design a unique sculpture (or an illustration for a sculpture) that includes sporks.

• Turn sporks into puppets. Write a play for your spork characters. Give your characters special names such as Spunky, Spavinaw, etc.

August 12
First Sewing Machine Patented

• • • • • • • • • • • • • • • • • • • •

Other Events This Day
- Katherine Lee Bates' (author of "America the Beautiful") birthday (1859)
- Thomas Edison invents the Edisonphone (a sound recording device) (1877)

Unless your school requires uniforms, you know your back-to-school outfit will make a statement about your personality and style. Thank Isaac Singer for the vast array of clothing now available, since he was the one who received the patent for the sewing machine on this day in 1851. He developed mass production capabilities and without them, we might have only one or two homemade outfits to wear.

Sewing can be traced back 20,000 years. The first sewing needles were made of bone or animal horns. The first thread was made of animal sinew. Iron needles were invented in the 14th century CE, and eyed needles were invented in the 15th century CE.

Who truly invented the sewing machine is still being argued. The idea of the sewing machine goes back to 1755 in London when Charles Weisenthal took out a patent for a needle to be used for mechanical sewing. However, there is no record of a machine to go with it. Then in 1830, Bartholomew Thimonnier invented a machine that within 10 years of the patent had him running a factory with 80 machines sewing uniforms for the French army. Unfortunately, a group of tailors, afraid they would soon be put out of work by Thimonnier's success, stormed the factory and destroyed every machine.

Isaac Singer's design was so close to that of a machine invented by Elias Howe that Mr. Howe was given rights to some of Mr. Singer's profits. Mr. Howe saw his income go from $300 to $200,000 a year. Both men died millionaires.

Response
Why can it be said that the sewing machine is one of the most important machines ever invented?

Fascinating Factoid: Isaac Singer's early passion was the theater. He did not get the acting parts or success he hoped for on the stage so he formed his own touring group. At the end of 14 years, claiming great success as a stage actor but having gone bankrupt in theater, he called it quits.

Word Play

Buying or wearing clothing usually involves coordinating at least three items of clothing: a shirt or blouse, pants or skirt, and shoes. Practice your coordinating skills by finding one word that the three given words have in common—a word that when combined with each of the three given words will form compound words.

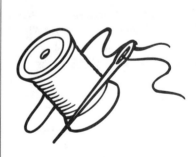

Word Trios	Common Word	Compound Words
1. drop stand off	_____	_____ _____ _____
2. man back craft	_____	_____ _____ _____
3. child read water	_____	_____ _____ _____
4. corn sweet winner	_____	_____ _____ _____
5. watch back short	_____	_____ _____ _____

Activities
- Design the next clothing fashion trend for students. Sketch several ideas, then let your classmates vote on which they like best.
- Brainstorm and list uses for a needle and thread. Be as creative as possible.

August 13
Annie Oakley's Birthday

Other Events This Day
- William Gray patented coin-operated telephone (1889)
- Alfred Hitchcock's birthday (1899)

Phoebe Ann Oakley Mozee was born August 13, 1860, in Drake County, Ohio. Her seven brothers and sisters called her Annie, but Chief Sitting Bull called her "Little Sure Shot" when she met him later in her life. Annie's father died when she was very young, and she had to spend time at the county poor farm because her mother couldn't provide for her family.

After returning to the family, Annie honed her shooting skills while hunting game to feed the family and to sell to others. She became a master marksman with a pistol, rifle, and shotgun. When she was 16, she went to Cincinnati to compete in a shooting contest with Frank Butler, a noted marksman. Annie not only won the contest, but she won his heart. They were later married and performed a traveling shooting act before they joined Wild Bill's Wild West Show in 1885. She was billed as Annie Oakley and became the star of the show. She was a legend in her own time, but she always had time to help orphans and widows.

Ms. Oakley was injured in a train wreck in 1901 and she was partially paralyzed for a while. After that, she toured less, but her shooting skills remained sharp. After 50 years of marriage, she and her husband both died of natural causes in 1926. Annie, however, lives on through movies, TV, books, and museums. The Broadway musical, *Annie Get Your Gun,* was a tribute to Annie Oakley, sharpshooter extraordinaire.

Response

Why do you think Annie liked to help orphans and widows?

Fascinating Factoid: Annie often gave out free passes to her shows. She did it so frequently that in the theater business, a free ticket is known as an "Annie Oakley."

Word Play

Find at least 10 story words that you can make into compound words by adding another word at the end of the story word.

Example: farmland

_____

_____

_____

_____

_____

_____

_____

_____

Activity

- Brainstorm, list, and describe shooting events that the public might pay to see. Give your show a name and make an advertising poster.

August 14

Is It Over Yet?

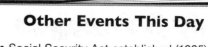

On this day in 1945, the Japanese surrendered to the Allied Forces, ending World War II. The day was proclaimed Victory over Japan (VJ) Day. Celebrations were held around the world.

Other Events This Day

- Social Security Act established (1935)
- Wiffle® Ball invented (1953)

Actually, one of three days—August 14, August 15, or September 2 could be considered VJ Day. August 14 was the day that Japan announced its surrender. Germany had already surrendered; the United States had dropped two atomic bombs on Japan, and there was a threat that the Soviet Union would invade Japan from the north. Japan saw its hope of winning the war falling rapidly. The Imperial Council met on the evening of August 9 to discuss the situation. When a vote was taken whether to stop the war, there was a tie vote: three to three. Emperor Hirohito cast the deciding vote, and he voted to end the war. Many of the Japanese citizens did not like the decision, and an unsuccessful attempt was made to take over the government and keep fighting.

The cease-fire order came on August 15. The Allied Forces (United States, England, France, Soviet Union, and other smaller nations) didn't trust the Japanese, so they kept a close watch on their activities. Luckily, time passed uneventfully. September 2 was the day that Japan signed the official document of surrender. The 23-minute ceremony took place aboard the USS *Missouri,* harbored in Tokyo Bay. It was broadcast around the world. Japanese General Yishijiro presented his sword to U.S. General Douglas MacArthur.

President Truman declared September 2 as the official VJ Day; however, it is usually observed on August 14, the day Japan announced its surrender.

Response

What might Emperor Hirohito been thinking when it was his responsibility to break the tie vote?

Fascinating Factoid: For years after the war ended, Japanese soldiers were discovered on islands throughout the Pacific region. In 1974 one soldier was discovered—28 years after the surrender. He refused to believe the war was over, and he would not surrender. His family had to convince him to come out of the jungle.

Word Play

Use the clues to decode the following cryptogram.

11 5   21 4 6   16 4 17   9 10 15   15 20 21   18 8

4   16 4 12   9 10 4 9   17 9 4 12 9 15 21

16 10 15 20   5 4 7 4 20   14 18(o) 1 14 15 21

7 15 4 12 26   10(h) 4 12 14 18 12   18 20

21 15 2 15 1 14 15 12   7, 1941.

Bonus Clues: E = 15 and T = 9

Activity

- Make a ladder mobile showing the major events of World War II in the proper sequence (e.g., Pearl Harbor, D Day, VE Day, VJ Day). Incorporate red, white, and blue into the project. (A ladder mobile is made of note cards or strips of cardboard strung one below the other.)

August 15
The Wizard of Oz Premiered

· · · · · · · · · · · · · · · · · · ·

The script for *The Wonderful Wizard of Oz* movie began in February 1938 at MGM Studios. The movie finally premiered on August 15, 1939, starring Judy Garland at the peak of her career.

The movie was based on the book, *The Wizard of Oz*, written by L. Frank Baum and published in 1900. The book is about a lonely, sad, Kansas farm girl, Dorothy, who dreams of a better place for her dog, Toto, and herself. She plans to run away, but during a Kansas cyclone, she is struck on the head and transported to a land beyond the rainbow. There she meets magical characters from her life who are transformed within her dream. Dorothy and Toto travel down a yellow brick road to the Land of Oz. With the defeat of the Wicked Witch of the West, the Wizard of Oz rewards Dorothy and her friends with their hearts' desire. So, Dorothy returns home.

Silent movies, stage plays, musicals, TV shows, ice-skating productions, and cartoons have been based on the book. It is movie magic at its best. Its filming technique of sepia color for the scenes in Kansas and beautiful Technicolor® in the Land of Oz were far ahead of its time.

Response
How much time elapsed between the beginning of the script and the premiere of this movie?

Fascinating Factoid: The budget for *The Wizard of Oz* movie was $3 million.

Word Play
A *cyclone* is a severe weather event. Find the names of other weather events by unscrambling each word. Then match the weather event to its definition.

_____ 1. NROAODT   a. small, weak tornado

_____ 2. IRACRUHNE   b. system that moves north along the Atlantic Coast

_____ 3. SNAUTMI   c. hurricane in western Pacific Ocean

_____ 4. ZILZRDBA   d. unusually large ocean wave

_____ 5. DANOTSUG   e. intense winter storm with blowing snow

_____ 6. OPHONYT   f. funnel cloud that touches ground

_____ 7. EATSRE'ORN   g. storm with swirling 150 mph wind

Activity
• Dorothy said, "There's no place like home." Write a descriptive paragraph about your home and why it is special to you. Use at least 15 different adjectives to describe it. Underline each adjective.

August 16
First Issue of
Sports Illustrated
• • • • • • • • • • • • • • • • •

The first issue of *Sports Illustrated* was dated August 16, 1954. It contained a 27-card insert, featuring many great baseball players such as Ted Williams, Willie Mays, and Jackie Robinson.

Each year, the magazine presents an annual award for Sportsman of the Year that recognizes a notable person in the world of sports.

Major League Baseball player Eddie Mathews was on the first cover. About a week later, he suffered a hand injury that forced him to miss several games. That was the beginning of the *Sports Illustrated* "cover jinx." Jill Kinmont was on the cover of the January 31, 1955, issue. A week later, she struck a tree while skiing and was paralyzed. On May 26, 1958, Pat O'Conner, a race car driver, was featured. Later he was killed in a crash in the Indy 500. The February 24, 1961, cover pictured figure-skater Laurence Owen. Two days later, she and the rest of the figure skating team perished in a plane crash. The Texas Longhorn football team was enjoying a 30-game winning streak when they made the cover on December 14, 1970. The next game, they fumbled nine times and lost to Notre Dame in the Cotton Bowl.

In spite of the jinx, *Sports Illustrated* has little trouble finding people or teams to feature on its cover.

Response

Why might a sports figure hesitate to accept an offer to be on the cover of *Sports Illustrated*?

Fascinating Factoid: About 23 million adults read *Sports Illustrated* each week.

Word Play

Unscramble the name of each sport. Then match the sport to the *Sports Illustrated*'s Sportsman of the Year player.

_____ 1. LOFG   a. Lance Armstrong

_____ 2. LALBSTEKAB   b. Chris Everett

_____ 3. SINNET   c. Tiger Woods

_____ 4. YEKCOH   d. Joe Montana

_____ 5. ABSELBLA   e. Sammy Sosa

_____ 6. NILCGYC   f. Michael Jordan

_____ 7. CARTK & DLFIE   g. Mary Decker

_____ 8. OFTOLABL   h. Wayne Gretsky

_____ 9. NIGXOB   i. Muhammed Ali

Activity

• Every year, *Sports Illustrated* presents an award for Sportsman of the Year. Write a letter to them, nominating someone you think should have this recognition. Your person can be a well-known sports figure or someone you know (someone in your family, on your favorite team, your own team, or classmate). Remember to be persuasive. The more good reasons you give, the better your nominee looks to the judges who select the Sportsman of the Year.

August 17

Happy Birthday, Davy Crockett

● ● ● ● ● ● ● ● ● ● ● ● ● ● ● ● ● ●

Other Events This Day

• Robert Fulton's steamboat began first trip up Hudson River (1807)
• Prospectors found gold in Alaska (1896)

It's hard to separate what is real about David Crockett and what is legendary. The real David Crockett was born on August 17, 1786, beside the banks of the Nolichucky River in Tennessee. He was a frontiersman, hunter, explorer, militiaman, and politician. He served in political office in his state as well as in the U.S. Congress. Davy Crockett was the model for the hero in a play, *The Lion of the West*. But it was probably a series of comic almanacs published under his name that helped create the outrageous tall tales about the adventures of Davy Crockett. After becoming disillusioned with politics, Mr. Crockett went to Texas to explore but ended up joining forces with Col. Travis to help defend the Alamo. It was there that Mr. Crockett was killed alongside other brave men.

The legendary Davy Crockett was born on a mountaintop in Tennessee. He killed a bear when he was only three. He defeated many enemies single-handedly. He fixed up the government, he took over Washington DC, and even patched the crack in the Liberty Bell. He wore buckskins and a coonskin cap.

A movie about Mr. Crockett's life was made in 1955. *The Ballad of Davy Crockett* was the number one song for several weeks. Young boys everywhere were seen wearing coonskin caps.

Response

Compare the real and the legendary Davy Crockett.

Fascinating Factoid: Davy Crockett didn't learn to read until he was nearly 18 years old.

Word Play

Find each word in the Word Box in the puzzle.

```
S H A R P S H O O T E R
I O L A D O U P R E T I
D N A E R T C Y O X A F
A D M I L I T I A A C L
V V O A L A M O E S A E
I C O L O N E I R T W V
D C O O N S K I N C A P
C O F R O N T I E R T D
R N L M K C D A R D E E
O G G H V P E E T T N Z
C R F Q A O I L K J N X
K E H U N T E R K E E A
E S H O N N I N I V S N
T S M O N I A T U A S N
T H R U H A M J B R E A
H F S G U T R O E B E A
E W S D G N K N A B U T
A R G U I U H E R O N N
R E T Y O O D F V B V A
D J K L P M F S A X C S
```

Word Box

CONGRESS
MILITIA
SHARPSHOOTER
TENNESSEE
MOUNTAINTOP
TEXAS
ALAMO
HUNTER
FRONTIER
BEAR
COONSKIN CAP
RIFLE
BRAVE
DAVID CROCKETT
SANTA ANNA

Activity

• David Crockett ran for political office several times during his lifetime. In most campaigns, politicians like to use slogans or jingles to advertise their candidacy. Write a catchy jingle or slogan that David Crockett might have used in one of his campaigns.

August 18
First English Child Born in the New World

• • • • • • • • • • • • • • • • • •

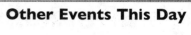

Virginia Dare was the first baby born to English parents in the new world. She was born on August 18, 1587, just 15 days after the Colonists arrived on Roanoke Island. Her parents were Eleanor and Ananias Dare, the daughter and son-in-law of Governor John White. When Virginia was only nine days old, Governor White had to return to England for supplies. He was worried about leaving his family and friends behind, but he knew they needed more supplies to survive until they could grow their own crops.

They worked out a secret code before he left. If the Colonists had to flee the fort, they were to carve their new location on a tree or post. If they had to leave because of an attack, they were to carve a distress signal in the form of a Maltese cross over the letters or name.

Because England was at war with Spain, Governor White could not return immediately. He eventually returned to find an abandoned fort. The only clue to be found was the word *Croatoan*, the Native American name for *Hatteras*, carved on a tree. The Colonists were never found. To this day, it is not known whether they went elsewhere or whether natives killed them.

Response
What do you think happened to Virginia Dare?

Fascinating Factoid: It took Governor White three years to return from England with supplies.

Word Play
Make a new, bigger word than the one above it, by following the directions.

A

A __   add a letter (little word used before words beginning with a, e, i, o, u)

__ __ __   add a letter (Ananias _____ Eleanor)

__ __ __ __   add a letter (_____, ahoy!)

__ __ __ __ __   substitute a letter, add letter (_____ the crops.)

__ __ __ __ __ __   substitute 2 letters, add a letter (Their new home was an _____ .)

Activity
• The first English baby born in the new world, Virginia Dare, was born on Roanoke Island. Where is Roanoke Island? Locate it on a map and write directions from your hometown using cardinal directions (North, South, East, West). Through which states must you pass? List the latitude and longitude for your home and for Roanoke Island.

August 19

First Indianapolis 500 Speedway Race

Other Events This Day

- Orville Wright born (1871)

- 42nd U.S. president Bill Clinton's birthday (1946)

Carl Fisher believed that auto research and development were hampered because the roads did not allow the cars to go fast enough. In 1906, he proposed a track of long straight-aways and sweeping turns to use for testing and occasional races. A two and one-half mile (4 km) rectangular track, known as the Indianapolis Motor Speedway, was built northwest of downtown Indianapolis in 1909.

The first race was held on August 19, 1909. That five-mile (8.1 km) dash was a disaster. The surface of the tracks didn't hold up. Two drivers, two mechanics, and two spectators were killed. After other unsuccessful car and motorcycle races, Mr. Fisher decided that a different plan was needed. Changes to the track were made and as a result, the extravaganza known as the Indianapolis 500 was born on May 30, 1911. Out of a field of 39 drivers, Ray Harroun was the winner.

Since that race in 1911, the Indy 500 has had its ups and downs. In 1916, the race was only 300 miles (482.8 km) long because Speedway management feared a shortage of cars due to the war in Europe. The races were not held in 1917 and 1918 because of World War I. Racing suffered hard times during the Depression years and then again during World War II when the track was shut down. Since 1957, after extensive upgrades, the racing spectacular has been an outstanding success. The races are televised nationally each year.

Response

What is meant by "ups and downs"? Explain how they affected the Speedway.

Fascinating Factoid: The winner's average speed for the race on August 19, 1909, was 74.59 (120 km) mph, and the race lasted 6 hours, 42 minutes, and 8 seconds.

Word Play

Can you find at least 18 little words in the big one?

INDIANAPOLIS

_____   _____
_____   _____
_____   _____
_____   _____
_____   _____
_____   _____
_____   _____
_____   _____
_____   _____

Activity

- Auto racing has become one of America's top sports. Race car driving is certainly an exciting career. What are the pros and cons of being a race car driver? Create a two-column chart listing all the positive things about being a racecar driver in one column, and all the negative things in the other column of the chart.

August 20
Radio Station 8MK
Is on the Air

• • • • • • • • • • • • • • • • • •

The early history of radio in the United States was not completely recorded. However, it is known that the first radio broadcasts began in the early 20th century.

On December 23, 1900, a speech by Professor Reginald Aubrey Fessenden was transmitted. He spoke the words, "One, two, three, four. Is it snowing where you are, Mr. Theissen? If it is, would you telegraph back to me?" The transmission was heard. It is believed that this was the first voice ever transmitted by radio waves heard by another person.

On August 20, 1920, a radio station, 8MK, in Detroit, Michigan, began to broadcast a daily radio program. It is believed that this is one of the first U.S. commercial radio stations. On that historic day, listeners tuned in to their homemade sets to hear, "This is 8MK calling," and recorded music was transmitted from the second floor of the Detroit News building in downtown Detroit.

Now there are thousands and thousands of radio stations. Some stations broadcast 24 hours a day.

Response

What might explain the long (20 years) time span between the first transmission and the first commercial radio station?

Fascinating Factoid: WWJ (8MK) was the radio station that broadcast Will Rogers' radio debut in 1922.

Word Play

The words shown at the end of the coded message below should provide enough clues for you to complete the entire cryptogram.

‾ ‾ ‾ ‾   ‾ ‾ ‾ ‾   ‾ ‾ ‾ ‾ ‾ ‾
Y Q T M   D V J T W   M Y V Y T W F

‾ ‾ ‾   ‾ ‾ ‾ ‾ ‾   ‾ ‾
X V M   K T D M Y   Y W

‾ ‾ ‾ ‾ ‾ ‾ ‾ ‾   ‾ ‾ ‾ ‾ ‾ ‾ ‾
O D W V J E V M Y   P U P E Y T W F

‾ ‾ ‾ ‾ ‾ ‾   O N
D P M B U Y M   W F

A U G U S T   31, 1920.
V B C B M Y

Activities

• Complete a survey about the radio listening habits of your classmates. Compile your results in a graph.

• Make a pie chart showing what you think the ideal radio station should air. How much of the day should be spent on music, talk, sports, interviews, call-ins, news, etc. Don't forget the advertising!

August 21
Hawaii Became a State

Other Events This Day
- William Burroughs patented first adding and listing machine (1888)
- Wilt Chamberlain, basketball great, was born (1936)

Princess Lili'uokalani, ruler of Hawaii, was overthrown, and Hawaii was annexed as a territory to the United States in 1898. Hawaii was admitted as the 50th U.S. state on August 21, 1959. Talk of statehood for Hawaii was heard as early as the 1930s, before World War II. Over the years, those who wanted statehood had to convince the residents of the islands, as well as U.S. citizens, that statehood was a good thing for everyone.

The benefits of statehood are many for both Hawaii and the mainland. The beautiful terrain and the wonderful climate make Hawaii an outstanding vacation destination for people all over the world. The people of Hawaii are welcoming and friendly.

In addition to the beauty, Hawaii is one of the major agricultural states. It is the nation's largest producer of sugar cane and pineapple. Hawaii is the only U.S. state where coffee and macadamia nuts are grown. Much of our ocean and energy research and development are centered in Hawaii. Hawaii is also of extreme importance to U.S. defense because it houses some of our best defense facilities.

Response

What could you add to the list of Hawaii's assets?

Fascinating Factoid: 'Iolani Palace, the only royal palace on American soil, is located in Hawaii.

Word Play

Unscramble each word associated with Hawaii.

1. ALUU _____

2. PELPEPINA _____

3. OULUNOHL _____

4. AMACMADAI _____

5. IAILON ALAPEC _____

6. OOLAVCN _____

7. GINFSRU _____

8. ELI _____

9. SAGRS KITSR _____

10. LUAH _____

Activity

- Create a travel poster or brochure for Hawaii. Be sure to show some of the things that would make people want to visit Hawaii. You may draw, paint, color, use pictures from magazines, or use a combination of media.

August 22
First America's Cup Race

• • • • • • • • • • • • • • • • •

Other Events This Day

- First international air race (1909)
- Gold discovered in Johannesburg, South Africa (1926)

The America's Cup, considered the most famous trophy for yachting, is the oldest active award in sports. The first race was on August 22, 1851, when a schooner named *America* raced 15 other yachts representing the Royal Yacht Squadron. *America* won by 20 minutes. The organization awarding The America's Cup became the namesake of New York Yacht Club's schooner, *America.* Commodore John Cox Stevens was the club leader.

In 1857, the organization was assigned to the New York Yacht Club through a Deed of Gift, which established the event and governs it to this day. The first challenge for the America's Cup came from James Asbury's *Cambria* in 1870. The New York Yacht Club retained the America's Cup Trophy for over 130 years, which is the longest winning streak in the history of the sport.

Racing enthusiasts spend millions of dollars to prepare for the race to challenge or defend the America's Cup, and their prize is the satisfaction and glory of winning such a prestigious event. Because of the great cost and preparation required, the race is held about every three years.

Response

Why do you think satisfaction and glory are suitable prizes for such a prestigious event? What is your opinion of these prizes?

Fascinating Factoid: The America's Cup winners receive no prize money.

Word Play

Unscramble each nautical term.

1. FAT_____
   (at, near, or toward stern)

2. YOAH_____
   (seaman's call to attract attention)

3. ERTBH_____
   (place to sleep)

4. OWB_____
   (forward part of vessel)

5. GIDRBE_____
   (location from which a vessel is steered)

6. CKED_____
   (any part of ship serving as a floor)

7. ALELYG_____
   (kitchen on a boat)

8. AMTS_____
   (large wooden pole that holds up sails)

9. ROPT_____
   (left side of ship when facing forward)

10. SNOCHORE_____
    (sailing ship with at least two masts)

11. RENTS_____
    (aft end of a ship)

12. YHEZPR_____
    (gentle breeze, the west wind)

Activity

- Go on a word search. Look for bigger words that have the word ship in them (e.g., *worship, shipwreck*). List as many as possible.

August 23
Blowing in the Wind
● ● ● ● ● ● ● ● ● ● ● ● ● ● ● ● ● ●

Today marks the birth of Hurricane Katrina, the costliest hurricane in U.S. history. It was the sixth strongest Atlantic hurricane ever recorded with an estimated $115 billion in damages.

After forming over the Bahamas on this day in 2005, Katrina crossed the southern tip of Florida as a moderate (Category 1) hurricane and strengthed as she moved into the Gulf of Mexico. Katrina made landfall again on August 29 in southeast Louisiana, with sustained winds of 125 miles (201.2 km) per hour. The hurricane-force winds caused devastation outward for 120 miles (193.1 km) from the center. There were at least 36 confirmed tornadoes associated with Katrina.

Not everyone could evacuate when Katrina headed for the coastlines of Louisiana, Mississippi, and Alabama. The official death toll as of May 19, 2006, was 1,836, with more than 750 people still unaccounted for. The wind and flood damage was catastrophic. Eighty percent of New Orleans was flooded. Ninety percent of the buildings along the Biloxi-Gulfport coastline were wiped out. Almost one-third of the state population of Mississippi was without power.

It will be years before some of the cities and towns complete the rebuilding process.

Response

In what ways, directly or indirectly, has Hurricane Katrina made an impact on your town and/or school?

Fascinating Factoid: The Great Hurricane of 1780 (Caribbean Islands) caused the most fatalities—22,000.

Word Play

In olden days, people relied on weather lore to predict the weather and often believed in weather superstitions. Following are some weather lore poems. Supply the missing word(s).

1. Cold is the night when the stars shine _____ .
2. When the dew is on the grass, / Rain will never come to _____ .
3. When grass is dry at morning light, / Look for _____ before the_____ .
4. If a cat washes her face o'er her ear, / 'Tis a sign the _____ will be fine and _____ .
5. If a circle forms round the moon, 'twill rain_____ .
6. Red night in the morning, sailors take_____, / Red night at night, sailor's _____ .
7. When clouds look like black smoke, / A wise man will put on his _____ .
8. Pale moon rains, red moon blows, / White moon neither rains nor _____ .
9. When clouds appear like rocks and towers, the earth will be washed by frequent _____ .
10. If salt is sticky and gains in weight, it will rain before too _____ .

Activities

- Research hurricane statistics. Create a Pocket Book of World Records for Hurricanes (e.g., fastest, strongest, spawned the most tornadoes, season/year for having the most).

- Research weather facts. Create a game that involves weather/storm trivia. You can design your own game format or use true/false questions.

- Make a map showing the locations of the top five hurricanes. Include a map key with the hurricane symbol. What conclusions can you draw?

August 24

Potato Chips Invented

• • • • • • • • • • • • • • • • • • •

Other Events This Day

• Mt. Vesuvius erupted and buried Pompeii (79 CE)

• Waffle iron invented (1869)

Potato chips are one of America's favorite snacks. It is interesting to note that they were not the product of someone's creative genius in the kitchen, but rather someone's revenge. It is believed that in 1853, a railroad executive by the name of Cornelius Vanderbilt was dining at a restaurant in Saratoga Springs, New York. French-fried potatoes were on the menu. Mr. Vanderbilt ordered them, but he was not happy because they were too thick. He returned them to the chef.

The chef that evening was George Crum. He didn't appreciate the complaint. The story goes that he cut and fried a thinner batch. Those, too, were not satisfactory. Irritated, Mr. Crum sliced the next batch of potatoes paper-thin, fried them crisp in boiling oil, and salted them. It is reported that Mr. Vanderbilt loved the "crunch potato slices" and from that day on, these Saratoga Chips became a restaurant favorite.

When you eat to the bottom of your chip bag and nothing is left but the crumbs, pause to thank Mr. George Crum, who is credited with inventing one of our favorite snacks.

Response

How did an unhappy, complaining customer turn out to be the best thing that ever happened to Mr. Crum?

Fascinating Factoid: Americans consume more potato chips than any other people in the world.

Word Play

Seek and find your favorite chips in the word search puzzle.

```
S T E S F R U B M S N I U N
E O R I G I N A L A Y S T O
L L S I R T L R M L N G O S
G D A H A B O B U T J V R O
N F L T D O W E R A A C F U
I A T X D D F C U N E D D R
R S A U E O A U F D E L L C
P H N L H U T E F V P E E R
C I D R C A N D L I N N S E
O O N I O N B J E N O O L A
H N H I V L M O S E V C R M
C E G R O O V Y C G Z A F D
R D F B A K E D L A N B V C
L D O S A L T A N R R B O M
```

BAKED
ORIGINAL
BARBECUE
ONION
BACON
CHEDDAR
SOUR CREAM
SALT & VINEGAR
OLD FASHIONED

Activity

• What do you find at the bottom of a package of potato chips? Crumbs, of course—because George Crum invented potato chips! Think of other food items and make up a funny or interesting name for its inventor or creator (e.g., peanut butter—Ima Nutt).

August 25
Can You Believe?

Other Events This Day
- New Orleans was founded by French settlers (1718)
- Paris, France, was liberated from Nazi occupation by Allied forces (1944)

Everyone loves a good story—the bigger and more outrageous, the better. Some newspapers are notorious for printing stories that stretch the truth. The stories, as wild as they usually sound, have just enough factual information that people are convinced they are true. It is such a story that made *The New York Sun* become the best-selling newspaper in the world in 1835. The first article of this six-part story was published on August 25, 1835. This story is now referred to as "The Great Moon Hoax."

The fictional author, Dr. Andrew Grant, was supposedly a traveling companion of Sir John Herschel, a well-known astronomer of the time. *Sun* reporter Richard Adams Locke is most likely responsible for publishing the articles. The articles described fantastic creatures and sights that Sir Herschel reportedly saw with a new powerful telescope. Bison, goats, unicorns, tailless beavers, and bat-like humans with wings were described in detail. *The New York Times* believed the reports were probable because new theories had recently been in the news. The news suggested the possibility of life on the moon, and a recently published book spoke of inhabitants in the solar system and on the moon.

As preposterous as "The Great Moon Hoax" seems to us now, many people were convinced it was true. When people finally learned it was a hoax, most seemed amused, not mad.

Response

Why do you think people were willing to believe a story that sounded so preposterous?

Fascinating Factoid: *The New York Sun* discussed the possibility of the story being a hoax, but it never admitted any guilt.

Word Play

The moon has been used in many familiar sayings or figures of speech. Supply a saying to match each definition. The word *moon* will appear in each saying.

1. __ __ __ __ __ __ __ __ __ __ __ __ __.
   (ask for something that is not possible)

2. __ __ __ __ __ __ __ __ __ __ __ __
   (to be extremely pleased about something)

3. __ __ __ __ __ __ __ __ __ __ __ __
   (long time ago)

4. __ __ __ __ __ __ __ __ __ __ __ __ __ __
   (very rarely)

5. __ __ __ __ __ __ __ __ __ __ __ __ __
   (to ensure something impossible)

6. __ __ __ __ __ __ __ __ __ __ __ __ __ __ __ __ __
   (try to achieve something that is very difficult)

7. __ __ __ __ __ __ __ __ __ __ __ __ __
   (aim high)

Activities

- Imagine that you are a reporter for your local newspaper. Create your own preposterous front-page news story about a recent discovery that is sure to boost circulation of your paper.

- Look through a current newspaper. Rewrite one of the stories to make it more exciting or outrageous.

August 26

Nineteenth Amendment Passed

Other Events This Day

• Houdini escaped from chains underwater in 57 seconds (1907)

• Charles Lindbergh died (1974)

Today commemorates the passage of the Nineteenth Amendment to the Constitution in 1920. It is also known as Women's Equality Day. This day is intended to focus attention on full equality for women in all walks of life.

The Women's Rights Movement was born on July 13, 1848, in New York when five women met for tea and discussed their plight in American society. As a result of this discussion, Elizabeth Cady Stanton and Lucretia Mott led a convention on July 19, 1848, in Seneca Falls, New York, to discuss the social, civil, and religious conditions and rights of women.

Attendees wrote a declaration of sentiments that began, "We hold these truths to be self-evident, that all men and women are created equal . . . ." One hundred men and women signed the declaration, but only one, Charlotte Woodward, was still alive at the end of the 72-year struggle, when women were finally given the right to vote nationwide. The Nineteenth Amendment is often referred to as the Susan B. Anthony Amendment, and it states "The right of citizens of the U.S. to vote shall not be denied or abridged by the U.S. or by any state on account of sex."

Although Susan B. Anthony and Elizabeth Cady Stanton devoted 50 years to the women's suffrage movement, neither lived to realize their right to vote. Their work and the work of many others contributed to the ultimate passage of the Nineteenth Amendment, which was only the beginning of the women's struggle for equality.

Response

Why do you think the Nineteenth Amendment is often called the Susan B. Anthony Amendment?

Fascinating Factoid: Martha Washington is the only woman whose portrait ever appeared on U.S. paper currency. It was on the face of the $1 silver certificate, issued in 1886 and 1891.

Word Play

Can you supply the missing letters to find words that are used when discussing this special day?

1. ◯ O T E

2. ◯ I G ◯ T

3. ◯ o ◯ E ◯

4. ◯ Q ◯ A ◯ I ◯ Y

5. A ◯ E ◯ D ◯ E ◯ ◯

6. ◯ o ◯ s ◯ I ◯ ◯ T I ◯ N

Activity

• In the past, many careers, such as doctors and engineers, were only associated with men. Women were housewives, secretaries, and nurses. Now, no job is just a "guy job" or a "girl job." Write about a career/job you think you want when you grow up. Tell why you are interested in it. Include a list of things you would like to know about this career.

August 27
Guinness Book of World Records First Published

• • • • • • • • • • • • • • • •

Other Events This Day

• Earliest recorded North American hurricane (Jamestown, Virginia) (1667)
• Mother Teresa's birthday (1910)

The *Guinness Book of World Records* came about when Sir Hugh Beaver, director of Guinness Brewery, was shooting plover (game birds) in Ireland. He and his party marveled at the speed of the plover and thought they must be the fastest game birds alive. Then in 1954, another argument arose as to whether grouse were even faster.

Sir Beaver and his friends thought there must be other questions that people would debate over and not be able to answer. The idea for a book of records was born. They hired employees to research records and opened an office in London. The first copy of the *Guinness Book of World Records*, 198 pages, was bound on August 27, 1955. It became such a surprise hit that many additional editions were printed. Now, one revision per year is published in October to coincide with Christmas sales.

New categories must be found constantly in order to keep the public interest. Some records still stand from earlier years. Nothing appears too trivial or obscure to be included in this amazing book.

Response

How did a discussion or argument lead to the idea of a book of records?

Fascinating Factoid: Ashrita Furman holds the Guinness World Record for the individual with the most Guinness World Records! Among his 111 official records he has held the most glasses balanced on his chin and he has the fastest time to pogo-stick up the CN Tower.

Word Play

Synonyms are words with the same meaning. Find a five-letter synonym for each story word.

1. debate _____

2. research _____

3. trivial _____

4. coincide _____

5. obscure _____

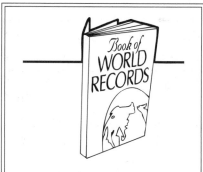

Activity

• New categories must be found constantly to keep people buying the *Guinness Book of World Records*. Create a list of possible new categories. You may want to look at a copy of the book before you start. If you come up with some really new and interesting ideas, you might forward them to the editor of the book.

August 28
First Steam Locomotive Raced a Horse

Other Events This Day

- Metal zipper inventor Whitcomb L. Judson's birthday (1890)
- Martin Luther King Jr. gave his "I Have a Dream" speech (1963)

When the locomotive was first in operation, many people thought that horses were still the best bet to get the job done. On August 28, 1830, a famous race took place in Maryland to try to prove which was best.

The *Tom Thumb* was the first American-built steam locomotive operated on a commercial track. Peter Cooper invented it. Mr. Cooper wanted to convince the owners of the Baltimore and Ohio (B&O) Railroad that they should use his steam locomotive, rather than horses.

The Baltimore and Ohio Railroad line suggested a race to prove that horses were faster and more dependable than the locomotive. The race was run on the B&O tracks near Baltimore. What a race it was! *Tom Thumb* huffed and puffed along the tracks pulling a wagonload of people. A horse ran alongside the locomotive. The locomotive led the race, and it seemed a sure thing it would win until it lost a part and had to slow down.

The horse won the race, but it actually lost out to the steam engine! The B&O officials were convinced that the future was in locomotives.

Response

Do you think that more people rooted for the locomotive or for the horse in the race? Explain.

Fascinating Factoid: Peter Cooper, inventor of the *Tom Thumb*, ran for U.S. president on the Greenback Ticket when he was 85 years old.

Word Play

How many three-, four- (or more) letter words can you make from the letters in the name *Tom Thumb*? If you need more space, use the back of this sheet.

T	O	M
B	☺	T
M	U	H

_____   _____

_____   _____

_____   _____

_____   _____

Activity

- The race between *Tom Thumb* and the horse looked like a sure thing for the locomotive; however, the horse never gave up. It kept racing and ended up the winner. Write a story, real or imaginary, about a time when it really paid off not to give up when things looked hopeless.

August 29
Chop Suey Invented

• • • • • • • • • • • • • • • • • • •

Other Events This Day

• Air Force Academy opened (1958)

• *Mary Poppins* movie released (1964)

The origin of chop suey is a big mystery! The story we love to believe is that the Chinese Ambassador to the United States, Li Hung Chang, had American guests to dinner on August 29, 1896, and that is when his chef supposedly invented chop suey. It is said that he devised the dish to appeal to both American and Asian appetites. The dish was composed of celery, bean sprouts, and meat in a tasty sauce. Word spread about this wonderful new dish. It became very popular in America and in China.

Another version of the story is that a Chinese man was invited to the White House for dinner and he didn't care for the food served, so he whipped up his own dish of whatever he could find in the kitchen.

However, chop suey may have been created by an angry Chinese cook who mixed together the garbage in a bit of broth and served it to clients in a restaurant in San Francisco. The diners, not knowing what they were eating, loved it and they came back and ordered it again and again.

Some credit a cook who whipped up a meal of leftover meat and vegetables for a group of drunken miners to keep them happy. Yet another version says that Chinese cooks who fed laborers on a railroad in California came up with chop suey when they had nothing to cook for dinner but leftovers. They mixed them all together and called it chop suey.

Response

Which version of the chop suey invention do you believe? Explain.

Fascinating Factoid: Not only is chop suey an American dish, so is its companion—the fortune cookie.

Word Play

X marks the place to start. Draw a continuous line through the ingredients you might find in chop suey. Your lines should not cross. Do not use the same letter twice. List the ingredients on the back of this sheet.

M	S	B	A	M	B	O	O
O	U	T	S	W	A	T	S
O	O	R	Y	O	N	E	H
R	R	E	M	E	I	R	O
H	P	L	**X**	A	O	C	O
S	S	E	C	T	N	H	T
U	N	A	E	B	S	E	S
M	S	T	U	N	T	S	✳

Activity

• Write another story about how chop suey was invented. Include information such as who created it and why, to whom it was first served, and when it happened. Include the recipe for your chop suey and give directions for making it.

Thurgood Marshall Became Supreme Court Justice

• • • • • • • • • • • • • • • •

Other Events This Day

• *Frankenstein* author Mary Shelley's birthday (1797)

• Max Factor, American makeup artist and cosmetic manufacturer, died (1938)

President Lyndon Johnson nominated Thurgood Marshall to the Supreme Court on August 13, 1967. He was confirmed by the U.S. Senate on August 30, 1967, and he received his commission on that date. Mr. Marshall was the first African-American appointed to the U.S. Supreme Court.

Justice Marshall was born July 2, 1908, in Baltimore, Maryland. He grew up to be one of the most well-known figures in U.S. Civil Rights history. He became an attorney upon graduation from Lincoln University and he received his law degree from Howard University. He served on the Supreme Court for 24 years, until June 28, 1991, when he retired.

As a lawyer, before taking the bench on the Supreme Court, he had argued 32 cases before them and won 29 of them. Mr. Marshall and his mentor, Charles Hamilton, developed long-term plans to rid segregation in schools. Bit by bit, and case by case, they tackled the education system in America. In 1954, the landmark decision of *Brown v. the Board of Education* was handed down. It declared segregation of public schools to be illegal.

Response

How would you summarize Justice Thurgood Marshall's career?

Fascinating Factoid: The movie *Simple Justice* was made about Thurgood Marshall and his efforts to integrate schools in the south.

Word Play

Make an acrostic of Thurgood Marshall's name using the letters in his name as a letter in another word. On another sheet of paper, write *Thurgood Marshall* vertically. Unscramble the story words below. Each word associated with Thurgood Marshall begins with the underlined letter. Fit each word in the proper place by or around the letters of his name. The word can come before or after a name letter.

DETP<u>A</u>PINO _____   GE<u>S</u>GERITANO _____

TO<u>A</u>NRYET _____   DANARMK<u>L</u> _____

TSIOR<u>H</u>Y _____   <u>L</u>CNINOL _____

GIHT<u>SR</u> _____   NA<u>S</u>TEE _____

MINAETDO<u>N</u> _____   RO<u>C</u>UT _____

YA<u>L</u>ERW _____   DYLRAA<u>MN</u> _____

RPEEMU<u>S</u> _____   ERCAMA<u>I</u>N _____

DWAOR<u>H</u> _____   OMER<u>B</u>LATI _____

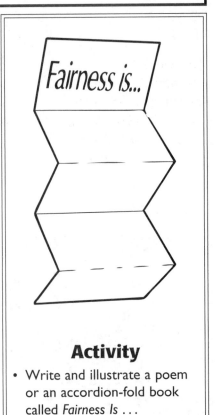

Fairness is...

Activity

• Write and illustrate a poem or an accordion-fold book called *Fairness Is . . .*

August 31
First Solar-Powered Vehicle

• • • • • • • • • • • • • • • • •

Other Events This Day
- First prestamped envelopes created (1852)
- Packard (type of car) completed early auto trip from San Francisco to New York City in 52 days (1903)

The need to develop vehicles powered by solar or other energy sources as alternatives is urgent because of the shortage of fuel supplies. Pollution problems are also cited in the need for alternative sources.

The very first solar-powered vehicle was introduced on August 31, 1955, at General Motors Powerama in Chicago. There was only one problem—it was only a 15-inch (38.1 cm) sun mobile built by W. G. Cobb of General Motors. It had 12 photoelectric cells. The light was converted by electricity that powered the small electric motor. A drive shaft was attached to the rear axle by a pulley.

Some solar-powered autos have been designed and built. The Bluebird is perhaps the first, totally solar-powered life-sized car. Ed Passerini built it in 1977. Other manufacturers have produced some solar cars, but they have not been well received by the public.

Perhaps one day solar-powered aircraft will be commonplace in our sky, along with solar-powered vehicles on the highways, and solar-powered boats on our waterways.

Response

Do you think the General Motors model should have been recognized as the first solar-powered car? Explain.

Fascinating Factoid: About 66 percent of the petroleum used in the United States is burned for transportation.

Word Play

Change only one letter at a time to get from the top word to the bottom word in each column. You may or may not need to rearrange the letters.

CARS

1. __ __ __ __
(used for grocery shopping)

2. __ __ __ __ (sour)

3. __ __ __ __ (tight)

AUTO

CARS

4. __ __ __ __ (pets)

5. __ __ __ __ (taps)

6. __ __ __ __ (cores)

TRIP

Activity

- Brew up tea at home or school for your classmates using solar power. Fill a large glass jar with water. Add two or three family-sized tea bags. Seal the jar with a lid and put it in the sun early in the day. Check on it occasionally to be sure it is still in the sunlight. Later in the afternoon, bring it in and serve the tea. Keep a journal about your observations throughout the day. Include the times you checked on it and a description of what you observed.

September

September 1
Wreckage of the *Titanic* Discovered

• • • • • • • • • • • • • • • • •

Other Events This Day

• Emma N. Nutt Day, which honors first woman telephone operator (1878)
• World War II began (1939)

April 14, 1912, was a cold, blustery night on the Atlantic Ocean. But inside the *Titanic*—a giant ocean liner that was thought to be unsinkable—the rich and famous were having a wonderful time as they sailed from England to New York. The ship hit an iceberg and over 1,500 people lost their lives.

In 1985, a joint French and American exploration team, headed by Dr. Robert Ballard, successfully located the *Titanic* resting on the ocean floor about 13,000 feet (4 km) below the surface. They had been searching 24 hours a day for six weeks with no success. They had only five days left before they would be forced to quit because of weather conditions. Then, in the early morning hours on September 1, they spotted something! Man-made objects were detected as they watched the screen for pictures being transmitted by *Argo*, a small submarine with lights and cameras. Then the hull of the *Titanic* came into view. They were the first people in 73 years to see the *Titanic*!

A year later, Dr. Ballard returned for further exploration inside the *Titanic*. At that time *Jason*, a robotic miniature submarine, was used to go into the different rooms to make video and photos. Dr. Ballard wanted the *Titanic* to remain untouched as a memorial to those who had died on that fateful night; but in 1987, another group gained salvage rights and began taking artifacts from the ship. As more teams have gone down to explore, many of the events of the night of April 14, 1912, have been pieced together, explaining how and why the ship sank.

Response

What do you think about Dr. Ballard's opinion that the *Titanic* should have been left undisturbed as a memorial to those who died?

Fascinating Factoid: The discovery of the sunken *Titanic* on September 1, 1985, was made around one o'clock in the morning—close to the same time the Titanic is believed to have sunk.

Word Play

The *Titanic* was supposed to be unsinkable. In the word *unsinkable*, the prefix *un-* and the suffix *-able* have been added to the base word sink. Unscramble each word and rewrite the word adding the prefix *un-* and the suffix *-able*. Write a short definition of each word to which you have attached the prefix and suffix. Use a separate sheet of paper.

1. TEBA _____

2. ELNAC _____

3. PEMYOL _____

4. CACETP _____

5. WALLO _____

6. NAILE _____

7. PARACHPO _____

Activities

• Imagine that you were a passenger aboard the *Titanic* on that fateful night. Write a message to be placed in a bottle and thrown overboard. What would you like your family, friends, and business associates to know?

• Research and list items recovered from the *Titanic*.

September 2
Time Begins Anew

Can you imagine going to bed one night and waking up 12 days later? That's exactly what happened to millions of people in England and its colonies on this day in 1752. Prior to this time, the British used the Julian calendar, and it was 11 days different from the calendar used in other parts of the world. The Julian calendar was named for the Roman ruler Julius Caesar who invented it. Although it was fairly accurate, it fell behind the solar calendar a few minutes each year. After centuries, the Julian calendar had fallen behind by several days. The solar calendar is based on the required seasonal changes Earth undergoes in its yearly orbit around the sun.

In 1582, Pope Gregory XIII devised a new calendar, throwing in a leap year every four years. It solved the problem of falling behind the solar calendar. His system, called the Gregorian Calendar, is what we still use. It differs from the solar year by only a few seconds. While the Gregorian Calendar was a big improvement, it took some countries many years to adopt it. The calendar change is responsible for the missing days back in 1752.

The months were named for Roman gods and goddesses in addition to Latin words: January (Roman god Janus); February (Roman festival of purification Februa); March (Roman god Mars); April (Roman calendar month Aprilis); May (Roman goddess Maia); June (Roman goddess Juno); July (Roman Emperor Julius Caesar); August (Roman Emperor Augustus); September (Latin word *septem* meaning "seven"— seventh month of Julian calendar); October (Latin word *octo* meaning "eight"—eighth month of Julian calendar); November (Latin word *nove* meaning "nine"—ninth month of Julian calendar); and December (Latin word *decem* meaning "ten"—10th month of Julian calendar).

Response

Why do you think it took some countries many years to adopt the new, more accurate calendar?

Fascinating Factoid: From the second century CE until 1925, astronomers counted days from noon to noon, rather than midnight to midnight.

Word Play

Starting with the (X), go around in a clockwise fashion to discover seven special words. **Hint:** You need to add vowels to make the words. What does each word have in common?

(X)	M	N	D	Y	T
D	Y	F	R	D	S
S	N	D	Y	Y	D
R	S			S	Y
H	Y	D	R	T	W
T	Y	D	S	N	D

_____

_____

_____

_____

_____

_____

_____

Activity

• Imagine that you lived in 1752 and your birthday was September 3. You went to sleep on September 2, eagerly awaiting your big day. Surprise! When you wake up, it is September 14! Write a journal entry about your lost birthday. What did you think? What did you do? Did you go ahead and celebrate on the September 14? Did you just skip it for that year? Tell about this extraordinary happening.

September 3
Treaty of Paris Signed

Other Events This Day
- First daily newspaper, *NY Sun*, began (1833)
- Unmanned U.S. spacecraft *Viking II* landed on Mars and took first pictures of planet's surface (1976)

The Treaty of Paris officially ended the Revolutionary War (the war between the Colonies and Great Britain). It was signed on September 3, 1783, and was ratified by Congress on January 14, 1784. The treaty called for ratification within six months. As late as January 12, only seven of the 13 states were legally represented at the convention. By January 13, they were still one vote short of a quorum. Richard Beresford of South Carolina left his sickbed and went to Annapolis where the convention was being held. With his arrival, a quorum was present and a vote was taken.

Under the terms of the treaty, Great Britain recognized the colonies as an independent nation. They agreed to remove all troops. The treaty set new boundaries for the country. The United States agreed to pay all debts to Great Britain and to allow troops to leave the country. They also agreed not to persecute loyalists in America and to allow them to leave.

After the signing of this treaty, the United States encompassed land from the Great Lakes on the North to Florida on the South and from the Atlantic Ocean to the Mississippi River.

Response

The treaty was signed September 3, 1783, but was not ratified until January 1784. Why do you think it took so long?

Fascinating Factoid: This is actually the second Treaty of Paris. The first Treaty of Paris was signed in 1763 to end the French and Indian War.

Word Play

As a part of the treaty, the colonies agreed to pay their debt to Great Britain. *Debt* is pronounced with a silent **b**. Write other words with a silent **b**.

_____   _____   _____

_____   _____   _____

Now list a word for each of the following silent letters.

A _____   C _____   D _____

E _____   G _____   H _____

I _____   K _____   L _____

N _____   O _____   P _____

R _____   T _____

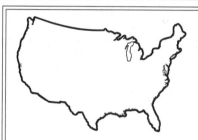

Activities

- Draw a map to show the United States territory after the Treaty of Paris was signed in 1783.

- Determine the number required for a quorum of representatives from the Thirteen Colonies. Research to find which colonies, in addition to South Carolina, were represented when a quorum was reached and a vote was taken on September 3, 1783.

September 4
Peter Rabbit Was Born
• • • • • • • • • • • • • • • • • • •

Other Events This Day
- Capture of Geronimo ended last major Indian War (1886)
- George Eastman patented first roll-film camera (1888)

"Once upon a time, there were four little rabbits. Their names were Flopsy, Mopsy, Cottontail, and Peter." Beatrix Potter is the author of the book that begins with these familiar words. The first version of *The Tale of Peter Rabbit* came about on this day in 1893, when she wrote and illustrated it in a letter to an ill five-year-old friend, Noel Moore. He was the son of her former governess.

Beatrix Potter was born to wealthy parents in London, England. She and her brother had little contact with other people. They had lots of pets, including rabbits, which she cared for, studied, and practiced sketching and painting.

The Tale of Peter Rabbit was printed in 1901, first privately, and then by Frederick Warne and Co., who had previously rejected it. This book is one of several for young children, written and illustrated by Ms. Potter. In her beautiful watercolor pictures, the animals are usually dressed as humans. For example, Peter Rabbit wears a little blue coat with a big silver button.

In her later years, she bought several farms, raised sheep, and enjoyed her life as a conservationist, landowner, lawyer's wife, and farmer. When she passed away in 1943, Ms. Potter left 14 farms to the national trust, along with her flocks of sheep.

Response
In what ways did Ms. Potter's early life influence her writing?

Fascinating Factoid: Beatrix Potter never attended school; governesses educated Beatrix.

Word Play
Unscramble each word below. Then find an antonym (opposite) for it from the story.

1. DLO _____
   _____

2. SALT _____
   _____

3. IGNTH _____
   _____

4. OPOR _____
   _____

5. SITRES _____
   _____

6. DLOS _____
   _____

7. YULG _____
   _____

8. DRE _____
   _____

9. GIB _____
   _____

10. ECTCAPDE _____
    _____

Activity
- Beatrix Potter sent the story of Peter Rabbit in a letter she had written to a sick friend. Practice your letter-writing skills by writing a friendly letter to someone you care about. Be sure to use correct letter-writing form, including heading, greeting, body, closing, and signature. You should also address an envelope in which your letter can be sent. If you don't have an envelope, just fold a sheet of paper into an envelope.

September 5
First Labor Day Celebration

• • • • • • • • • • • • • • • • •

Other Events This Day

• First Continental Congress met (1774)
• World's longest auto tunnel opened in Swiss Alps (1980)

Labor Day is dedicated to workers who have contributed to our country with the highest standard of living and the greatest production of products in the world. It is not known for sure who proposed the first Labor Day. Some records show that the General Secretary of the Brotherhood of Carpenters, Peter J. McGuire, was the one who proposed the holiday. But other sources say that it was Matthew Maguire, a machinist, who should be remembered for founding Labor Day.

The first Labor Day holiday was celebrated on September 5, 1882, in New York City. Through the years, Labor Day has been celebrated in other parts of the country as well. In 1894, Congress passed an act making the first Monday in September a legal holiday in the United States and its territories.

The first proposal for the holiday in New York called for a street parade to be held and then afterward fun and games for amusement and entertainment. After a few years, speeches by prominent men and women became a traditional part of the holiday celebrations.

Response

In what ways did the first Labor Day celebration differ from the ways we celebrate today?

Fascinating Factoid: In 1890, the average yearly income for a family of four was $380.

Word Play

Unscramble each story word below. Use letters from these words to make new words to fit in the spaces provided.

1. EBRECTADEL	2. TREFAWRDA
_____	_____
_	_
_ _	_ _
_ _ _	_ _ _
_ _ _ _	_ _ _ _
_ _ _ _ _	_ _ _ _ _

Activity

• Many people like to spend Labor Day relaxing at the lake, at the beach, or camping in the mountains. What is your ideal day of relaxation? Make a schedule showing times and activities. Be specific.

September 6
The *Mayflower* Left Port

• • • • • • • • • • • • • • • •

Other Events This Day
• First American lighthouse built (1716)
• First westbound train arrives in San Francisco (1869)

One hundred two passengers left England on September 16, 1620, on the *Mayflower* heading for the new world. They were expecting a long journey, but never in their wildest imaginations did they dream of that storm-tossed, 66-day voyage across the wintry Atlantic Ocean.

Although we don't know for certain how big the *Mayflower* was, it is believed that it was no larger than 100 feet (30.5 m) long and 25 feet (7.6 m) wide, with two decks that ran the length of the ship. There were quarters and a galley for the crew of 30. On this trip to the new world, it was crowded with men, women, and children and all the supplies they thought they needed to start a new life. It is a mystery how over 100 passengers and crew found room to sleep.

This trip was not a fun cruise. There was no privacy; there was not enough fresh water for cleanliness or for washing clothes. Because of the tossing waters, there was a lot of seasickness among the travelers. There were no lavish meals—only cold food such as hard biscuits, cheese, and salted beef or fish. Because there were no fresh fruits and vegetables, many came down with a disease known as scurvy.

Just imagine the happiness, excitement, and apprehension as the Pilgrims spotted land!

Response

Which living condition on the *Mayflower* would you find most horrid? Explain your answer.

Fascinating Factoid: The first thing the women did in the new world was wash dirty clothes.

Word Play

Unscramble each story word. Then use it to make a compound word by adding another word before or after.

Story Word	Compound Word
1. NO	_____
2. FILE	_____
3. VREO	_____
4. WREC	_____
5. GONL	_____
6. OT	_____
7. NALD	_____
8. ERWTA	_____
9. NOWD	_____
10. STOLHEC	_____
11. SEEHCE	_____

Activities

• When you think of May, you think of flowers. Do you suppose the ship name combined these two words? Create ship names by combining other month names and the name of something associated with that month.

• If you had to leave the United States to live in another country, what would your choice be? Support your answer with at least three reasons.

September 7
First Miss America Pageant

The first Miss America pageant was held in Atlantic City, New Jersey, on this date in 1921. It started as an idea to boost business. Two reporters suggested a contest where readers could send photos of beautiful girls in swimsuits. Winners of the photo contest would then travel to Atlantic City and compete. The winner would become "Miss America."

At the first pageant, contestants wore wool bathing dresses with baggy tops over leggings or bloomers. They posed in wicker chairs and paraded on the beach. The first Miss America was Margaret Gorman. She was a 16-year-old chosen for her good looks and potential for becoming a good homemaker and mother.

A few years later, the pageant was discontinued, but started again in 1930. Ms. Lenora Slaughter is responsible for establishing the pageant as we know it today. It is now a weeklong event with a contestant from each state.

Originally, contestants were judged on their figures and looks; however, after about 1940, judging began in four categories: talent, swimsuit, evening gown, and interview. There are several scholarships and prizes for finalists and semifinalists. The winner makes her famous walk down the runway of the stage while a celebrity sings the well known "There she is, Miss America. . . ."

Response

If you were in charge of creating the judges' ballot, what percent would you assign each of the four categories?

Fascinating Factoid: Miss America 1995, Heather Whitestone, was deaf.

Word Play

Solve this puzzle with words from the story. Hint: Fill in the longest row and the longest column first. They both are two words.

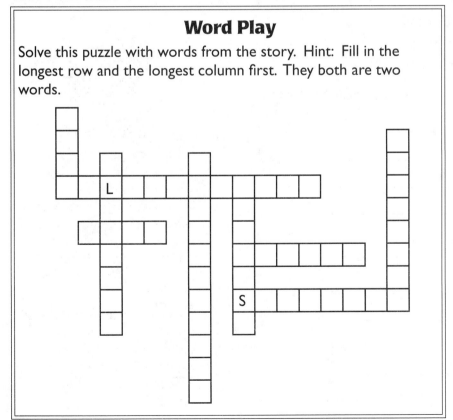

Activity

- The winners and runners-up of the Miss America Competition win scholarships for college. Estimate the cost of a four-year college/university degree at one of your state colleges or universities to see how much the prizes may be worth.

Pledge of Allegiance First Published

Other Events This Day

- ESPN premiered (1979)
- *The Oprah Winfrey Show* airs nationally for first time (1986)

The Pledge of Allegiance to the U.S. flag first appeared on this day in 1892 in a magazine, *The Youth's Companion*. It was meant to be used at the 400th anniversary of Columbus claiming the discovery of America. Francis Bellamy is given credit for writing it. He was an educator involved in the planning of the Columbus Day celebration.

The original pledge read: "I pledge allegiance to my Flag, and to the Republic for which it stands: one Nation indivisible, with Liberty and Justice for all."

In 1923, a slight adjustment was made and it read: "I pledge allegiance to the **Flag of the United States** and to the Republic for which it stands: one Nation indivisible, with Liberty and Justice for all."

Just one year later, in 1924, another slight change was made. It then read: "I pledge allegiance to the Flag of the United States **of America** and to the Republic for which it stands: one Nation indivisible, with Liberty and Justice for all."

The last change in the wording came in 1954 when Congress passed a resolution and President Dwight Eisenhower signed the measure into law. It now reads: "I pledge allegiance to the Flag of the United States of America, and to the Republic for which it stands: one Nation **under God,** indivisible, with Liberty and Justice for all."

Response

Why do you think it was important to make those wording changes to our pledge?

Fascinating Factoid: The original salute intended for the flag was to be made with the right arm extended.

Word Play

Count off every third letter, starting with S, filling in the blanks in order as you go. Keep repeating the rows until all the letters have been used and the message has been decoded.

```
S F G A L A L A T U G A T W T E
I T T T E H H N E H T F A I L N
O A D N G O F B V A Y E C S R I
T H N A E G N A T D R H I T E N
```

———— ———— ——— ———

—— ——————

—— ——————————,

—————— ———— ————,

—————— ———— ————— —————.

Activity

- What is the purpose of the Pledge of Allegiance? Why do you think it is important for school children to recite the pledge every morning? Why do you think that the hand is held over the heart during the pledge? Write your thoughts on this matter.

September 9
A New Name for Our Country

Other Events This Day

• American Bowling Congress established (1895)

• Elvis first appeared on the *Ed Sullivan Show* (1956)

On September 9, 1776, the United Colonies got a new name—the United States of America.

Have you ever thought what it might be like to choose a new name for a country? Well, that was the job of the Second Continental Congress when it met in Philadelphia in 1776. Thomas Jefferson, Benjamin Franklin, John Adams, Samuel Adams, and John Hancock were just a few of the notable American historical figures present when the Congress met. They wrote the Articles of Confederation to govern our new country.

Article I of the Articles of Confederation stated that this confederacy shall be "The United States of America." Congress adopted the Articles of Confederation on November 15, 1777. They were ratified in 1781.

In addition to picking a new name for the country, the Second Continental Congress wrote and signed the Declaration of Independence. They elected George Washington to lead the Continental Army, and they made the decision to print paper money.

Response

In addition to naming the country, what other important decisions did the Second Continental Congress make?

Fascinating Factoid: Under the Articles of Confederation, each state only had one vote.

Word Play

Make words to fit in the spaces below from the letters in the word given in the center of the puzzle. You can use a letter only once in each word unless it is used more than once in the center word.

```
               __
             __ __
           __ __ __
         __ __ __ __ __
       __ __ __ __ __ __
     __ __ __ __ __ __ __
 U N I T E D   S T A T E S
     __ __ __ __ __ __ __
       __ __ __ __ __ __
         __ __ __ __ __
           __ __ __ __
             __ __ __
               __ __
                __
```

Activities

• Give our country a nickname as some of the states have. *Examples:* New Mexico is nicknamed "The Land of Enchantment," Oklahoma is "The Native State," and Texas is the "Lone Star State."

• List as many states in the United States as you can without looking at a map or in a book. When you have completed your list, check your answers.

September 10
First TV Dinner Sold!

Other Events This Day
• John Smith elected president of Jamestown Colony Council (1608)
• Baptist minister, Rev. Jonathan E. Scobie, invented rickshaw in Yokohama, Japan (1869)

Food distributor Swanson made it easier for the housewife to call "Dinner is served!" On September 10, 1953, Swanson is reported to have sold its first TV dinner—a frozen meal that could be ready for the table in a mere 25–30 minutes, with no advance preparations.

The story of the development of TV dinners is not really clear. As is the case of many other products, several people and companies played a role in the development of frozen dinners commonly called TV dinners. It is believed that Maxson actually made the first frozen meal in 1945, but this was not available to the public. Maxson's frozen meats were served on airline and military flights. FridgiDinners by Jack Fisher came along in the late 1940. They were sold only to bars and taverns. The Berenstein Brothers sold frozen dinners in the Pittsburgh area. But it was the Swanson Company that made the frozen meals a common household word. They were the ones who coined the term *TV dinners*. Even within the Swanson Company, it is not clear who invented the TV dinner. The American Frozen Food Institute honored Gerry Thomas, a salesman for Swanson, as the inventor of the TV dinner, while others say it was the Swanson Brothers, Gilbert and Clarke, who actually invented the TV dinner.

Regardless of who invented the product, it has played an important role in American culture. In 1987, to commemorate that role, an original aluminum tray was placed in the Smithsonian Institution. In 1999, Swanson even received a star on the Hollywood Walk of Fame.

Response
What food would you like to see frozen?

Fascinating Factoid: The first TV dinner consisted of turkey, cornbread dressing with gravy, buttered peas, and sweet potatoes.

Word Play
Often figures of speech about a food item are used to make comparisons or describe someone or something. Match each figure of speech with the corresponding food.

_____ 1. cool as a   a. fruitcake

_____ 2. of my eye   b. bacon

_____ 3. like two in a pod   c. peas

_____ 4. bring home the   d. cucumber

_____ 5. nutty as a   e. apple

_____ 6. sizeable nest   f. egg

_____ 7. full of   g. bologna

Activities
• Write the meaning of each figure of speech listed in the Word Play.
• Conduct a survey about TV dinners with your classmates. Graph the results.

September 11
Collapsible Tube Invented

Other Events This Day

• Henry Hudson discovered Manhattan Island (1609)

• 9-11 Day/Patriot Day (2002)

• • • • • • • • • • • • • • • • • •

John Goffe Rand, an Englishman, invented the collapsible tube on this day in 1841. The first tube was a metal tube and it wasn't made for toothpaste—it was for artists' paints. Although the tube was successful, Mr. Goffe gave up his patent to settle bad debts.

The origin of toothpast dates back to 300–500 BCE in the civilizations of India and China. Early Egyptian toothpaste recipes called for ashes from oxen hooves, myrrh, powdered burnt eggshells, and pumice. In ancient Persia, toothpaste recipes consisted of burnt hartshorn, burnt shells of snails and oysters, and burnt gypsum. These tooth-cleaning products were kept in pots.

Dr. Washington Sheffield made and sold a crème cleanser far closer to modern toothpaste than all the other recipes. His creation was sold in costly jars; but his son, Lucius, went to Europe in the 1890s and saw painters with their paints in tubes. He thought this would be perfect for his dad's tooth cleanser. Dr. Sheffield began selling his product in a collapsible tube in 1892. In 1896, Colgate® Dental Cream was packaged in collapsible tubes, imitating Dr. Sheffield's tubes.

Response
How did ancient toothpaste recipes and containers differ from today's?

Fascinating Factoid: The forerunners of toothbrushes were probably twigs with cloth wrapped around the end.

Word Play
Use a little math to squeeze lots of new words from **tube**.
Hint: The letters may need to be re-arranged to form the new word.

1. TUBE – TU + BA =
_____
(a very special pig)

2. TUBE – B + N =
_____
(music)

3. TUBE – TU + EN =
_____
(was)

4. TUBE – TU + GNI =
_____
(start)

5. TUBE – TU + AD =
_____
(part of a necklace)

6. TUBE –UBE + AOST =
_____
(breakfast food)

7. TUBE – E + TRE =
_____
(eat on Toast)

8. TUBE – TBE + LYG =
_____
(not pretty)

9. TUBE – UB + TEH =
_____
("better to bite you with, my dear")

10. TUBE – B + R =
_____
(not false)

11. TUBE – ET + RHS =
_____
(this has bristles)

12. TUBE – UBE + ISR =
_____
(mix)

13. TUBE – E + N =
_____
(small hit)

14. TUBE – UB + I =
_____
(fasten together)

Activity
• Toothpaste and cake icing come in tubes. What other things come in tubes? Brainstorm and make a list. Can you think of other things that could be packaged in a tube that would make life easier or more fun? Make a list of things you would like to see in a tube.

September 12
5, 4, 3, 2, 1–Blast Off!

● ● ● ● ● ● ● ● ● ● ● ● ● ● ● ● ● ●

Dr. Mae C. Jemison was chosen for the NASA astronaut program in June 1987. With the launch of *Endeavor* on September 12, 1992, Dr. Jemison made history. She was the first African-American woman to go into space.

Dr. Jemison was born October 17, 1956, in Decatur, Alabama. She graduated from high school in Chicago, Illinois, in 1973. She received a degree from Stanford University in 1977 and a doctorate degree in medicine from Cornell University in 1981.

She has both an engineering and medical research background. From January 1983 through June 1985, Dr. Jemison worked as the Area Peace Corps Medical Officer in Sierra Leone and Liberia in West Africa. After her tour with the Peace Corps, she worked as a family doctor. When she was selected for the space program, she enrolled in engineering classes to better prepare herself for her mission.

Her job on the eight-day mission of *Spacelab-J* included 44 science and materials processing experiments. She logged 190 hours, 30 minutes, and 23 seconds in space.

Response
What was Dr. Jemison's background before she became involved with the space program?

Fascinating Factoid: Christa McAuliffe was the first teacher admitted to the space program.

Word Play
Unscramble each story word. Then on the grid below, make an acrostic using the letters in *astronaut* to substitute for one of the letters in each unscrambled word.

				A					
				S					
				T					
				R					
				O					
				N					
				A					
				U					
				T					

BALAAMA	APECS	RETMEPESB	URTCEDA
VEDEANRO	ASAN	MAOWN	CHUNAL
FONADTSR			

Activities
- Illustrate some dreams that you may have for your future.
- Design your own experiment to be conducted in space. Start by stating your hypothesis (what you think will happen). Then explain the testing necessary to prove or disprove your hypothesis.

September 13
Uncle Sam's Birthday

• • • • • • • • • • • • • • • • • • •

Uncle Sam is one of America's most beloved patriotic symbols. It is believed that he was named for Samuel Wilson, a businessman from Troy, New York. During the War of 1812, Mr. Wilson supplied beef in barrels to the Army. These barrels were labeled "U.S." Which probably caused someone to say the initials stood for "Uncle Sam." This might have led to the idea of Uncle Sam being a U.S. symbol.

Thomas Nast, who also drew Yankee Doodle, did many of the earliest cartoons of Uncle Sam. It is hard to distinguish this Yankee Doodle from Uncle Sam since both figures wore suits of red, white, and blue. However, Yankee Doodle usually wore a feather in his hat and Uncle Sam did not. Uncle Sam is nearly always seen with a goatee but Yankee Doodle is not. Throughout the years, Uncle Sam has undergone many changes. The Civil War era brought about the development of an Uncle Sam image that looked somewhat like Abraham Lincoln.

James Montgomery Flagg is responsible for the most famous picture of Uncle Sam, which was released in 1917. He appeared on an Army poster designed during World War I and was used again in World War II. The caption read: "I Want You for the U.S. Army." It is rumored that Mr. Flagg served as his own model for this drawing.

Response

How did the idea of Uncle Sam come from beef in barrels?

Fascinating Factoid: The figure of Uncle Sam dates back to the War of 1812 although most people think it came about during World War I.

Word Play

Start in the largest bordered box. Write a word from the story by placing a letter in each box in the direction of the arrows. Each word begins with the last letter of the previous word. Dark boxes indicate word beginnings and endings.

Hint: The first word begins with an **a**.

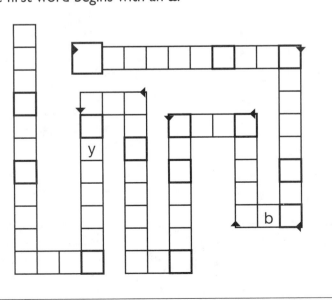

Activities

• Uncle Sam's theme is "I Want You." What can you, as a young person, do for your country? Make a list and check with your classmates to see if they can offer additional suggestions.

• Draw Uncle Sam with an updated look.

September 14
"The Star-Spangled Banner" Written

Other Events This Day

- Nobel Prize winner Ivan Pavlov's birthday (1849)
- Graf Zeppelin II, world's largest airship, makes maiden flight (1938)

Every country has a national anthem. America has "The Star-Spangled Banner." A 35-year-old poet/lawyer named Francis Scott Key wrote the words of this famous song on September 14, 1814.

Mr. Key was actually opposed to the war, but he did serve in the Light Field Artillery. In 1814, Mr. Key's friend, Dr. William Beanes, was taken prisoner. Mr. Key wanted to secure his release, so he went immediately to Baltimore to get Colonel John Skinner, a prisoner of war exchange agent, to go with him. Together, they sailed on a truce ship to meet the British fleet in an effort to secure Dr. Beanes's release. Dr. Beanes was released; however, they were detained by the British until after the attack on Baltimore.

Mr. Key's boat was anchored about eight miles (12.9 km) from the battle under the watchful eye of a British warship. It was from this site that Mr. Key watched the British attack Fort McHenry. They fired off several hundred bombshells and rockets that exploded in the air. The rockets red glare and the bombs bursting in air were such an awesome sight that Mr. Key's heart compelled him to write words describing the valiant efforts of the defenders of our country. He began the poem, which he called *The Defence of Fort McHenry*, on the back of an old letter and finished it later at his hotel.

Response

Why was Francis Scott Key an observer, rather than a participant, in the battle that inspired his song?

Fascinating Factoid: "The Star-Spangled Banner" did not become our official national anthem until 1931.

Word Play

Find each word in the puzzle.

ANTHEM
AMERICA
FRANCIS
RED GLARE
ROCKETS
WAR
STAR
BATTLE
FORT MCHENRY
KEY
POET
LAWYER
BOMBS
SHIP
SONG

```
G F P O G P K O V Y S
A A N T H E M S T R T
B F A U Y T W O S N A
E R C P I H S E O E R
R A I L K I B O N H W
A N R E P O E T G C R
L C E D K N L P K M A
G I M R E Y W A L T W
D S A S Y D N R E R Y
E J B O M B S K C O Q
R O C K E T S W S F A
T E R R A R U B R A B
C D R F E L T T A B G
```

Activities

- The sight of bombs bursting in air awed Mr. Key. Write a story, poem, or song about a sight that has awed you.
- What other U.S. or flag songs do you know? Create a script for a patriotic musical to celebrate our flag and country. End it with "The Star-Spangled Banner."

September 15
USA Today First Published

Even though *USA Today* started with less than an enthusiastic welcome, it changed the shape of newspapers everywhere. It was first published on September 15, 1982. At that time, it was very different from other newspapers. Critics called it too colorful, too splashy, and too glitzy. They even called it "News McNuggets" and "The Nation's Comic Book."

USA Today was not profitable for a long time. It survived because someone was willing to put a lot of money into it to get it through the first difficult years. They did not give up publishing with the style and manner in which they strongly believed. Now, there are over five million readers. It can be purchased on the same day of publication across the United States. It even has print sites in London, Hong Kong, Frankfurt, and Belgium.

USA Today's success is partially due to the creative use of color and graphics, which was unheard of at that time in the newspaper industry. The newspaper itself has a maximum of 64 pages, 20 of them in color. However, a fifth bonus section can add up to 24 additional pages.

Response
Why do you think people called this newspaper such names as "News McNuggets" and "The Nation's Comic Book"?

Fascinating Factoid: In 2003 alone, there were nearly 5,000 pages of advertising in *USA Today*.

Word Play
Unscramble each story word. Then write an antonym (opposite) for each word.

1. RIFTS _____ _____

2. REFIEDTNF _____ _____

3. GLNO _____ _____

4. TLO _____ _____

5. VEIG _____ _____

6. SCUCSES _____ _____

7. ADY _____ _____

8. EROV _____ _____

9. XAMMIUM _____ _____

10. DDA _____ _____

Activities

• Check out today's newspaper. Find an article that you think might deserve national attention. Use the *Who, What, Where, When, How,* and *Why* words or sentences in a poem.

• Write an article about yourself, your teacher, or your class that could appear in *USA Today*. It can be real or imaginary. Remember to include the *Who, What, When, Where, Why,* and *How* when writing your article.

September 16
Going to Great Heights

Other Events This Day

• Words to "Jingle Bells" registered under title of "One Horse Open Sleigh" (1857)
• Mexican Independence Day

The Empire State Building in New York City was completed in 1931 and topped out at 1,454 feet (443.2 m) tall with an airship-docking facility at the top. One of the floors was devoted to a lounge and ticket offices. However, the planners did not take into account the steel and glass canyons of Manhattan, which became a nightmare of air currents. They did not consider that a dirigible would have to dock without the help of a ground crew, and it could only be tethered at the nose with no ground lines to stabilize it. In addition to these problems, if a dirigible docked there, passengers would have to walk a narrow, open walkway near the top and then go down steep ladders inside before being able to get to an elevator.

It was on this day in 1931, that a small privately-owned dirigible momentarily docked atop the Empire State Building in New York City. It dropped a long rope to three building crewmen. It took about 30 minutes, but they finally caught the rope and moored it to the building— for only three minutes. It was only long enough to deliver a bundle of newspapers by rope. After that, the dirigible docking idea was abandoned, but the mast atop the building remained as a radio and TV transmitter.

The building celebrates holidays and other major events with light displays. There is a foot race up its 86 floors—1,576 stairs—every year. People get married there on the 80th floor on Valentine's Day. The building has been featured in several movies, including the popular *King Kong* movies.

Response

If taller skyscrapers are built, do you think the Empire State Building will lose some of its fascination? Why or why not?

Fascinating Factoid: The Empire State Building was designed to serve as a lightning rod. It is struck by lightning about 100 times a year.

Word Play

List eight compound words (a word made up of two or more small words) from the story.

_____   _____

_____   _____

_____   _____

_____   _____

Unscramble the following story words and add another word to each to form a new compound word.

1. CARE _____   _____
2. SLAGS _____   _____
3. CHIWH _____   _____
4. GHLIT _____   _____
5. WREC _____   _____
6. THIW _____   _____
7. YAD _____   _____
8. LKAW _____   _____

Activities

• Use straws, tape, and other common materials to create a tower. Be creative!
• Research famous buildings and structures of the world. Create a list of the top 10 tallest buildings; include interesting facts about each building (e.g., height, location).

September 17
United States Constitution Signed

• • • • • • • • • • • • • • • • • •

Other Events This Day

• First 33⅓ recording released (1934)

• Camp David Accords signed by Egyptian President Sadat and Israeli Prime Minister Begin (1978)

September 17 celebrates the oldest working constitution in the world; it is the anniversary of the signing of the U.S. Constitution in 1787. Today is also designated as Citizenship Day and Constitution Day, commemorating the signing of the Constitution. Citizenship Day is for honoring both native-born and naturalized citizens. *Native-born* means being born in America or of American parents. *Naturalized citizen* is the term given to people who were not born Americans but have become citizens.

Back in 1939, newspapers owned by William R. Hearst gave a lot of publicity to recognizing and honoring naturalized citizens. In 1940, Congress designated the third Sunday in May as "I Am an American Day" to honor newly naturalized citizens.

In 1952, President Harry Truman signed a bill that changed both the name and the date of this special day, designating September 17 as Citizenship Day. To become a naturalized citizen, one must be 18 years old and have lived in the United States for five years. A form must be completed and submitted to the Immigration Office, along with a fingerprint chart, photographs, and a filing fee. Applicants are required to read and write simple English and to have a basic knowledge of U.S. government and history.

Response

What two U.S. celebrations occur on this day and how are they related?

Fascinating Factoid: From 1905 until 1914, an average of more than a million foreigners entered the United States each year.

Word Play

Make words to fit in the spaces below from the letters in the word shown. You can use the letter only once in each word unless it is used more than once in the center word.

```
              __
           __  __
        __  __  __
     __  __  __  __
  __  __  __  __  __
__  __  __  __  __  __
    N A T U R A L I Z E D
  __  __  __  __  __  __
     __  __  __  __  __
        __  __  __  __
        __  __  __  __
           __  __  __
           __  __
              __
```

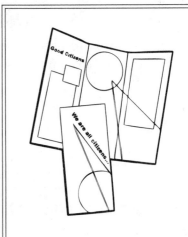

Activities

• Create a "Kid's Guide to Good Citizenship" booklet or brochure. Illustrate each idea.

• Design and make a poster or mural promoting America. Illustrate why America is the best place in the world.

September 18
Almond Hershey's® Kisses® Introduced

● ● ● ● ● ● ● ● ● ● ● ● ● ● ● ● ● ● ●

"Remember this, a kiss is still a kiss" are those unforgettable words of a song in the vintage movie *Casablanca*. Many other songs have been written about a kiss. So, how about a big, big kiss?

Hershey's® Food Corporation chose a unique way to introduce the world to its new kiss with almonds. On September 18, 1990, they lowered a six-foot (1.8 m), 500-pound (226.8 kg) Hershey's Kiss® from a 60-foot (18.3 m) flagpole atop One Times Square in Manhattan. But the question is—was that kiss still a kiss? The giant kiss had an aluminum interframe and was covered with gold-colored aluminum and sequins. Hershey's chose Manhattan for this spectacle because the original Hershey's Kisses were introduced there in 1907—the same year that the first New Year's Eve ball dropped on Times Square. The giant replica of the kiss is displayed in the Hershey Museum in Hershey, Pennsylvania.

The kiss remains the same as it was in 1907 when it was hand-wrapped in silver foil. Hershey's Kisses probably got their name from the sound or motion of the chocolate being deposited by the machinery during the manufacturing process. The tissue plume was included in the silver foil wrap in 1921. Starting in the early 1960s, red and green wrappings were added for the holiday season. The new chocolate treat with almonds was the first new kiss to be offered since the original kiss in 1907.

Response
Why do you think Hershey's didn't make a real chocolate kiss to lower from the flagpole?

Fascinating Factoid: For its 90th anniversary, Hershey's launched the Hershey Kissmobile®.

Word Play
The Hershey's Kisses introduced in 1990 had almonds in the chocolate. The **l** in almond is silent. Write a silent **l** word to match each clue.

1. __ __ __ __ (baby bovine)

2. __ __ __ __ __ (underside of hand)

3. __ __ __ __ __ __ (teachers write with it)

4. __ __ __ __ __ (chatter)

5. __ __ __ __ __ __ __ __ (a U.S. president)

6. __ __ __ __ __ __ __ (a type of fish)

7. __ __ __ __ (freedom from turmoil)

8. __ __ __ __ (perambulate)

9. __ __ __ __ __ (to refuse abruptly)

10. __ __ __ __ __ (one of two equal parts)

Activities
- In writing, describe Hershey's Kisses to someone who doesn't know about them. Include in your description information about how they look, feel (in your hand and in your mouth), smell, and taste. (Do not use the word candy in your description.)

- Carefully unwrap some Hershey's Kisses. Flatten out the foil and measure it. What is its perimeter? What is the area? Estimate how many kisses you would have to eat to cover a notebook page with flattened wrappers. Now check it out. You might try eating that many kisses to use the wrappers, or you could just use one wrapper.

September 19
Bissell® Sweeper Patented

Other Events This Day

- President James Garfield died of gunshot wounds (1881)
- National Butterscotch Pudding Day

Melville Bissell patented the Bissell® carpet sweeper on this day in 1876. He and his wife, Anna, ran a crockery shop in Grand Rapids, Michigan. Mr. Bissell was allergic to dust. Anna worked hard to keep the dust out of the shop, but it was a losing battle. The harder she swept, the more dust filled the air. Finally, she asked her husband for ideas on how to cut down on the dust.

Mr. Bissell developed a sweeper, which became known as the Bissell sweeper. He used tufts of hog bristles for the brushes in the sweeper. Ladies in the neighborhood put together the inner workings of the sweeper. Anna and Melville assembled the sweeper in a room above the shop. Mr. Bissell demonstrated it by throwing dirt on the rug and using his invention to clean it up. After that, sales were very easy.

In 1883, the Bissells established a sweeper business. It burned down, and they had to take out loans to rebuild. Through the years, other companies have made sweepers, but none seemed to work as well as the Bissell sweeper. It was lighter and seemed to pick up the dirt without stirring up a lot of dust. Mr. Bissell died of pneumonia in 1889. Mrs. Bissell then took over the business and became a successful businesswoman. She became the first female CEO (Chief Executive Officer) and ran the company until she died in 1934.

Response

What was the involvement of Anna in Mr. Bissell's invention?

Fascinating Factoid: In 1907, William H. Hoover produced the first commercial bag-on-a-stick upright vacuum cleaner.

Word Play

Start with the circled box. Write a word from the story by placing a letter in each box in the direction the arrows point. Dark borders denote word beginnings and endings.

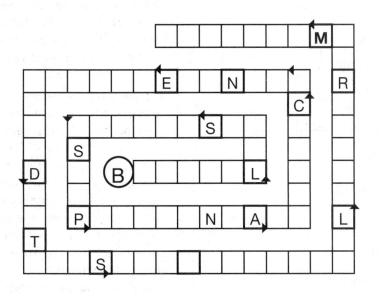

Activity

- A sweeper uses suction to pick up dust and other items. Try a variation of this idea. See what you can pick up using suction from your mouth through a drinking straw. Keep a record of your experiments. What is the heaviest item you could lift? **Caution:** Don't try this with tiny items that could go up the straw into your mouth. Only use items larger than the circumference of the straw.

September 20
Magellan Set Sail

• • • • • • • • • • • • • • • • • •

Other Events This Day

- Electric range patented (1859)
- First Cannes Film Festival held in France (1946)

Ferdinand Magellan was a great explorer. He was born in 1480 in Portugal. His Portuguese name was Fermao deMagalhaes.

On September 20, 1519, Magellan set sail on a voyage financed by the King of Spain. He left with 240 men and 5 ships: *Concepcion, San Antonio, Santiago, Trinidad,* and *Victoria.* The trip was long and hard. For more than a month, they battled through what is now known as the Strait of Magellan. One ship was wrecked, and another was damaged and sailed back to Spain. In November, Magellan finally reached the ocean that Balboa had discovered a few years earlier. Food ran low; there was little drinking water, and many of the crewmembers died. But they kept on sailing.

During the voyage, Magellan was killed. Only about half of the original crew survived. There weren't enough men to sail the three ships so they abandoned the *Concepcion.* The remaining two ships made it to the Spice Islands. They loaded up the ships with goods for the return trip to Spain. The *Trinidad* tried to sail eastward across the Pacific to the Isthmus of Panama. More than half the crew died. The rest returned to the Spice Islands and were arrested.

Nearly three years after the voyage began, the remaining ship, *Victoria,* made it back to Spain with less than 20 survivors. This trip around the world was considered to be the greatest feat of navigation that has ever been performed because it provided the first positive proof that the world was indeed round.

Response

Do you think the surviving crewmembers understood the significance of their trip? Explain.

Fascinating Factoid: Magellan's crew had to eat rats, ox hides, and sawdust to stay alive after their food and water was gone.

Word Play

Circle every third letter, starting with T, filling in the blanks in order as you go. Keep repeating the rows (from left to right) until all the letters have been used and the message has been decoded.

T	F	N	H	P	T	I	R	H	S	O	A	B	V	T	I
I	T	G	D	H	V	E	E	O	D	W	Y	T	O	A	H
R	G	E	L	E	F	D	B	I	W	Y	R	A	M	S	S
A	T	R	G	P	O	E	R	U	L	O	N	L	O	D	A

— — — — — — — — — — — — — —

— — — — — — — — — — — — —

— — — — — — — — — — — — —

— — — — — — — — — — — — —

Activity

- Back in Magellan's day, it was not unusual to be told that monsters roamed the seas. Create your own sea monster. Give it a name. Describe and illustrate your sea monster.

September 21
My Weekly Reader Debuted

Other Events This Day

• *The Hobbit,* written by J. R. R. Tolkein, published (1937)

• UN International Day of Peace

On September 21, 1928, *My Weekly Reader* made its debut. This publication brings world news and current events to elementary school children at their level. *My Weekly Reader* was the creation of Eleanor Johnson, an educator from Pennsylvania. The presidential election was featured in the first issue. The headlines read: "Two Poor Boys Who Made Good Are Now Running for the Highest Office in the World!" The two poor boys were Herbert Hoover and Al Smith.

To date, an estimated 18 billion copies have been distributed. It is still going strong today, providing school children with up-to-date news and other interesting information.

The staff spends a large amount of time trying to decide what to include in each issue. Special attention is given to the graphics and pictures as well to develop educational experiences for the readers. *My Weekly Reader* provides a fun way for children across the country to keep up on the current news while enjoying the stories and other features such as puzzles, and pictures.

Response

What are the three major areas of consideration for staff members of *My Weekly Reader?*

_____   _____   _____

Fascinating Factoid: *My Weekly Reader* serves more than seven million elementary-age children.

Word Play

"Do the math" with the word *reader* to make new words by unscrambling the letters.

1. READER – A + D =

   _____
   (more of a color)

2. READER – RE =

   _____
   (loved one)

3. READER – RE + NIG =

   _____
   (decoding words)

4. READER – DRE + S =

   _____
   (the better to hear you with, my dear)

5. READER – RD + T =

   _____
   (ant-)

6. READER – ER + M =

   _____
   (some are sweet)

7. READER – E + Y =

   _____
   (drab)

8. READER – RER + LYD =

   _____
   (dangerous)

9. READER – ER + INGD =

   _____
   (not looking forward to)

10. READER – EER + OGN =

    _____
    (fire-breather)

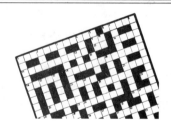

Activities

• Write a one-page "Daily Reader" about your class. It should include at least one news item, a puzzle of some type, a graph, a picture/cartoon, and anything you think your classmates might be interested in.

• Write a letter to the editor of *My Weekly Reader,* giving a few suggestions for features you think kids would enjoy. Remember to include all elements of a good letter.

September 22
Ice-Cream Cone Patented

Other Events This Day

• Last person hanged for witchcraft in America (1692)

• U.S. Post Office established (1789)

Italian Italo Marchiony is credited with inventing the ice-cream cone because he applied for a patent on September 22, 1896. He reportedly sold his ice-cream cones from a pushcart in New York City. There is, however, controversy as to who really invented the ice-cream cone.

One story is told of a Syrian vendor, Ernest A. Hamwi, who sold a crisp, waffle-like pastry at the 1904 St. Louis World's Fair in a booth near an ice cream vendor who ran out of dishes. Mr. Hamwi solved the problem by rolling up one of his wafer-like waffles in a cone shape and giving it to the ice cream vendor—thus the birth of the ice-cream cone.

Another vendor at the 1904 World's Fair, Abe Doumar, said that he created the cone and sold it nightly at the fair. Yet another vendor, David Avayou, claimed to do the same. He said that he learned about the cones in France.

It certainly is possible that several vendors began using ice-cream cones at the same time. Each in his own way helped the cone evolve into the ones eaten today. As to which came first—no one can say for sure except that Marchiony did patent his version, while the others didn't.

Response

How many people claim to be the inventor of the ice-cream cone, and how was it determined who got credit for the invention?

Fascinating Factoid: Baskins-Robbins™ once made a ketchup flavored ice cream.

Word Play

How about a double dip ice-cream cone? Unscramble the letters below. Each group has at least one set of double letters.

Example: POOCS = SCOOP

1. NAVLILA _____
2. YSREBRARWT _____
3. SISWS MLNAOD _____
4. TCHLOCAOE LWAMHRMASOL _____
5. PNUAET BTUTRE NDA CHTCAOOEL _____
6. PCACUCINOP_____
7. OCOHCATLE TEFOFE _____
8. GEGOGN _____
9. KOCESOI DAN MEARC_____
10. LCOHCTAEO OETRTMAA _____
11. YERHRC _____
12. UTITT TRUTFI _____
13. NIVLALA DUGFE _____
14. FECOEF_____
15. DUGEF PLERPI_____
16. ETRUBT CNAPE _____
17. ULERBRYEB CCESKAHEEE _____
18. TUNYT NOCOTUC _____
19. EPEPIPNTMR_____

Activities

• Imagine that you work in an ice cream shop and need to make a sign showing all the possible combinations of double dip ice-cream cones available at your shop. You sell 10 different flavors. Decide what flavors to sell. Make a chart showing the combinations.

• What's your favorite way to eat an ice-cream cone—lick it or bite it? Conduct a survey of your schoolmates to determine how they eat an ice-cream cone. Graph the results of your survey.

September 23
Happy Birthday, Mr. McGuffey

• • • • • • • • • • • • • • • • • • •

Other Events This Day

• John Paul Jones declared, "I have not yet begun to fight!" (1779)
• Neptune discovered (1846)

September 23, 1800, is the birthday of William Holmes McGuffey, author of the reading books that your great-great-grandparents probably used to learn to read. They were called *McGuffey's Readers*. There was one book for each grade level.

The primer started off with the letters of the alphabet to be memorized in order. Then came the building blocks of language to form and pronounce words. Each page of these small books had a word list, a short story, and a rule about an honest way to live. Material in the readers was taken from other writings that explained, promoted, and illustrated virtues such as honesty, charity, thrift, hard work, courage, patriotism, respect for parents, and reverence for God.

Mr. McGuffey was inspired to write these readers because of his love of children. They were first published in 1836. More than 100 million copies were printed and sold before 1890. It is believed that no other books influenced so many children over such a long period of time.

Response

What are some ways the *McGuffey Readers* differ from school reading material today?

> **Fascinating Factoid:** During the 50 years after the readers were first published, over 125 million were sold.

Word Play

Mr. McGuffey's first-grade reader listed many word families. How large a word family can you build from each of these word endings by adding a consonant or consonant blend at the beginning? If you need more space, use the backside of this sheet.

at	in	og	ig
___	___	___	___
___	___	___	___
___	___	___	___
___	___	___	___
___	___	___	___
___	___	___	___
___	___	___	___
___	___	___	___
___	___	___	___
___	___	___	___

Activities

• Make an ABC book for a small child you know or for a kindergarten class. Illustrate each page with corresponding drawings.

• Material in *McGuffey's Readers* promoted honesty, charity, thrift, hard work, courage, patriotism, respect, and reverence. Choose one of these virtues and write 10 rules that might help people attain that particular virtue.

September 24
Jim Henson's Birthday

• • • • • • • • • • • • • • • • •

Other Events This Day

• Dirigible (airship) first demonstrated (1852)

• *60 Minutes* premiered (1968)

The creator of Elmo and other characters of *Sesame Street®*, Jim Henson, was born on September 24, 1936, in the small town of Leland, Mississippi. During his childhood he moved to a suburb of Washington DC.

While in high school, Jim and a friend got a job at a local TV station on a children's program. They used a puppet named Pierre, the French rat. Although the job was not long term, it helped him land another puppeteer job at a different station. *Sam and Friends,* a five-minute show, aired twice a day for six years. During this time period, he attended the University of Maryland where he studied art and theater design.

Mr. Henson produced the highly successful *The Muppet Show®*, which ran from 1976 to 1981. The careers of Miss Piggy and her friend Kermit were launched on this show. The puppet characters he created were not always sugar-and-spice nice. Although Elmo is a sweetie, Bert and Ernie fuss at times. Miss Piggy sometimes behaves badly. But it is these little quirks in their personalities that endear the characters to millions of children and adults alike.

In 1990, Jim became sick with a very dangerous form of pneumonia and passed away. His puppets live on, and they will continue to be a strong influence to many generations.

Response
How did Mr. Henson get his start with puppets?

Fascinating Factoid: *Sesame Street* has won over 22 Emmy® Awards.

Word Play
The "Vowel Monster" ate all the vowels in the following words. Write in vowels at the right place to name *The Muppet Show* characters.

1. MSS PGGY _____

2. KRMT_____

3. NML_____

4. BKR _____

5. FZZ BR_____

6. GNZ_____

7. RZZ _____

8. SWDSH CHF _____

9. SCTR _____

10. RWLF _____

Activities
• Create a puppet. Give it a name, voice quality, personality, and some idiosyncrasies. Draw and color its picture.

• Write a script for a puppet play for a new *Sesame Street* character and/or the old familiar ones. Talk with your teacher about a time that you might perform your play for the class.

September 25

First U.S. Newspaper Published

Other Events This Day

• First printing press in North America (1639)

• Sandra Day O'Connor was sworn in as first female justice on Supreme Court (1981)

Benjamin Harris published the first newspaper, *The Publick Occurences Both Foreign and Domestick*, in Boston, Massachusetts, on September 25, 1690. The newspaper had only four pages, each about 7½ by 11½ inches (19.1 x 29.2 cm), with two columns of text on each page. The backs were left blank, and there were no advertisements.

Mr. Harris was a former publisher of Whig books, pamphlets, and a newspaper in London, England. Mr. Harris and his family came to the Colonies because of trouble in England over his publications. In Boston, he ran a successful bookstore, coffeehouse, and printing business, which gave him the money to begin his newspaper business.

Publick Occurrences was intended to be published monthly; however, it only lasted for one issue before being shut down. He had once again offended the government with his publication. Four days after distribution of the paper, the governor shut it down because of its content. Although *Publick Occurrences* was the first newspaper in America, John Campbell's *Boston News-Letter* in 1704 became America's first successful newspaper.

Response

How would you describe Benjamin Harris as a businessman—successful, shrewd, or foolish? Explain your reasoning.

Fascinating Factoid: One reason newspapers were not very successful during the Colonial period was that many people did not read well.

Word Play

List at least six compound words from the text. (If you need more space, use the back of this sheet.)

_____ _____

_____ _____

_____ _____

Then make compounds words by using a story word and a word below.

_____ born	_____ ward
_____ book	_____ self
_____ out	_____ out
_____ hand	_____ all

Activities

• Make a list of the parts/features of a current newspaper. Think about what newspapers in the Colonial period might have been like. Do you think any of today's parts or features were in the Colonial papers? Explain your thoughts.

• To commemorate this date in history, cut words from a newspaper and glue them onto construction paper to make a collage. Arrange the words in an interesting design or message.

September 26
Johnny Appleseed's Birthday

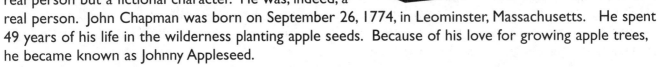

Other Events This Day
- First public appearance of John Philip Sousa's Band (1892)
- National Pancake Day

Many people believe that Johnny Appleseed was not a real person but a fictional character. He was, indeed, a real person. John Chapman was born on September 26, 1774, in Leominster, Massachusetts. He spent 49 years of his life in the wilderness planting apple seeds. Because of his love for growing apple trees, he became known as Johnny Appleseed.

Mr. Chapman wore sack clothing and a cooking pot as a hat when he planted apple seeds. It is said that Johnny Appleseed was a gentle and kind man who slept outdoors and walked barefoot everywhere he went. He was a friend to everyone he met—even the animals. His favorite book was the Bible.

Because of the tales associated with him, it is easy to see why people would think that Johnny Appleseed is just a fictional character. One story is that a rattlesnake tried to bite him, but the snake couldn't get his fangs into Johnny's feet because they were as tough as an elephant's hide. Another tale exists about Johnny playing with a bear family.

Response
What did you find out about Johnny Appleseed that surprised you?

Fascinating Factoid: The biggest apple on record weighed over three pounds (1.4 kg).

Word Play
Here are just a few kinds of apples: Golden Delicious, Red Delicious, Jonathon, Ginger Gold, Idared, McIntosh, Winesap, Pink Lady, Paula Red, Jonagold, and Fuji. Fill in the grid below. Start with *Ginger Gold* in the first column.

Activities
- Estimate how many apples it would take to fill you up. As a class, check your estimate by having a student trace around your body on a large piece of paper. Then cut out apples from red construction paper and glue them inside the body outline. How many apples did it take?

- Using the kinds of apples listed in the Word Play, write an alliteration for each kind of apple. (*Alliteration* is the "repetition of the initial consonant sound in all the words in a sentence.")

September 27
Matchbooks Patented

● ● ● ● ● ● ● ● ● ● ● ● ● ● ● ● ● ●

A patent for matchbooks was awarded on this date in 1892 to Joshua Pusey, a patent attorney in Pennsylvania. Until Mr. Pusey's invention, there was not an easy way to carry around matches. They were big and bulky. Mr. Pusey's idea for a smaller and lighter match came about as he was dressing for a fancy dinner party. He wanted to carry along matches for an after-dinner smoke, but noticed if he put them in his pockets, they ruined the looks of his best suit.

While he was busy working on his "flexibles," others were working on the matchbook idea at the same time. After several years of battles over the patent, he finally won the war and received his patent. He sold his rights to Diamond® Match Company and worked there the rest of his life.

At first, not many people were interested in matchbooks, but then an opera company bought several boxes of blank matchbooks and placed their advertisement on the cover. Everyone became interested and matchbooks were sold as quickly as they were made.

Response

What caused matchbook sales to rise quickly after a slow start?

Fascinating Factoid: Matchbook collecting is a popular hobby. A couple in Canada has collected over 5,000 matchbooks.

Word Play

Mr. Pusey had an idea to make matchbooks. Use the letters in the word idea and the scrambled letters surrounding it in each line to find the word suggested by the definition in parentheses.

1. MEA IDEA LBR = _____
   (deserving high esteem)

2. HV IDEA SE = _____
   (sticky)

3. M IDEA = _____
   (TV, newspapers, radios)

4. CL IDEA M = _____
   (type of number)

5. DIT IDEA NOC = _____
   (tribute to someone)

6. TRI IDEA OL = _____
   (opinion article in newspaper)

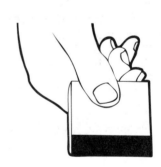

Activities

• In the past, politicians handed out matchbooks with their ads on them. Design a matchbook cover advertising the campaign of someone who is running for governor of your state or mayor of your city.

• Make a list of phrases or sayings with the word *strike* in it. Example: "Strike up the band."

The Big Tomato Controversy

Other Events This Day
- Confucius's birthday (551 BCE)
- Answering machine patented (1950)

Tomatoes have stirred up quite a story over the years. Even the pronunciation of the word itself has been debated. A song was even written that included this phrase, "You say to-may-toe and I say to-mah-toe." The word *tomato* is of Yematasi origin, meaning "sharp biting berry."

As early as the 16th century, many Europeans believed tomatoes were poisonous because they are in the poisonous nightshade plant family. But in the last part of the 18th century, people began eating tomatoes in Italy and France. Thomas Jefferson was a pioneer in growing tomatoes in America.

Doubts lingered whether they were safe to eat or not. An almost unbelievable tomato-related event is said to have taken place at noon on September 28, 1820. Colonel Robert Gibbon Johnson announced that he would eat a bushel of tomatoes in front of the courthouse in Salem, Massachusetts. A huge crowd is said to have turned out to see this poor man die after eating the poisonous tomato and they were shocked when he lived.

Just as people have argued over how to pronounce the word, people have argued for years as to whether a tomato is a fruit or a vegetable. The U.S. Supreme Court settled the controversy in 1893 by declaring the tomato a vegetable because it is used as a vegetable and not a dessert.

Response

Why were people afraid to eat tomatoes many years ago?

Fascinating Factoid: Robert Johnson supposedly ate a bushel of tomatoes at one time—that's 53 pounds (24 kg) of tomatoes!

Word Play

Use each clue to make a new word that has the letters **mat** in it.

1. __ __ mat __
   (red vegetable in this story)

2. __ __ __ mat
   (form or style)

3. __ __ __ __ __ mat __ __
   (operates without human help)

4. mat __
   (school subject)

5. __ __ __ __ mat __
   (someone you share a room with)

6. mat __ __ __ __
   (bullfighter)

7. __ __ mat __ __ __
   (lacking complete development)

8. __ __ mat __
   (person confined in jail)

9. mat __
   (partner)

10. mat __ __ __
    (married woman)

11. mat __ __ __ __
    (afternoon movie)

Activity

- Imagine that you and your friends have opened a brand new restaurant called "The Royal Tomato." Your restaurant serves a full-course dinner for tomato lovers. Create a menu with appetizers, salads, and main courses (and possibly desserts!) that feature tomatoes.

September 29
Gene Autry's Birthday

Other Events This Day
- U.S. Army established (1789)
- Scotland Yard formed in England (1829)

One of the most famous of America's singing cowboys, Gene Autry, was born on this day in 1907 near the small town of Tioga, Texas. Orvon Gene Autry was one of the most popular entertainers in the world in the early 1940s. He was a movie star, a radio star, a recording star, an Academy Award®–nominated songwriter, a rodeo entertainer, and the owner of both a music publishing company and a rodeo company.

When Gene was young, his family moved to Oklahoma. He began working for the railroad when he was around 16. It was while he was working at the railroad depot in Chelsea, Oklahoma, that Will Rogers heard him singing and playing the guitar and urged him to go into show business.

He became known as "Oklahoma's Yodeling Cowboy" while he worked for a radio station in Tulsa, Oklahoma. Mr. Autry went to Hollywood and starred in many western movies—about eight per year. World War II interrupted his career. He served as a flight officer in the Army. After returning from the Army, his singing career was greater than ever. His theme song, "Back in the Saddle Again," seemed quite appropriate.

Mr. Autry bought 1,200 acres of land near Berwyn, Oklahoma, in 1938 to keep his rodeo livestock. The town renamed itself Gene Autry, Oklahoma, in 1941.

Mr. Autry wrote more than 200 songs. Although it has been over 50 years since he recorded his biggest single hit, "Rudolph, the Red-Nosed Reindeer," it is still a favorite Christmas song.

Response

Why do you think the saying "Everything he touched turns to gold" is a good way to describe Gene Autry?

Fascinating Factoid: Gene Autry has five stars on the Hollywood Walk of Fame—Recording, Movies, TV, Radio, and Live Theatre.

Word Play

Suffixes are syllables added to the end of a root word to make a new word. Prefixes are syllables added before a root word. Find a story word to use with the given common suffixes and prefixes. Write the new word.

Story Word	Suffix	New Word	Prefix	Story Word	New Word
_____	ing	_____	re	_____	_____
_____	es	_____	al	_____	_____
_____	ly	_____	pre	_____	_____
_____	ed	_____	a	_____	_____
_____	est	_____	to	_____	_____

Activity

- "Rudolph, the Red-Nosed Reindeer" has alliteration. That simply means repetition of the initial sounds of two or more neighboring words or syllables. Brainstorm and list similar alliterative titles for songs that could possibly become big hits. Choose your favorite and write one verse of the song.

September 30
Kaleidoscope Patented

Other Events This Day

• First surgical anesthetic use of ether (1846)

• The *Flintstones* premiered (1960)

The name for *kaleidoscope* came from the Greek words *kalos* (beautiful), *eidos* (form), and *scopos* (watcher). Charles G. Bush is responsible for the popularity of kaleidoscopes in America. However, they were invented and patented in Scotland in 1816 by David Brewster.

Mr. Bush was born in Prussia. He came to Massachusetts in 1847. While working in the rope business, he started experimenting in optics. On September 30, 1873, Mr. Bush obtained a patent for his innovative kaleidoscope. These kaleidoscopes were not toys, but expensive gadgets bought by adults to entertain guests in their home. There were large table models, as well as the smaller hand-held ones. For about 30 years, Mr. Bush was the leading producer of parlor kaleidoscopes in America.

Amazing reflections fall into place as the scope turns. The interior of a kaleidoscope can have two or more mirrors fastened together at angles that run the length of a tube. The size of the angles of the mirrors determines the number of reflections viewed at one time (the smaller the angle, the more reflections become visible). A transparent container filled with colored pieces of glass or beads is at the end of the mirrored tube.

Response

Compare early kaleidoscopes with today's versions.

Fascinating Factoid: An early kaleidoscope sold for over $2,000.

Word Play

Make a kaleidoscope of words by using the letter combinations found in *kaleidoscope* and adding other letters to fill the spaces. The letters do not have to be used in the same order shown.

— — — —

— — — —

K A

L E   I D

— — —   — — —

— — — —   — — — —

O S   C O

— — —   — — —

— — — —   — — — —

P E

— — —

— — — —

— — — —

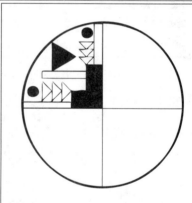

Activity

• Draw and color a kaleidoscope design. Draw a large circle on paper and divide it into four equal parts. Make a design in one of the sections and color it with bright colors. Repeat the exact design in each of the other three sections of the circle.

October

October 1
First World Series Baseball Game

• • • • • • • • • • • • • • • • • • •

Other Events This Day

• Yosemite National Park established (1890)

• Walt Disney World® opened in Orlando, Florida (1971)

The first World Series baseball game was played October 1, 1903, in Boston, Massachusetts. A crowd of more than 16,000 showed up for the big event. The name, World Championship Series, arose when promoters and newspaper writers tried to get the interest of the public.

The American League formed in 1901 and it became the rival of the older and more established National League. Bad feelings existed between the two leagues. Feuds were halted temporarily in 1903 when the Boston Club and the Pittsburgh Club agreed to play a best-of-nine series after the regular season.

The Boston Pilgrims led by Cy Young, one of the greatest pitchers of all time, lost the first game but they won the series five games to three. In game one, right fielder Jimmy Sebring of the Pittsburgh team hit the first home run in the World Series and led his team to victory. Thousands of fans came by train between the two cities, and the players didn't disappoint them.

There was no series in 1904, but the extreme popularity of the 1903 series brought about an official World Series starting in 1905.

Response

Why do you think this series of championship games is called the World Series when only U.S. teams play in it?

Fascinating Factoid: A baseball has 108 stitches.

Word Play

One of these baseball words is hidden in each sentence: *base, bat, ball, run, hit, tag, win, home, out, catcher.* Circle each answer.

1. The plants grew in the greenhouse.
2. The teacher said, "Get with it, John!"
3. Steve asked, "Do I have to hear that again?"
4. The coach yelled, "Great catch, Ernie!"
5. Mr. Johnson wanted a fish omelet for breakfast.
6. The caribou tried to hide from the lion.
7. The player was penalized for unnecessary roughness.
8. Reba sent her friend a letter.
9. Kimbal left the party early.
10. Take that tuba to the band room, please.

Activity

• Create a personal trading card similar to baseball trading cards. Include a drawing of yourself on one side. On the reverse side, include such information as height, eye color, hair color, and any other statistics you wish to share. Other information to include might be hobbies, favorite foods, games, and other identifying characteristics. The cards can be used to play the game, Who Am I?

October 2
"Peanuts®" Debuted

Other Events This Day
- President Woodrow Wilson suffered a stroke (1919)
- Gene Autry, the singing cowboy, died at age 91 (1998)

"Good grief!" Charlie Brown is over 50 years old! Charles Schulz taught at the same art school where he had previously learned to draw cartoon characters. While there, he met many of the people who inspired his future work, including a friend named Charlie Brown and a red-haired girl who broke his heart. He sold some single comic panels and even did a weekly comic feature called "L'il Folks" for the St. Paul *Pioneer Press*. These are the comics in which he created Charlie Brown and Shermy.

United Feature Syndicate Inc. publishers liked Mr. Schulz's cartoons, but they suggested that he change the format to a four-panel comic strip. Mr. Schulz signed his first five-year contract with them. They had to change the name because a comic strip was already named "Little Folks." The Syndicate named the comic strip "Peanuts®." Mr. Schulz was not happy with that name, but he went along with it. "Peanuts" was first printed on October 2, 1950, in seven newspapers.

The comic strip became very popular, probably because of those unforgettable characters and their unique personalities. Over the years, "Peanuts" grew into more than a comic. There are now books, calendars, toys, T-shirts, wristwatches, bedding, and much more to honor these characters!

Response
How did Mr. Schulz's background contribute to the "Peanuts" comic strip?

Fascinating Factoid: Charles Schulz was the only American comic-strip artist to have an exhibition at the Louvre in Paris.

Word Play
Some of the "Peanuts" gang are playing hide-and-seek and have hidden behind five large oak trees all in a straight row. Use these clues to find out which tree Snoopy is hiding behind. In order to do that, you must first determine who is behind each of the other four trees.

Lucy is hiding behind the tree that is next to Charlie Brown.

Pigpen is behind the middle tree.

There are no trees to the right of Charlie Brown.

Charlie and Schroeder are as far apart as they can be.

Snoopy is hiding behind tree #_____.

Activity
- Create a new "Peanuts" character. Lucy is the fussbudget. Pigpen is the messy, happy kid who walks around in a cloud of dust. Schroeder is the piano player. What will your new character look like? Create a personality for him or her and tell how your new character will fit in with the gang.

October 3
The Andy Griffith Show Premiered

Other Events This Day

• Myles Standish, Plymouth Colony leader, died (1656)

• Last Thursday in November was declared Thanksgiving Day (1863)

The Andy Griffith Show centered around Andy Taylor (played by Andy Griffith), who was the sheriff of a little town called Mayberry. He used a lot of reverse psychology on people and he had a knack for making people feel good about themselves. The core cast consisted of Andy, Opie (his young son), Aunt Bee, and Deputy Barney Fife. Other eccentric characters became regulars such as Gomer Pyle, Goober Pyle, and Ernest T. Bass.

In 1960, the first episode began with Andy's housekeeper getting married and moving away. Andy's Aunt Bee moved in to keep house and take care of Opie. Viewers immediately felt a connection with the widowed sheriff and his family. In addition to some corny, nitwit antics, there was also an occasional crime to be solved, a storyline of a serious nature and, of course, a little romance.

The show was set in and around a fictional town in North Carolina. Some thought it was patterned after Andy's hometown of Mount Airy, North Carolina. The fictional town of Mayberry was located near Mt. Pilot and Siler City. It was synonymous with charm and goodness. In reality, every episode was shot on a 40-acre (.2 sq. km) lot on the RKO Pictures back lot. Even the fishing hole scene that opened each show was shot near Los Angeles. Although this show ended in 1968, the episodes are still enjoyed as reruns.

Response

Why do you think viewers like to watch the old episodes of this show over and over again?

Fascinating Factoid: In the series, Barney Fife was supposedly Andy's cousin, but it was only mentioned in three episodes during the first season.

Word Play

Mayberry is a little town in the South. People in the Old South often used a dialect that was different from other parts of the country. Match each Southern word to its meaning.

_____ 1. crick   a. valley

_____ 2. tote   b. longing

_____ 3. britches   c. animal

_____ 4. cotton (to)   d. courting

_____ 5. purtneer   e. like

_____ 6. polecat   f. creek

_____ 7. fetch   g. pants

_____ 8. poke   h. carry

_____ 9. holler   i. skunk

_____ 10. sparkin   j. bag

_____ 11. hankerin   k. bring

_____ 12. varmint   l. almost

Small Town	Big City
1.	
2.	
3.	
4.	

Activities

• Would you prefer to live in a small town or a large city? Make a list of advantages and disadvantages for both and explain your preference.

• Imagine that you were a writer for *The Andy Griffith Show*. Create a new character that would fit right in with the others. Give him or her a name. Describe the character's looks and personality.

October 4
Sputnik I Launched

In October 1954, the International Council of Scientific Unions adopted a resolution calling for artificial satellites to be launched to map Earth's surface. In July 1955, the United States announced plans for a satellite.

The Space Age, however, arrived on October 4, 1957, with the launch of the Soviet Union's *Sputnik I.* It was the first satellite ever launched. This launch was significant because it was the start of the U. S. and Soviet Union space race. *Sputnik I* weighed about 183 pounds (83 kg). It took nearly 100 minutes for it to orbit Earth. *Sputnik I* sent back radio signals for 21 days.

Today, there are hundreds of satellites in varying shapes and sizes orbiting Earth. They may look like balls, boxes, or even drums. Each is sent into orbit to do a special kind of work. Some transmit radio and TV signals while others gather weather data. Some help ships and planes find their way.

The National Aeronautics and Space Administration (NASA) was created in 1958 as a direct result of the *Sputnik I* launch. Since then, NASA has been responsible for many successful experimental launches and space adventures.

Response

What are some of the purposes of satellites?

Fascinating Factoid: A Russian dog, Laika, was the first living creature to orbit Earth.

Word Play

Use the last letter in each word to begin the next word in the following chain of story words.

1. _ _ _ _ _ _ _ _ _ E   celestial orbiter

2. _ _ _ _ _ _ _ _ _ _ _ _   for testing purposes

3. _ _ _ _ _ _ _ _   sent off

4. _ _ _ _ _ _ _   nonstop route

5. _ _ _ _ _ _ _   send off

6. _ _ _   part of speech called an article

7. _ _ _ _ _ _ _ _ _ _ _   looking for something

8. _ _ _ _ _ _ _ _   pertaining to a nation

Activities

- Take a space adventure of your own. If you could go anywhere in space, where would you go? What would it be like there? Write about your adventure.

- Create your own satellite. Make a model, give it a name, and describe its purpose.

October 5
National Storytelling Festival Began

Other Events This Day
- Chief Joseph surrendered, ending Nez Perce War (1877)
- President Truman made first televised presidential speech from White House (1947)

On October 5, 1973, the first National Storytelling Festival was held in Jonesborough, Tennessee, a 200-year-old town in the Appalachian Mountains.

A high school teacher was listening to his car radio with a group of students when they heard a funny tale by storyteller Jerry Clower. The teacher, Jimmy Smith, decided to start a local storytelling festival. Around 60 people showed up for the first festival.

Now more than 10,000 visitors go to Jonesborough each October for the festival. Storytellers come from all over the world. Those who attend the festival can hear funny tales, myths, poetry, and more.

In days past, storytelling was the way people were educated and entertained. Stories were told to explain, honor, or record special moments in history. We owe much of what we know about the history of the world, and even the history of our family, to this kind of communication.

Response
What were the main purposes of storytelling in the past and today?

Fascinating Factoid: Since time began, the world has been full of mysteries. People have tried to explain the unexplainable through stories.

Word Play

Unscramble each type of story and match it to the corresponding definition.

_____ 1. TMYH _____

_____ 2. AFBEL _____

_____ 3. GELNED _____

_____ 4. IARFY AELT _____

_____ 5. KLFO ELAT _____

_____ 6. LATL AELT _____

a. exaggerated story

b. short moral story not based on fact, using animals as characters

c. story about gods and heroes, explaining the workings of nature

d. story about imaginary folks such as elves, giants, and fairies

e. story based on the life of a real person in which events are depicted larger than life

f. story in which ordinary people gain special insight, enabling them to overcome extraordinary obstacles

Activity
- Choose one type of story identified in the Word Play and write your own story of that type.

October 6
American Library Association Founded

• • • • • • • • • • • • • • • • • •

Other Events This Day

- First U.S. train robbery (1866)
- *The Jazz Singer*, the first full-length talking picture, debuted (1927)

The American Library Association was founded on this day in October 1876 in Philadelphia, Pennsylvania, and chartered in Massachusetts in 1879. Its head office is now located in Chicago, Illinois. The purpose of the association is to promote reading and make information available to everyone by providing leadership for libraries across the country. Anyone can join if they are willing to pay dues; however, most of the members are libraries.

When we think of libraries, we think first of all the books that are housed there. However, a library is much more than books. People can find such things as maps, artwork, microfilm, microfiche, audio and videotapes, CDs, DVDs, magazines, and newspapers. Most libraries have a place where the public can work on computers and access the Internet.

Colleges and universities offer courses of study in Library Science. They teach people about all the different aspects of a library, such as how to organize resources, classify the information, and preserve books and other materials.

Response

How many services of a library have you personally used? Name them.

Fascinating Factoid: The world's libraries now store well over 100 million original volumes.

Word Play

What title would you search for if you wanted to find each book below in the library?

1. Dorothy was whisked away from Kansas in a tornado.

   _____

2. Seven little people share their cottage with a pretty young girl. _____

3. These two kids get lost in the woods.

   _____

4. Charlie explores Willy Wonka's factory.

   _____

5. Harriet keeps a diary about her classmates and neighbors.

   _____

6. The family cat and dog think the new pet bunny is a vampire.

   _____

7. A little girl is friends with an incredible pig and a beautiful gray spider. _____

8. Billy makes a yucky bet to eat worms.

   _____

Look there-
In that large
Building...
R
A
R
Y

Activities

- Write an acrostic poem about libraries using the beginning letters in the word *library* as the beginning for each line.

- Design and create a thank-you card for your school librarian.

October 7
Rose Became National Flower Emblem

• • • • • • • • • • • • • • • • • • • •

Other Events This Day

• First double-decked steamboat, the *Washington,* arrived in New Orleans (1816)

• Poet Edgar Allan Poe died (1849)

In 1985, the U.S. Senate passed a resolution to make the rose America's national floral emblem. On September 23, 1986, the House of Representatives passed a joint resolution to also name the rose as America's national floral emblem.

The resolution was then sent to President Ronald Reagan. He signed it into law on October 7, 1986, in a ceremony held, appropriately, in the White House Rose Garden. From that day on, the rose has been our national flower emblem.

There are many varieties of roses, and some grow all over the country. They come in almost every size, shape, and color. They have wonderful aromas and are extremely beautiful, but most roses have thorns in order to protect themselves. Many people are named Rose, either as a given name or last name. Songwriters often choose to write about a rose, such as in the song, "The Yellow Rose of Texas."

A directional finder on a map is also called a rose—a compass rose. Is there any other flower that is more popular and beautiful to represent the United States?

Response

Why do you think the rose is a good choice as the national flower emblem for the United States?

Fascinating Factoid: Men give red roses to their sweethearts to declare their love; however, in the Victorian Age (many years ago), love was declared with red tulips, not roses.

Word Play

Complete the flower chain with some of the flowers in the Word Box. You must use the last letter in each word to begin the next flower word.

_ _ _ _ _ A

_ _ _ _ _

_ _ _ _ _ _ _ _ _ _ _ _

_ _ _ _ _ _ _ _ _ _

S _ _ _ _ _ _ _

_ _ _ _ _ _ _

_ _ _ _ _ _ _ _ _

_ _ _ _ _ _

Word Box

lilac	alyssum
marigold	nasturtium
zinnia	narcissus
rhododendron	magnolia
salvia	ajuga
aster	dianthus
daffodil	iris
coreopsis	lilies
sedum	rose
morning glory	monarda
phlox	

Activity

• Sometimes parents name their children with flower names because flowers are so beautiful. What do you think about a girl named Chrysanthemum? Kevin Henkes wrote the book *Chrysanthemum* about a little girl who loved her name until she started school and children made fun of it. What flower name would you choose for yourself? Select one and write about why you chose that particular flower. Do you think your classmates would treat you any differently if you had a flower name? Explain.

October 8
R. L. Stine's Birthday

Other Events This Day
- Franklin Pierce, 14th U.S. president, died (1869)
- New York Yankees baseball player Don Larsen pitches first perfect game in World Series history (1956)

Have you ever read a book that gave you goose bumps? If so, you've probably read some of the books written by R. L. Stine. He was born on this day in 1946 in Columbus, Ohio. He began writing stories, jokes, and comics for his friends when he was nine.

While in school at Ohio State University, Mr. Stine was the editor of the university's humor magazine. When Mr. Stine graduated, he moved to New York City. After moving to New York, he worked as editor of numerous magazines, and for 10 years, he was editor-in-chief of *Bananas*, a humor magazine for children. Mr. Stine started writing scary books in 1986 when he wrote a scary novel for teenagers. He was surprised at its success. Next, he created *Fear Street*, a young adult horror series. Then in 1992, he launched *Goosebumps* with Scholastic Inc.

Goosebumps is a series of scary, but funny stories for school children (ages 8 to 12). The books were an instant hit. Mr. Stine became the best-selling author in America with this series.

Response

Why do you feel that *Goosebumps* books are so popular?

Fascinating Factoid: The *Goosebumps* series has sold more than 220 million copies worldwide.

Word Play

Write each word that you might find in a scary book. Synonyms are listed below each space.

1. E __ __ __ __
   (bizarre, strange, peculiar)

2. S __ __ __ __ __
   (scream, shout, squeal)

3. H __ __ __
   (bay, yelp, roar)

4. __ E __ __
   (shout, whoop)

5. __ __ R __ __ __ __
   (alarm, scare)

6. T __ __ __ __ __ __ __ __
   (frighten, scare)

7. __ __ __ E __ __ __ __
   (ghastly)

8. G __ __ __ __ __ __
   (grim)

9. O __ __ __
   (sign, mark)

Activity

- Write about the scariest thing that ever happened to you. Describe it in detail and tell why it scared you.

October 9
Great Chicago Fire

Other Events This Day
• Woodrow Wilson became first U.S. president to attend a World Series baseball game (1915)
• First electric blanket manufactured; it sold for $39.50 (1946)

Chicago was a city in flames on October 9, 1871. The fire actually started on the previous evening. It burned all day and night on the 9th. It ended the morning of the 10th when rain began to fall. Chicago was a boomtown in the early 1870s. The area outside the downtown area consisted of miles and miles of rickety wooden structures.

Legend attributes the start of the fire to Mrs. O'Leary's cow. Mrs. O'Leary ran a milk business from a barn behind her home. The story is that she left a lantern in the barn and her cow kicked it over, igniting the hay in the barn. Others say "Pegleg" Sullivan, who first reported the fire, started it when he ignited some hay in the barn while he was trying to steal milk. Others believe that Louis Cohn may have started the fire since he confessed to it in a lost will. No one knows for sure how the fire started, but it is known that the fire did break out in the vicinity of the O'Leary home on the west side of Chicago. Over 300 people died, and another 100,000 lost their homes or shelters. Ironically, the O'Leary home survived the fire.

This great fire is probably responsible for Fire Prevention Month, which is observed every year in October. Fire Prevention Day began on the 40th anniversary of the Great Chicago Fire and it was sponsored by the Fire Marshals Association of North America. It expanded from a week in 1922 to an entire month. The United States Fire Administration, a branch of the Federal Emergency Management Agency (FEMA), asks that all Americans update and practice their fire evacuation routes at home, school, and work during this month. They also remind us to test smoke detectors and inspect our homes for fire hazards.

Response

Which version of the start of the fire do you believe? Why?

Fascinating Factoid: This great fire burned more than 2,000 acres (8.1 sq. km) in 27 hours.

Word Play

Make a compound word using the word *fire* for each definition.

1. weapon _____
2. paper cylinder filled with explosives _____
3. striking display _____
4. sphere of fire _____
5. resistant to fire _____
6. bird with bright orange or red plumage _____
7. ship with fire equipment on board _____
8. hydrant _____
9. barrier _____
10. fuel _____
11. fights fires _____
12. a bug with a light _____
13. near the hearth _____

Activities

• Explain in writing your family's escape plan from your house or apartment in case of fire. If you don't have one, write a plan.

• Being a firefighter is a dangerous profession. Do a pros and cons chart about this profession. Under the Pros sign list the positive things and under the Cons sign, list the negative things about chosing this career.

• Make posters about fire prevention and display them in your classroom.

October 10
Tuxedo Debuted in America

The tuxedo made its debut in America on October 10, 1886, at the Autumn Ball at Tuxedo Park in New York. Until 1886, the "White Tie" was the only accepted form of formal evening dress for men. It consisted of a tailcoat (tails) with peaked lapels, silk facings, and a white tie.

Traditions changed and a slightly less formal attire became acceptable. Black tie properly consists of a black short coat with silk lapels, and peak or shawl collars and no vents. The black pants have braid or ribbon on the outside seam of each leg, no belt loops (meant to be worn with suspenders), and no cuffs. A white shirt and black silk bow tie are part of the outfit. A low-cut waistcoat (vest) or a cummerbund is usually worn with the tuxedo. Black socks and black shoes finish the outfit.

It is believed that the tuxedo was designed by Poole and Co., in London, for the Prince of Wales in 1865. James Potter of Tuxedo, New York, visited England and was invited to a ball. The Prince of Wales recommended his tailor, who fitted Potter with the short black jacket and tie. One story says that Potter took the design back to New York and introduced it to his friends there. Other sources say that Pierre Lorillard, wealthy tobacco magnate, was the first to wear the outfit in America. The tuxedo was named for the Tuxedo Park Country Club, which was named by the Lenape Native Americans who called the largest lake in the area *tucseto*.

Response

Why do you think a penguin is sometimes described as wearing a tuxedo?

Fascinating Factoid: Today colored bow ties, waistcoats, and cummerbunds are sometimes worn at parties but are not acceptable at more formal occasions.

Word Play

The tuxedo is a special type of clothing. Match each item of clothing to its description.

_____ 1. braces   a. tight-fitting trousers with extra material layer on the inside of the legs

_____ 2. bisht   b. Arabic cloak

_____ 3. culotte   c. suspenders

_____ 4. gauntlet   d. diaper

_____ 5. knickers   e. boy's baggy knee trousers

_____ 6. nappy   f. shoe accessory used in the late 19th century

_____ 7. spat   g. long, ankle-length, T-shaped robe with long, full sleeves

_____ 8. jerkin   h. skirt-like traditional Celtic clothing

_____ 9. jodhpur   i. glove that covers wrist, hand, fingers, and forearms

_____ 10. kimono   j. man's short close-fitting, sleeveless jacket worn in 16th and 17th century

_____ 11. kilt   k. coat worn by horsemen, usually made of canvas and split up the back to hip level

_____ 12. duster   l. split skirt

Activity

• The tuxedo was named for the Tuxedo Park Country Club, which was named for Tuxedo, New York. Imagine that you are about to introduce a new item of clothing. Draw your creation and give it a name that would represent your city such as the tuxedo did. Explain why you think this item of clothing will make a fashion statement.

October 11
Eleanor Roosevelt's Birthday

• • • • • • • • • • • • • • • • • •

Other Events This Day
- Meriwether Lewis died (1809)
- Space shuttle Challenger astronaut, Kathryn Sullivan, became first American woman to walk in space (1984)

Anna Eleanor Roosevelt was born on October 11, 1884, in New York City. Her parents were Anna Hall and Elliott Roosevelt, brother of Theodore Roosevelt. She lived with her Grandmother Hall after her parents died when she was a child. Eleanor went to school in England. She returned to the United States for her debut. She met, fell in love with and married a distant cousin, Franklin Delano Roosevelt, in 1905. Her uncle, President Teddy Roosevelt, gave the bride away.

Eleanor Roosevelt became a political helpmate to her husband. She was active in the Women's Democratic Committee to help keep her husband interested in politics after he became ill with polio. Mrs. Roosevelt devoted her life to being a trusted advisor to her husband as he served as senator, assistant secretary of the Navy, governor of New York, and president of the United States.

When she became the first lady of the land, she changed that role into something it had never been. She entertained graciously, held her own press conferences, traveled all over the world, gave lectures and was even brave enough to express her own opinions. She became a champion for the downtrodden, working constantly to improve their lot in life. After her husband's death in 1945, she served as the American spokesperson at the United Nations.

Response

What are some things for which Eleanor Roosevelt will be remembered?

Fascinating Factoid: Eleanor Roosevelt was the first wife of a U.S. president to refuse the guard of Secret Service men except when she was with the president.

Word Play

Eleanor Roosevelt was an American First Lady. Unscramble each last name below to learn the names of other First Ladies.

1. MARTHA SHWINTGAON _____
2. DOLLEY IDAMONS _____
3. ROSYLN RACERT _____
4. BETTY DORF _____
5. NANCY NRAEAG _____
6. BARBARA SUHB _____
7. JACKIE NEKENYD _____
8. LUCRETIA FRAGEIDL _____
9. LOU OHVORE _____
10. PATRICIA XINNO _____
11. LAURA UBHS _____
12. HILARY NCILOTN _____

Activities

- Write "Who Am I" riddles about famous First Ladies. Include at least four important facts. (You can share these cards with the teacher for a class social studies lesson.)
- Eleanor Roosevelt once said, "No one can make you feel inferior without your consent." Rewrite her quotation in your own words, without changing the meaning. Illustrate your saying on a banner or poster.

October 12
Columbus Sighted a "New World"

Other Events This Day

• Charles Macintosh of Scotland began selling raincoats (1823)

• Confederate General Robert E. Lee died (1870)

It was on October 12, 1492, that Christopher Columbus sighted the "New World." Columbus was born in Genoa, Italy, in 1451. His father was a merchant and weaver. Columbus became a cartographer (mapmaker) in Lisbon, Portugal. He was intrigued with the idea of finding a westward route to Asia. Finding no one in Portugal to fund his voyage, he moved to Spain. Finally, monarchs Isabella and Ferdinand backed him.

Columbus made four voyages during 1491 to 1504. His first trip is the one that made him famous. There were three ships in the expedition—the *Nina*, captained by Vicente Pinzon, the *Pinta,* owned and captained by Martin Pinzon, and the *Santa Maria,* which Columbus captained.

They landed on an island that Columbus later renamed San Salvador. Columbus thought that they had reached Asia, so he called this area "The Indies" and the people there "Indians." On the return trip to Spain, the *Santa Maria* was wrecked. The captain of the *Pinta* sailed off on his own. Columbus returned to Spain on the *Nina.* He was convinced that he had found a new route to Asia and never gave up this belief. He never knew that he had discovered the land later to be called North America.

Response

How do you think Columbus might have reacted had he known the truth about his discovery?

Fascinating Factoid: The first gold brought back by Christopher Columbus from the Americas was used to gild the ceiling of Santa Maria Maggiore Church in Rome.

Word Play

Write the category for each word triplet.

1. *Nina, Pinta, Santa Maria* _____

2. Cuba, Haiti, San Salvador _____

3. ball, circle, orange _____

4. houses, apartments, duplexes _____

5. chocolate, lollipops, bars _____

6. bus, truck, auto _____

7. apples, blood, hearts _____

8. meow, woof, moo _____

9. pies, cakes, cobblers _____

10. juice, tea, milk _____

11. birds, airplanes, mosquitoes _____

Activity

• Plan a cruise from Spain to America. Plot a course of travel. Explain the route, including oceans, cardinal directions, continents, etc.

Compare your route to that of Columbus.

October 13
Construction Began on White House

Other Events This Day
- Continental Congress authorized the construction of a naval fleet (1775)
- First military use of trained dolphins (1987)

The Residency Act authorized President George Washington to choose a site for the nation's capital on the Potomac River. A square area, 10 miles (16.1 km) on each side, which was part of Maryland and Virginia, was surveyed and became known as the District of Columbia. President Washington and city planner Pierre L'Enfant chose the site that is now 1600 Pennsylvania Avenue for the president's house.

Construction on the White House began when the first cornerstone was laid on October 13, 1792. President Washington oversaw the building of the White House, but he never lived in it. President John Adams and his wife, Abigail, were the first official residents of the White House. They moved there in 1800.

The White House has survived two fires: one during the War of 1812 when the British set fire to it and another in the West Wing in 1929 when Herbert Hoover was president. It has been through major renovations. During Harry Truman's presidency in the 1940s, the inside was gutted and redone. The outside basic stones are still those that were put in place over 200 years ago.

Response

What part of the White House has remained virtually unchanged for over 200 years?

Fascinating Factoid: John Adams, the first president to live in the White House, only lived there four months. Soon after moving in, John Adams lost the election to Thomas Jefferson.

Word Play

Start on the **X** and draw one continuous line through the names of the last 14 presidents who have lived in the White House. (Hint: There will also be an **E** at the end of the puzzle.)

E	H	O	W	E	R	T	R	U	M
G	N	R	D	N	I	X	O	N	A
D	E	O	B	U	S	H	R	J	N
I	S	F	N	U	S	H	E	O	R
L	I	R	O	B	**X**	C	A	H	O
O	E	E	T	N	I	L	G	N	O
O	Y	T	R	A	C	N	A	S	S
C	D	E	N	N	E	K	N	O	E
R	E	V	O	O	H	T	L	E	V

_____ _____ _____ _____

_____ _____ _____ _____

_____ _____ _____ _____

Activities

- Imagine that you are the new president and your grandchildren are coming to visit on a regular basis. Change one of the rooms into a playroom. What colors will you use, and what kind of furniture and games will you include? Draw a sketch of the new playroom.

- Imagine that your father or mother has just been elected president of the United States. Make a two-column chart listing the good things and the bad things about being the child of a U.S. president and about living in the White House.

October 14
Sound Barrier Broken for First Time

• • • • • • • • • • • • • • • • • • •

It was on October 14, 1947, that Charles E. (Chuck) Yeager became the first human to fly faster than the speed of sound, breaking the sound barrier. He was test-flying the XS-1 (later called X-1). The XS-1 streaked past the speed of sound that morning with Mr. Yeager at the controls near Victorville, California. The X-1 was a plane unlike any before it. The nose was shaped like a bullet, and its high-strength aluminum body was only a little over 10 feet (3.1 m) high and 30 feet (9.1 m) long.

The X-1 was attached to the underside of a B-29 for its lift off. Prior to the flight of the B-29, the X-1 pilot had to take off in the B-29 and, in flight, climb down a ladder and snake his way into the small X-1 cockpit. At some point in the air, the X-1 was released from the B-29. As the X-1 soared in the air, its own power system engaged.

On the day of this memorable flight, all went well. The X-1 was dropped from the B-29, its engines started, and all systems were go. The airplane accelerated until .965 was indicated on the Mach meter. That is the magical speed when the sound barrier is broken. The meter stopped momentarily and then jumped to 1.06. The hesitation was assumed to be caused by the effect of shock waves. There was no jolt or shock to the pilot, but on the surface, a loud boom took place. The supersonic flight had lasted only 18 seconds, but it was this short flight that launched America into the second great age of aviation development.

Response

What took place at the instant Mr. Yeager broke the sound barrier?

> **Fascinating Factoid:** The X-1 in which Mr. Yeager first broke the sound barrier was called Glamorous Glennis after his wife, Glennis.

Word Play

Fill in the blanks and circles to make new words. You may change only the circled letter in the previous word to make the next word.

1. (B) O O M — loud noise
2. ___ ___ Ⓞ ___ — fate, ruin, death
3. ___ ___ ___ Ⓞ — college living area
4. Ⓞ ___ ___ ___ — flat-bottomed boat
5. ___ ___ ___ Ⓞ — blood and guts
6. Ⓞ ___ ___ ___ — pierce with a horn
7. ___ Ⓞ ___ ___ — greater amount
8. ___ Ⓞ ___ ___ — female horse
9. ___ ___ Ⓞ ___ — bog down; to sink
10. Ⓞ ___ ___ ___ — distance measurement
11. Ⓞ ___ ___ ___ — a stack
12. ___ ___ ___ ___ — arrange papers in a cabinet

Activities

• A *simile* is a comparison between two things using the words *like* or *as*. Example: Mr. Yeager flew as fast as the speed of sound. Write at least 10 "as fast as" similes of your own.

• Design a better paper airplane. Have a contest with a friend. Experiment with distances your planes will fly. Record your results on a graph.

October 15
Special Letter to the President-to-Be

Other Events This Day

- U.S. Department of Transportation created (1966)
- Mikhail Gorbachev awarded Nobel Peace Prize (1990)

On October 15, 1860, an 11-year-old girl named Grace Bedell wrote a short letter to presidential candidate Abraham Lincoln. In that letter she expressed her desire for Mr. Lincoln to become the next U.S. president and thought his chances would greatly improve if he grew a beard. She told him that his face was too thin and whiskers would make him look better. She also told him that all the ladies liked men with whiskers, and they would tease their husbands into voting for him.

Lincoln actually took time to answer Grace's letter, telling her about his family and that he wasn't really sure about the beard. However, he began to let his beard grow and must have liked the looks of it because by the time he left Springfield for the White House in February 1861, he was fully bearded.

On the way to the White House, Lincoln's train stopped in Westfield, New York, which was Grace's home. From the platform of the train, he called out for his friend Grace Bedell. She came up and Lincoln lifted her onto the platform and gave her a kiss.

The original letter from Grace to President Lincoln is in the Burton Historical Collection of the Detroit Public Library. Lincoln's letter to Grace is privately owned. Copies of both letters can be seen on display in the History Center in Westfield. A statue in Westfield also commemorates the event.

Response

Did the beard help Mr. Lincoln become president?

Fascinating Factoid: Colonel Jacob Schick invented an electric razor in 1928 and first sold one in 1931 for $25—that's more than $320 in today's money!

Word Play

Unscramble each name to discover a president who had a beard.

1. YSULESS S NGTAR _____

2. RDFTORUREH YSHAE _____

3. MAJENNIB RAORNHIS _____

4. SJMEA LAIFEGDR _____

5. RABMAHA CNNILOL _____

Unscramble each name to identify a fictional character with a beard.

6. HTEARF EMIT _____

7. TAANS USLCA _____

8. CNELU MSA _____

Activities

- Make copies of pictures of several other presidents. Draw a beard on each. Do you think the beard improved their looks or detracted from their looks? Explain.

- Write a letter to the current U.S. president and send it to the White House. Share a national concern you may have, along with a possible solution.

October 16
Noah Webster's Birthday
• •

What one book can help us find answers to those baffling word questions? The dictionary, of course! October 16 is Dictionary Day in honor of Noah Webster, who is known as the father of the dictionary. He was born on this day in 1758 in Hartford, Connecticut. He and his two brothers helped their father on the farm. His two sisters helped their mother with the housework. It was a typical Colonial family.

Mr. Webster began writing the dictionary when he was 43, and it took him more than 27 years to write it. He decided to compile and publish a list of words and their meanings because Americans in different parts of the country spelled, spoke, and used words differently. He thought that all Americans should speak the same way. He also thought that Americans should not speak and spell like the British.

Lexicography is the term used for editing or making of a dictionary. Noah Webster was a *lexicographer,* a person who does this type of work.

Response
How old was Webster when he finished writing the dictionary?

Fascinating Factoid: The longest word in the Oxford English Dictionary is *pneumonoultramicroscopicsilicovolcanoconiosis,* alleged to be a lung disease caused by the inhalation of fine silica dust.

Word Play
A common suffix is *-graphy.* Match each word to its definition.

_____ 1. lexicography

_____ 2. demography

_____ 3. stenography

_____ 4. choreography

_____ 5. floriography

_____ 6. areography

_____ 7. cartography

_____ 8. oceanography

_____ 9. geography

_____ 10. cryptography

_____ 11. cardiography

_____ 12. photography

a. editing or making a dictionary

b. study of population dynamics

c. method of writing in shorthand

d. process of recording electric activity of the heart

e. dance composition

f. study of Earth's oceans

g. technique of recording images

h. map making

i. study of Earth's physical and human phenomena

j. method of writing and studying coded messages

k. study of physical features of Mars

l. the language of flowers

Activities
• The dictionary entry spells a word and then shows how to pronounce it. Write a couple of your favorite jokes, using the pronunciation guide spellings and markings.

• Choose a letter and create a crossword puzzle using words that start with that letter.

October 17
Mother Teresa Awarded Nobel Peace Prize

● ● ● ● ● ● ● ● ● ● ● ● ● ● ● ● ●

Other Events This Day
• Albert Einstein arrived in United States, a refugee from Nazi Germany (1933)
• President Carter signed a bill restoring Confederate President Jefferson Davis's citizenship (1978)

On October 17, 1979, Mother Teresa received the Nobel Peace Prize for her humanitarian work. Mother Teresa was born in 1910 in Skopje, Yugoslavia. By the time she was 12, she knew that her role in life would be to help the poor. When she was 18, she taught in a convent school in Calcutta, India. She became a nun and took her final vows in 1937. She left the convent to work alone in the slums in 1948. During that same year, she found a woman lying in the street in front of a Calcutta hospital. She stayed with that woman until she died. This was probably how she got the name "Saint of the Gutters."

Mother Teresa founded an order of nuns called the Missionaries of Charity in Calcutta. This order is dedicated to serving the poor. She founded the House for the Dying in 1952 in a former temple in Calcutta. The sisters care for the dying people found on the streets. Mother Teresa didn't care about the reasons why they were dying; she wanted them to die in peace and with as much dignity as possible.

Mother Teresa's work showed respect for the human being and his or her innate value. Her philosophy of life was firmly rooted in her faith and her love for Calcutta and the people there.

Response
What was Mother Teresa sometimes called? How did she earn that name?

Fascinating Factoid: Mother Teresa's real name was Agnes Gionxha Bojaxhiu.

Word Play
Some story words begin and end with the same letter. Fill in the blanks below with these words.

1. N _ _

3. D _ _ _

2. T _ _ _

4. S _ _ _ _ _ _

5. D _ _ _ _ _ _ _ _ _

Think of some other words that begin and end with the same letter and fill in the blanks.

A _ _ _ A   P _ _ P   E _ _ _ E

D _ _ _ D   F _ _ _ F   H _ _ _ _ H

N _ _ N   G _ _ _ G   K _ _ K

R _ _ R

Activities
• Mother Teresa helped other people all of her life. Brainstorm and list ways you can help other people.

• Mother Teresa knew by the time she was 12 that she wanted to dedicate her life to helping the poor and downtrodden. Right now, what do you think you want to do with your life when you grow up? Explain.

October 18
Alaska Purchased

• • • • • • • • • • • • • • • • • • •

Beginning in 1725, Russia had a keen interest in the area that is now known as Alaska. As the United States expanded westward, it soon found itself competing against Russian explorers and traders. However, Russia didn't have the financial resources to support settlements or safeguard that area.

Other Events This Day

• Disney film *The Jungle Book* released (1967)
• Former First Lady Bess Truman died (1982)

Russia offered to sell Alaska to the United States in 1859. The Civil War postponed the purchase, but when the war was over, Secretary of State William Seward quickly renewed interest in the purchase. He agreed to pay $7.2 million. The U.S. Senate approved the purchase on April 9, and President Andrew Johnson signed the treaty on May 28. Alaska was officially transferred to the United States on October 18, 1867.

Although this purchase ended Russia's presence in this part of the world, many people did not understand spending that much money for a worthless piece of land. They called the purchase "Seward's Folly." The United States ignored Alaska for a long time, finally setting up a civil government in 1884. A major gold deposit was discovered in the Yukon in 1896. After that, things were quite different!

Response

Why was this purchase considered by many as "Seward's Folly"? What would you consider a good term for it today?

Fascinating Factoid: The price paid by the United States for Alaska, although it seemed like a lot, was really only about two cents an acre (4,046.9 sq. m).

Word Play

Unscramble each word in the box. Then fill in the puzzle with names of some of Alaska's largest cities.

ENCOAGRAH
SFRKANIAB
LILASAW
KITEHCNAK
UANUEJ
KITAS
BOARWR
KDAOKI
LETEHB

Alaska

Activities

• When the United States bought Alaska, people thought it was a mistake. However, after gold was discovered there, it turned out to be a good deal. Write about a situation that you thought would be bad but turned out well.

• Design a T-shirt for an Alaskan souvenir shop.

October 19
Lord Cornwallis Surrendered

● ● ● ● ● ● ● ● ● ● ● ● ● ● ● ● ● ●

Other Events This Day
- U.S. stock market crashed on "Black Monday" (1929)
- Basketball introduced to the 1936 Olympic Games by Berlin Organization Committee (1933)

A combined army of French and American troops numbering around 17,000 surrounded British General Cornwallis and his 8,000 British soldiers and seamen at Yorktown, Virginia. This maneuver proved to be the beginning of the end of the American Revolution. Lord Cornwallis, who had previously driven General Washington out of New Jersey and General Gates out of South Carolina, led his weary troops toward the Virginia coast where he thought reinforcements would come to him. After several raids of towns and plantations in Virginia, he settled in Yorktown in August and started fortifying the city.

Offshore, the French fleet blocked Lord Cornwallis's aid and reinforcements. On land, the American and French troops surrounded the city of Yorktown and subjected the British troops to three weeks of shelling. With supplies dwindling and no reinforcements, Lord Cornwallis realized that his only choice was to surrender. Lord Cornwallis surrendered his men, cannons, galleys, frigate, and transport ships on this date in 1781. The British troops marched to surrender as their instruments played "The World Turned Upside Down." Some insignificant battles followed this surrender, and the Colonies finally won their independence.

Response

Lord Cornwallis thought settling in Yorktown was a good idea; however, it turned out to be a nightmare. Have you ever had a good idea that turned out poorly? Explain.

Fascinating Factoid: During the siege of Yorktown, Lord Cornwallis had few options left. He sent smallpox-infected men across the lines in hopes of infecting the French and Americans.

Word Play

An *oxymoron* is a figure of speech using two contradictory words. (Examples: fine mess, virtual reality, unbiased opinion.) There is one oxymoron in the story. Find and write it below.

_____

Now match the first part to the second part of each of the following oxymorons.

_____ 1. paid	a. much
_____ 2. least	b. volunteer
_____ 3. wise	c. fool
_____ 4. climb	d. favorite
_____ 5. nothing	e. crook
_____ 6. old	f. shorts
_____ 7. melted	g. news
_____ 8. long	h. down
_____ 9. honest	i. ice

On the back of this sheet, write several oxymorons of your own.

Activity

- Imagine that Lord Cornwallis had kept a diary of his last week before surrender. What would he have written in this diary? Create diary entries for each day of that last week of the battle, describing what Lord Cornwallis was thinking, feeling, etc.

October 20
P. T. Barnum's Circus Opened

Other Events This Day
- U.S. Senate ratified Louisiana Purchase (1803)
- John F. Kennedy's Presidential Library dedicated in Boston (1979)

P. T. Barnum's Circus opened on this day in 1873. Mr. Barnum was born July 5, 1810, in Bethel, Connecticut. His beginning in show business came in 1835 when he paid $1,000 to exhibit Joice Heth, a woman who claimed to be 161 years old! She also said she had been George Washington's nurse. Because of Mr. Barnum's talent for publicity, this exhibit was a great success. Mr. Barnum is responsible for the first Circus Parade, which was held in Rochester, New York.

Mr. Barnum purchased Scudders American Museum and changed its name to Barnum's American Museum, which he packed with dozens of peculiarities and performances. He introduced Charles Stratton, a 25-inch (63.5 cm) tall man and he called him General Tom Thumb. General Tom Thumb was on exhibit at the museum, along with the Feejee Mermaid.

In 1881, Mr. Barnum joined with two London circus promoters, James Bailey and James Hutchison, to create P. T. Barnum's Greatest Show on Earth. Mr. Barnum then invited James Bailey to become a full partner. It became the new Barnum & Bailey Circus, which was later sold to Ringling Brothers in 1907.

Response

What is something in your classroom that is about the same height as General Tom Thumb? How does his height compare to your height?

Fascinating Factoid: The Feejee Mermaid, displayed in Mr. Barnum's museum, was really an embalmed monkey sewed into an embalmed fish's body.

Word Play

Alliteration is repetition of the beginning sounds in two or more words next to each other. Use each circus word to write an alliteration sentence or phrase on the back of this sheet.
Example: Tom Thumb tried to toot the trumpet.

acrobat

clown

sideshow

elephants

lions

caravan

circus

sword swallower

tent

tightrope

trapeze

jugglers

Activities

- Mr. Barnum got his start with exhibits of unusual persons and things. Imagine that you are opening an exhibit of odd and unusual animals. Combine animal parts from two different animals to make a new creature for your exhibit. Draw your animal and give it a name. Describe what it eats, whether it is tame or wild, and its characteristics.

- Which job would you apply for at a circus? Explain why you would like this job and what makes you qualified for it. What would you expect your day to be like?

October 21
Edison Invented Lightbulb

• • • • • • • • • • • • • • • • • •

Other Events This Day
• Magellan entered the strait that now bears his name (1520)
• Solomon R. Guggenheim Museum of Modern and Contemporary Art, designed by Frank Lloyd Wright opened in New York City (1959)

In 1878, the best source of lighting was gas lamps—and at best—they were bad! Gas lighting was dirty and dangerous. It used the oxygen in the air, and it caused fires and explosions. For years, inventors had tried to find a better way to light up our lives. They had a working electrical model, but it didn't work for very long. There was a filament in a vacuum tube. When electricity passed through the filament, it would glow. The big problem was that they couldn't find a filament that wouldn't burn up.

The story of the electric lightbulb goes back to 1811 when Sir Humphry Davy, an Englishman, found that an electrical arc could make light by passing between two poles. He actually invented the first lightbulb. In 1878, Sir Joseph Wilson Swan, an English physicist, developed a longer-lasting lightbulb. His lightbulb burned up to 13½ hours. However, it was an American, Thomas Alva Edison, who finally succeeded in coming up with the right filament that lasted the longest. His invention was based on a lightbulb patent of 1875, which he purchased from Henry Woodward and Matthew Evans.

Finally, on October 21, 1879, Mr. Edison announced that he had carbonized a piece of sewing thread to make a filament that lasted 40 hours. Then by changing the shape of the filament, he increased the burning time to 100 hours.

Response

Based on information in this story, would you call Mr. Edison the true inventor of the lightbulb? Why or why not?

Fascinating Factoid: Today, the average lightbulb burns for about 1,500 hours.

Word Play

Homophones are words that sound alike but are spelled differently. In the first column, finish the story word. In the second column, write a word that is pronounced the same as the word in the first column.

1. A _r_ _c_   _Ark_   6. B __ __ __ __   _____

2. T __   _____   7. W __ __ __ __   _____

3. W __ __   _____   8. T __ __ __   _____

4. B __   _____   9. P __ __ __ __   _____

5. T __ __ __ __ __ __   _____

Activities

• Thomas Edison was often referred to as a genius (incredibly smart), but he once said, "Genius is 1% inspiration and 99% perspiration." Explain what you think he meant by that statement.

• Lightbulbs are used in comics above a character's head to indicate a bright idea. Draw an outline of a lightbulb. Inside the outline of the lightbulb, write about the best idea you've ever had.

October 22
First National
Horse Show Held

• • • • • • • • • • • • • • • •

Other Events This Day

• Princeton University chartered (1746)
• Charles King who discovered Vitamin C born (1896)

America's oldest horse show, the National Horse Show, was first held on this day in 1883 at the original Madison Square Garden in New York City. In 1909, the show became international when the president of the show, Alfred G. Vanderbilt, invited British cavalry officers to compete. In 1983, the show celebrated its 100th anniversary with 100 horse-drawn carriages parading through Central Park in New York City.

The show moved to New Jersey's Meadowlands Arena in 1989. The larger facilities allowed for more competition divisions. The National Horse Show returned to Madison Square Garden in 1996. In 1997, a special celebration was held at Rockefeller Plaza for the show's 114th year. In 2002, the show moved to Wellington, Florida.

Today more than 50,000 spectators attend this annual event. The competition takes place over several days. About 400 horses are involved in this show produced by the National Horse Show Association. The competition is always at the highest level. Over the past 120+ years, proceeds from the event have benefited many worthwhile charities.

Response

Why do you think the National Horse Show moved to Wellington, Florida?

Fascinating Factoid: Normally, an adult horse has 40 teeth.

Word Play

Several breeds of horses are listed in the Word Box. Find each word in the puzzle.

| ARABIAN |
| LUSITANO |
| LIPIZZAN |
| MORGAN |
| APPALOOSA |
| MUSTANG |
| PALOMINO |
| PINTO |
| CRIOLLO |
| ANDALUSIAN |
| HANOVERIAN |
| TRAKEHNER |
| CLYDESDALE |

```
M I L R N A I R E V O N A H
N A I B A R A T Y Y U N A A
O N P R T S P O L L O I R C
L D I K I U P I N T O K R O
U A Z H J K A L M N G F E V
S L Z N D Z L X C V B N N A
I U A A G H O F R E S K H N
T S N G Y U O I O L K J E K
A I N R M U S T A N G W K E
N A T O G C A D T A B H A U
O N I M O L A P P Y J M R M
X V E L A D S E D Y L C T B
```

Activities

• Choose from one of the following "horsey" sayings and illustrate its literal meaning. Then explain in writing what it actually means: "That was a horse of a different color." "Quit horsing around." "Don't put the cart before the horse."

• Hands, not feet, are used to describe the measure of horses. Estimate how many hands tall you, your teacher, and a classmate are. Then check to see how good an estimator you are.

October 23
First Miniature Golf Tournament Played

Other Events This Day
- Blanche S. Scott became first female aviator to fly solo in an airplane (1910)
- Famous soccer player, Pelé, born (1940)

After playoffs in each state, over 200 players, representing 30 states, played for the top prize of $2,000 in the first National Miniature Golf Tournament on this date in 1930. This tournament was held on Lookout Mountain in Chattanooga, Tennessee. Since that date, national playoffs have been held, and they have been televised for the last few years. Miniature golf is scheduled to be part of the World Games in 2009.

Miniature golf started off as Garden Golf in the early 1900s. It was a shortened version of real golf, and it played with a putter on real grass. In the 1920s and 1930s, rails or bumpers appeared to keep the ball in a given area. The playing surface was hard-pressed cottonseed hulls. Other changes have been made over the years.

During the 1930s, there were about 30,000 miniature golf courses in America. Why did it become so popular? Perhaps because most people looked at it as a game in which everyone in the family could play and enjoy together.

Response

Compare early miniature golf with today's version.

Fascinating Factoid: About four million Americans played miniature golf in the 1930s.

Word Play

Find at least five story words that can make new words when written backward.

1. G __ __ __   _____

2. K __ __ __   _____

3. W __ __   _____

4. T __ __   _____

5. O __   _____

Now write a few reverse word pairs of your own.

_____   _____

_____   _____

_____   _____

Activities

- Create a board game about golf. Remember to include sand traps. Write the rules for your game.

- Design your own miniature golf course or an interesting hole for a miniature golf course. Make it challenging and interesting. Explain how it works.

October 24
United Nations Founded

Other Events This Day

- World's first soccer club, Sheffield F. C., founded in England (1857)
- Anna Taylor became first woman to go over Niagara Falls in a barrel (1901)

The United Nations (UN) was founded on October 24, 1945, when representatives from 50 countries met to draw up a charter. In 1947, this date was proclaimed by the General Assembly to be United Nations Day. United Nations Day is an international observance to commemorate the founding of this organization.

The idea of a United Nations organization was to save mankind from future horrible wars, focus on fundamental human rights, and promote better standards of living for all. The idea of a special day is to focus on the organization, its aims, and achievements. UN Day is now observed in nearly 200 member countries—large and small.

United Nations International Children's Emergency Fund (UNICEF) is one of the family of organizations within the United Nations. UNICEF was organized in 1946 during the first session of the UN General Assembly. It was intended to provide relief for millions of children involved in World War II. UNICEF was originally intended to be temporary; however, it became permanent in the 1950s.

Response

What is the purpose of the United Nations?

Fascinating Factoid: Although the United Nations provides measures for security and peace, the majority of its resources are devoted to economic, social, and sustainable development.

Word Play

Use the telephone dial to decode the name of each country that is a member of the United Nations. The first letter of each country is given.

2 ABC	3 DEF	4 GHI
5 JKL	6 MNO	7 PQRS
8 TUV	9 WXYZ	

a. 263-7422   A _____

b. 526-2422   J _____

c. 336-6275   D _____

d. 235-4486   B _____

e. 473-5263   I _____

f. 287-8742   A _____

g. 346-5263   F _____

h. 437-6269   G _____

i. 378-6642   E _____

Activities

- Write a motto for the United Nations, incorporating the goals and purposes of the organization.
- Make a detailed drawing of a sculpture that could be exhibited at the UN Building, representing world peace.

October 25
Pablo Picasso's Birthday

Not many painters are recognized while they are alive; that is not the case with Picasso. Pablo Ruiz Picasso (pee-kah'-soh) was born October 25, 1881, in Malaga, Spain. Picasso was an extremely intelligent and sensitive youngster. His parents, Jose Ruiz Blanco and Maria Picasso Lopez, encouraged him in his artistic talents. Pablo chose to adopt his mother's name, Picasso, because it was better known in the area.

At age 14, Picasso moved to Barcelona, Spain, to continue his studies in art. Later, he went to Paris, like many other aspiring artists. Life was hard in Paris. He roomed with another young man; and because they were so poor, they burned Picasso's drawings for warmth in the cold winters.

While in Paris, Picasso became very depressed. This is the time that was called his "Blue Period," and it produced his first independent art style. Next came the "Rose Period," which was inspired by a young woman. It was during this time period that his paintings sold well, and he was no longer poor. Working with another artist, Georges Braque, Picasso developed what is known as the Cubist style of art.

Response

How was Picasso's art influenced by his life circumstances?

Fascinating Factoid: Picasso produced over 20,000 paintings, prints, drawings, sculptures, ceramics, theater sets, and costumes during his lifetime.

Word Play

Analogies are comparisons. Complete the following analogies with story words.

Example: Paris is to France as Beirut is to Lebanon.

1. Statue is to sculptor as painting is to _____ .

2. Rome is to Italy as Barcelona is to _____ .

3. Plenty is to needy as rich is to _____ .

4. Knives are to carvers as hammers are to _____ .

5. **Z** is to **A** as last is to _____ .

6. Colts are to horses as children are to _____ .

7. Girl is to boy as woman is to _____

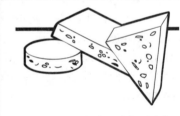

Activity

• Imagine that you have been hired to create a fabric design for a new line of children's clothing.

Create a geometric fabric design on a large sheet of paper. If supplies are available, use geometric-shaped sponges dipped in various colored paints. When it is dry, cut out the shape of a blouse, shirt, or dress from your fabric design. If paints are not available, use crayons or markers.

October 26
International Red Cross Organized

• • • • • • • • • • • • • • • • •

Other Events This Day

• First Continental Congress adjourns (1774)

• Erie Canal opened (1825)

The Red Cross was organized on October 26, 1863, as part of an international humanitarian effort that began in war-torn Europe. The idea for the Red Cross came from Henry Dunant, a young man from Switzerland. In 1859, he witnessed a bloody battle in Italy that left about 40,000 dead and dying on the battlefield. Mr. Dunant organized the local people to feed and tend the wounded.

Mr. Dunant's book, describing what he witnessed on the battlefield, reached many and led to the formation of the International Committee of the Red Cross. The organization's purpose was to provide neutral and impartial care to the sick and wounded in times of war. Today there are Red Cross chapters in about 175 countries, including the United States, which make up the International Federation of Red Cross and Red Crescent Societies. Headquarters are in Geneva, Switzerland.

While the International Red Cross was being established in Europe, the American Civil War was in progress. Clara Barton from Massachusetts helped care for the wounded on those battlefields. After the Civil War, Ms. Barton learned more about the Red Cross when visiting Europe. Upon returning home, she helped persuade the U.S. government to participate. The American Red Cross was established in May 1881. In 1900, Congress granted the American Red Cross a charter, making it responsible for services to the U.S. Armed Forces and relief to disaster victims at home and abroad.

Response
What are some of the functions of the American Red Cross today?

Fascinating Factoid: Today, more than 1,200,000 trained and dedicated volunteers serve in the American Red Cross.

Word Play
Use 2 five-letter story words that have a common letter and form a word cross. Then on the back of this sheet, make up and write your own three-letter word cross. Then try a seven-letter word cross.

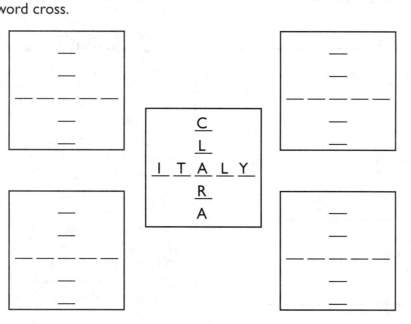

C
L
I T A L Y
R
A

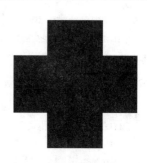

Activities
• Make a list of things you would like to ask a speaker from the American Red Cross should you have the opportunity.

• Write about a time when you or your family or friends have been helped by the American Red Cross or how you, your family, or friends have helped the American Red Cross.

October 27
Theodore Roosevelt's Birthday

• • • • • • • • • • • • • • • • • •

Other Events This Day

• World's first subway opened in New York City (1904)

• Du Pont announced that it would name its new synthetic yarn *nylon* (1938)

The 26th U.S. president, Theodore (Teddy) Roosevelt, was born on October 27, 1858. In 1902, he and a group went to Mississippi to settle a border dispute. While there, they went on a hunting trip. After several days with no luck, members of President Roosevelt's party tied a black bear cub to a tree for the president to shoot. He refused to harm the defenseless bear.

The next day, a political cartoon about this event appeared in newspapers across the country. It sparked the imagination of many Americans. In Brooklyn, New York, shopkeeper Morris Michtom asked his wife to make two stuffed bears for his display window—and you know the rest of the story! The bears were an instant success. Mr. Michtom got permission to call the stuffed bears "Teddy bears." Over the years, the teddy bear has become a symbol for love, friendship, care, and comfort. They were popular 100 years ago and they are equally popular today.

After reading a book about a man who dedicated his life to giving teddy bears to children in the hospital, James Ownsby organized a group called *Good Bears of the World*. This organization began in Bern, Switzerland, in 1973. It was established to bring the caring power of the teddy bear to people of all ages in need of a little hug.

Response

How do you think President Roosevelt would have felt about the fame of the teddy bear?

Fascinating Factoid: Sales of teddy bears by Mr. Morris Michtom allowed him to start the Ideal Toy Company.

Word Play

Insert spaces between the words to discover some interesting facts about Theodore Roosevelt. Rewrite the sentences on another sheet of paper, inserting the proper spaces, capitals, and punctuation.

1. Hewasthefirstpresidenttoflyinanairplane
2. Hewasthefirstpresidenttoownacar
3. Teddyfounded51birdsanctuaries
4. Hefoundedthefirst18monumentsinthecountry
5. Hehadakittennamedtomquartz
6. Hispetgardensnakewasnamedemilyspinach
7. Hisbluemacawwasnameddeli
8. Teddyrooseveltwasthefirstamericanaswellasfirstpresidenttowin anobelprize
9. Helikedroastbeefmashedpotatoesandstringbeansforsunday dinner
10. Itissaidthathedrankaboutagallonofcoffeeeachday
11. Hewasborninnewyork
12. Hischildrennamedtheirpetsafterrealpeopletheyadmired
13. Presidenttheodorerooseveltoncesaid"speaksoftlyandcarry abigstick"

Activities

• Make a list of 10 good reasons everybody needs a teddy bear.

• Create a Teddy Bear Award using a teddy bear or button. The Teddy Bear Award for the day or week goes to a student who gives special care or comfort to another person.

October 28
Statue of Liberty Dedicated

Other Events This Day
- Dr. Jonas Salk's birthday (1914)
- U.S. Congress passed Volstead Act, leading the way to Prohibition (1919)

• • • • • • • • • • • • • • • • • • •

The Statue of Liberty was dedicated on this day in 1886. It was a gift of international friendship from the people of France to the people of the United States. It stands for freedom, democracy, and diplomacy. The friendship between France and the United States was forged when the Colonies began their quest for independence.

The statue itself was the brainchild of Edouard Rene Lefevre de Laboulaye of France. His idea was to honor the friendship and the commitment to liberty between the two countries. The project was a joint effort; the American people built the pedestal and the French people built the statue.

French sculptor Auguste Bartholdi and structural engineer Gustave Eiffel (designer of the Eiffel Tower) finished the project in Paris, and the statue was presented to the United States on July 4, 1884, in Paris. The statue was then dismantled into 350 pieces, packed in over 214 crates, and shipped to the United States on board the French frigate *Isere*.

Lady Liberty was re-assembled on Liberty Island, originally Bedloe's Island, as a welcoming site to all immigrants arriving in New York Harbor.

Response

Why was the Statue of Liberty created?

Fascinating Factoid: Winds of 50 miles (80.5 km) per hour can cause the torch on the Statue of Liberty to sway 5 inches (12.7 cm).

Word Play

Decode this puzzle to learn the official name of the Statue of Liberty. (The four-letter-shift pattern of coding was used—does that give you a clue?)

I = E

___ ___ ___ ___ ___ ___ ___
P   M   F   I   V   X   C

___ ___ ___ ___ ___ ___ ___ ___ ___ ___ ___
I   R   P   M   K   L   X   I   R   M   R   K

___ ___ ___   ___ ___ ___ ___ ___
X   L   I   A   S   V   P   H

Activity

- The Statue of Liberty welcomes people to the United States. Are there statues that symbolize your town or city? Describe them and what they symbolize. If your town doesn't have a statue, design one that would symbolize your town to newcomers.

October 29
First Ballpoint Pen Sold

Other Events This Day

- William Penn landed in present-day Pennsylvania (1682)
- John Glenn, first American to orbit Earth, returned to space at age 77 (1998)

On October 29, 1945, about 5,000 people were lined up outside Gimbels Department Store waiting to buy ballpoint pens for $12.50 each. The entire stock of 10,000 was sold out that first day.

It all started in 1888 when John J. Loud of Massachusetts applied for a patent on a pen having a round marking point that would revolve in all directions—in other words, a ballpoint pen. The 1888 patent was unused and expired. In 1935, Hungarian Laszio Biro and his brother George developed a new tip that consisted of a ball that was free to turn in a socket. They manufactured the pens in Argentina. The pens were not very good at first because the ink was either too thick or too thin and did not flow well. The pens had to be held upright for the ink to flow at all. World War II pilots liked the pen because it worked well at high altitudes and it did not have to be refilled often. The U.S. government urged companies in America to make them. Eberhard Faber paid the Biro brothers $500,000 for the rights to manufacture their ballpoint pen in America. Meanwhile, Milton Reynolds saw the pen in Argentina and because many of the patents on them had expired, he began manufacturing the pens. He made millions of pens and millions of dollars!

Response

What is one thing you learned about the ballpoint pen?

Fascinating Factoid: The first ballpoint pen went on sale 57 years after it was first patented.

Word Play

Use each clue to find a word that contains *pen*.

1. PEN __ __ __ __
   (punishment)

2. PEN __ __ __ __ __ __ __
   (antibiotic)

3. PEN __ __ __ __
   (not finished)

4. PEN __ __ __ __
   (flag)

5. PEN __ __ __ __
   (flightless bird)

6. PEN __ __ __ __ __ __ __ __ __
   (jail)

7. PEN __ __ __
   (writing instrument)

8. __ __ __ __ PEN
   (place where pitcher warms up)

9. __ __ PEN
   (type of tree)

10. __ PEN __
    (use money)

11. __ PEN
    (not closed)

12. PEN __ __ __ __ __ __ __
    (top floor of tall apartment building)

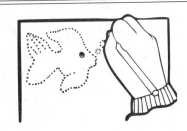

Activities

- Using felt pens, create a pointillism picture. A pointillism picture is made by dots only. There are no markings other than the dots made by pen points.

- We use pens to tell our diaries all about our lives each day. What if at the end of a day, a pen wrote in its own diary? What would the pen say about its day? Write a day's entry using the pen's point of view.

October 30
The Day the Nation Panicked

Other Events This Day
- President John Adam's birthday (1735)
- Daniel Cooper patents a time clock (1894)

On October 30, 1938, millions of Americans tuned in to a very popular radio program that featured plays; many of which starred Orson Welles. The play selected for broadcast that evening was called *The War of the Worlds,* written by H. G. Wells. It was a science fiction play about an alien invasion. Orson Welles directed the play to be reformatted into a newscast format, thinking that it would heighten the drama. An explanation of the play's content was given at the beginning and again about 40 minutes into the play.

As the play progressed, dance music was interrupted by news bulletins reporting a huge flaming object landing on a farm in New Jersey. Additional news flashes described the spaceship and even aliens emerging from the spaceship. For some reason, thousands of listeners did not hear the announcement about it being a play. They thought they were actually hearing a news account! People panicked. They flooded the newspaper and radio stations with telephone calls. They packed the roads, hid in cellars, and wrapped their heads in wet towels thinking it would keep the poisonous gas from killing them. Some listeners even had to have medical attention.

This radio program was produced with such vividness that it caused mass hysteria, and many listeners thought this was the beginning of a war of the worlds. This event spurred many studies into the phenomenon of mass hysteria.

Response
If you heard a broadcast such as this, what would you think? What would you do?

Fascinating Factoid: *The New York Times* took nearly a thousand calls on that night. One caller actually wanted to know what time the world would end.

Word Play
The root word for *panicked* is *panic.* Notice that a **k** was inserted before **ed** was added. Words ending in **c** almost always have the letter **k** inserted after the **c** when a suffix beginning with **e, i,** or **y** is added. Write the word, which ends in **c**, for each definition below. Add the **K** before the proper endings.

1. played about happily_____

2. went on an outing with food _____

3. a state of overpowering fright _____

4. having abdominal pain _____

5. taste given off by pungent bulbous herb _____

On the back of this sheet, write a list of all the words you can think of that end with **c.** Then write if a suffix beginning with **e, i,** or **y** can be added.

Activity
- Write your own science fiction story in a play format suitable for a radio broadcast. Be sure to include instructions for sound effects.

October 31

Happy Halloween

● ● ● ● ● ● ● ● ● ● ● ● ● ● ● ● ● ● ●

Other Events This Day

• Birthday of Girl Scout founder Juliette Gordon Low (1860)
• Nevada admitted as 36th U.S. state (1864)

Halloween is one of America's oldest holidays. It started thousands of years ago. Of course, it wasn't the Halloween that we know today.

Today's Halloween has been influenced by many cultures over the centuries, from the Roman's Pomona Day to the Celtic festival of Samhain (pronounced *sow-in*) to the Christian holidays of All Saints and All Souls Days. Over the years, the customs from these holidays became mixed. It was known as All Hallow Even, then All Hallow's Eve, Hallowe'en, and now Halloween.

Irish immigrants probably brought the custom of Halloween to America in the 1840s. The Irish used turnips as their "Jacks lanterns," but when they came to America, they found that pumpkins were more plentiful, and so the Jack-o-lantern became a hollowed-out pumpkin.

Response

When Halloween came to America in 1840, what big change was made to Americanize it?

Fascinating Factoid: About 99 percent of all pumpkins marketed are used at Halloween time.

Word Play

Write the question for each answer to a Halloween riddle.

1. _____ ?
   (spookhetti)

2. _____ ?
   (boo-berry pie)

3. _____ ?
   (witch watch)

4. _____ ?
   (boo jeans)

5. _____ ?
   (boo booms)

6. _____ ?
   (I scream)

7. _____ ?
   (day scare center)

8. _____ ?
   (scare spray)

9. _____ ?
   (ghoulie)

Activities

• Brainstorm and list as many scary Halloween characters as you can. Then write a tongue twister using each. Example: witch = Wanda Witch went wacky when walking with Waldo.

• Write and solve five Halloween math word problems.

November

November 1
Motion Picture Ratings Began

● ● ● ● ● ● ● ● ● ● ● ● ● ● ● ● ● ●

Other Events This Day
- U.S. Weather Service established (1870)
- Diphtheria vaccine discovered by Dr. Roux of Paris, France (1894)

Have you been to a good movie lately? What was it rated? The rating of motion pictures began in the United States on November 1, 1968. Ratings are an effort to give moviegoers an idea of the suitability for different age groups. Ratings are not mandated by law. They came about as a voluntary action by the movie industry to avoid government regulations.

In the 1960s, movies were being made that were explicit and violent, and often with undesirable language. After meetings between the government and representatives of the movie industry, a rating system was scheduled. Movies are submitted to the Classification and Rating Administration of the Motion Picture Association of America before they are released to the public. If the moviemakers are not happy with the rating given to them, they can edit the film to come in compliance with the rating they are seeking.

When you go to a G-rated movie, you are seeing a movie suitable for all ages. A PG-rated movie means that there is some material that may not be suitable for children, and parental guidance is suggested. PG–13 means that parents should be strongly cautious; some material in the movie may be inappropriate for children under 13. A parent or adult guardian must accompany children under the age of 17 to see an R-rated movie. The NC17 rating means that no one under 17 is admitted.

Response

Do you think the motion picture rating system is effective in protecting children? Explain.

Fascinating Factoid: In Australia, a governmental body decides movie ratings.

Word Play

There are many different genres (types) of movies and even many subgenres. Match each genre to the corresponding description.

_____ 1. horror	a. horses, dusty towns, trails
_____ 2. crime	b. high energy, stunts, chases
_____ 3. drama	c. criminals, mobsters, bank robbers
_____ 4. adventure	d. realistic characters, settings, and situations
_____ 5. science fiction	e. lavish costumes, legendary figures, extravagant settings, grandeur
_____ 6. action	f. amusing, funny, usually with happy endings
_____ 7. war/antiwar	g. travels, conquests, explorations
_____ 8. comedy	h. terrifying, shocking, scary
_____ 9. musical	i. songs and choreography integrated into story line
_____ 10. western	j. visionary, imaginative, heroes, aliens, planets
_____ 11. epic/historical	k. horrors and heartbreak of conflicts between countries

On the back of this sheet, write the title of a movie to fit in each genre.

Activities

- Devise a rating system for books you have read—such as LK, which could mean suitable for Little Kids. Your rating system can be based on reading difficulty, interest level, subject matter, etc.

- Brainstorm and list movies you have seen or heard about, and explain if you agree or disagree with their ratings.

November 2
The Spruce Goose Was Airborne

• • • • • • • • • • • • • • • • • • • •

Other Events This Day

• Daniel Boone's birthday (1834)
• Martin Luther King Jr. Day established (1988)

The largest airplane ever built took to the air on November 2, 1947. Made of laminated birch and spruce lumber, it was designed and built by Howard Hughes, a successful Hollywood movie producer and owner of Hughes Aviation. It was Mr. Hughes who sat at the controls when this giant seaplane took to the sky for a mile-long (1.6 km) flight. The airplane was known as Hughes Flying Boat.

This giant of the sky, also known as Hercules, was often called the "Flying Lumberyard" and "The Spruce Goose." It was designed to carry 750 fully equipped troops and two Sherman tanks. The airplane was made of lumber because the United States was in World War II and it needed to divert all of the available metals to the war effort. This plane had a wingspan of over 300 feet (91.4 m), and it was powered by eight strong engines with 17-foot (5.2 m) propellers. It weighed about 300,000 pounds (136,077.7 kg).

Although construction of this plane was begun during World War II, it was not ready for testing until the war was over. At that point, there was no longer a need for this type of aircraft. So, the Spruce Goose is the only one of its kind ever built. Although it never flew again after its maiden flight, Mr. Hughes kept the plane maintained and flight ready until his death.

Response

Compare the size of a football field with the wingspan of the Spruce Goose.

Fascinating Factoid: Mr. Hughes paid $1 million per year to store the Spruce Goose from the 1940s until he died in 1976.

Word Play

Spruce Goose is a rhyming word pair. Supply the words to make a rhyming word pair for each clue.

1. glove for a little cat _____ _____

2. bashful secret agent _____ _____

3. badly behaved young person_____ _____

4. corner library shelf _____ _____

5. uncommon twosome_____ _____

6. animal educator_____ _____

7. feisty primate _____ _____

On the back of this sheet, write several pairs of rhyming words similar to the pairs above.

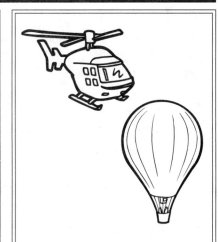

Activities

• Use Venn Diagrams to compare the following: an airplane and a glider; a helicopter and a hot air balloon; a kite and a seed.

• Research Bernouilli's Principle and summarize how it relates to the flight of an airplane.

November 3
Happy Birthday, Sandwich!

• • • • • • • • • • • • • • •

November 3 marks the birthday of John Montague, the Fourth Earl of Sandwich, born in 1718. Montague gets credit for discovering the sandwich. Sandwich Day is celebrated each year on the anniversary of John Montague's birth. This English nobleman loved to gamble. He participated in gambling marathons in different pubs in England. It is said that in 1762, he had been gambling in a London Men's Club for at least 24 hours and apparently having a run of good luck. He was hungry, but he didn't want to risk leaving the gambling table to go out for dinner. He asked someone to bring him some meat between two slices of bread.

Other gamblers kept asking for the same meal that the Earl of Sandwich was having. The concept of meat between two pieces of bread caught on quickly. People started calling for a *sandwich*.

The French disagree with this account of the first sandwich. They say that long before 1762, people were taking meat between bread to the fields to eat as they worked. Although the English and the French may have been the first to eat a sandwich, it is the Americans who have taken it to new heights. We have perfected the art of sandwiching. We are accustomed to sandwiches of all sizes, shapes, and flavors. The all-time favorite of most younger people is the peanut butter and jelly sandwich.

Response
What is your favorite kind of sandwich? Describe how to make it.

Fascinating Factoid: According to the *Great Food Almanac*, the average American eats 193 sandwiches a year.

Word Play
The word *sandwich* is an eponym. An *eponym* is a word derived from someone's name. Unscramble each word to discover the eponym for a person.

1. _ _ _ _ _ _ _ _
   CANRAHDI
   (Arachne, a girl who turned into a spider in a myth)

2. _ _ _ _ _ _
   AEGOBNI
   (Michael Begon)

3. _ _ _ _ _ _ _ _ _ _
   GSGE DETEBCNI
   (Commodore E. C. Benedict)

4. _ _ _ _ _ _ _ _ _ _ _ _
   EPASIRUTZITONA
   (Louis Pasteur)

5. _ _ _ _ _ _ _ _ _
   SOSPHNEUAO
   (John Phillip Sousa)

6. _ _ _ _ _ _ _ _
   RMOSE DEOC
   (Samuel Morse)

7. _ _ _ _ _ _ _ _ _ _
   FFEILE WETOR
   (Alexander Gaston Eiffel)

8. _ _ _ _ _ _ _ _ _ _
   RERFIS ELEHW
   (George Washington Gale Ferris)

9. _ _ _ _ _ _
   LORATDE
   (Jules Leotard)

10. _ _ _ _ _ _ _ _ _
    SPITNOIETA
    (Joel Roberts Poinsett)

11. _ _ _ _ _
    NIZNIA
    (John Gottfried Zinn)

12. _ _ _ _ _ _ _ _ _
    DTEDY REAB
    (Theodore Roosevelt)

Activity
- Imagine that you are going to cater a party with sandwiches. The supplies you have on hand are wheat bread, white bread, and three kinds of meat—ham, beef and turkey. You have two kinds of cheese—American and Swiss. Make a list showing all the different combinations for sandwiches you can make from your supplies.

November 4
First Election Day Observed Nationwide

Each state used to have its own election day, ranging from October to December. This didn't work well because a dishonest person could vote in one state on a certain day and then travel to another state to vote again.

Eventually, Congress passed a law, establishing Election Day as the Tuesday after the first Monday in November. Americans observed their first uniform election day on November 4, 1845. Every year since that time, even-numbered years have congressional elections, and presidential elections take place every four years in years that are divisible by four.

November was probably chosen as Election Day because that is a time when the crops were harvested and the weather wasn't too bad yet for people to get out to the polls and vote. Tuesday was probably chosen because that would give voters a day to travel to their polling places after their day of rest on Sunday. In early days, polling places were usually in the county seats—not in every town. People had to walk, ride horses, or travel in wagons to vote.

Response

Why is it important to have a single day for elections in our country?

Fascinating Factoid: Gerald Ford was the only man who held both the presidency and the vice presidency and was not elected to either post.

Word Play

Begin with the word *Vote*. Use addition and subtraction to complete each new word. The first letter for each new word has been provided for you.

VOTE

1. + R = V __ __ __ __

2. + E = R __ __ __ __ __

3. – E + L = R __ __ __ __ __

4. + AG – R = V __ __ __ __ __ __

5. + U – OLT = V __ __ __ __

6. + RD – UV = R __ __ __ __

7. – RD + V = G __ __ __

8. – V = A __ __

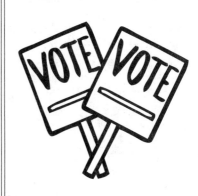

Activity

• Think of a school position that you would like to hold such as student council president or class officer. Create a slogan, jingle, and short speech on why people should vote for you. Create a strategy for getting elected.

November 5
Shirley Chisholm Elected to Congress

Other Events This Day
- Susan B. Anthony arrested for trying to vote (1872)
- First U.S. patent for automobile issued to George Selden (1895)

On November 5, 1968, Shirley Anita St. Hill Chisholm became the first African-American woman to be elected to the U.S. House of Representatives. Before serving as a U.S. Representative, she served in the New York Assembly.

Born in Brooklyn, New York, on November 30, 1924, Shirley Chisholm spent several years with her grandparents in Barbados. She received a degree from Brooklyn College in 1946 and a Master's Degree from Columbia in 1952. Upon graduating from Brooklyn College, Ms. Chisholm taught in a nursery school and later became a childcare center director.

After gaining support from local Democrats in Brooklyn, Ms. Chisholm was elected as a state assemblywoman in 1964. She became known as one of the best female speakers in the country. While serving in the House of Representatives until 1982, her most notable causes were childcare issues and minimum wage legislation. She cosponsored an act that would have guaranteed a minimum wage. In 1971, she announced plans to seek the Democratic nomination for U.S. president. In her unsuccessful campaign throughout the country, she addressed educational issues. Until she retired, Ms. Chisholm continued to fight for labor, women's rights, and public education.

Response
Explain why you think Shirley Chisholm should have an important place in American history.

Fascinating Factoid: Although Shirley Chisholm was the first African-American woman to run for president, she was the second woman to seek that office. Victoria Woodhull ran in 1872 on an equal rights platform.

Word Play
Listed below are other "firsts" for African-American women. Unscramble each name. (Hint: The letters shown in bold print are the first letters in each name).

1. **M**RIANA **A**ERNSODN _____
   (first African-American singer at the Metropolitan Opera)

2. THAEL**A** BSIN**G**O _____
   (first African-American tennis player to win Wimbledon Singles)

3. HU**R**T ORAL**C** AY**T**LOR _____
   (first African-American airline stewardess)

4. PRH**O**A FIN**W**EYR _____
   (first African-American woman to own a TV production company)

5. ATLAEI**N** EL**C**O_____
   (first African-American to win a Grammy® for Best New Artist)

6. LALE**H** RE**B**RY_____
   (first African-American woman to win an Oscar® for Best Actress)

Chisholm for President

Activities
- Shirley Chisholm wanted to be a U.S. president. Her platform was labor, women's rights, and public education. If you were running for president, what three things would you choose to include in your platform? Explain your choices.

- There's a wonderful poem, "If I Were in Charge of the World," by Judith Viorst. Write a poem about how things would be in the United States if you were in charge.

November 6
John Philip Sousa's Birthday

Other Events This Day
- Founder of basketball, James Naismith's birthday (1861)
- Jacob Schick patented first electric razor (1928)

John Philip Sousa was born November 6, 1854, in Washington DC. His father played trombone in the U.S. Marine Band. He started his study of music around the age of eight. He eventually became known as the March King because over 100 of his musical compositions were marches. Many were written especially for the U.S. Marine Band, with which he signed on as an apprentice at age 13. At 26, he became the leader. In his 12 years as the leader of the U.S. Marine Band, Mr. Sousa transformed it into the country's premier band, known as The President's Own. He served under five different presidents—Hayes, Garfield, Cleveland, Arthur, and Harrison.

After resigning from the Marines, he started his own band that successfully toured the world. Mr. Sousa was elected to the Hall of Fame for Great Americans in 1976.

His composition, "The Stars and Stripes Forever," was designated as the national march of the United States in 1987. It is probably his most popular composition, and it also happened to be the last piece he conducted before he died in 1932 at age 77.

Response
Why do you think one of Mr. Sousa's compositions became the national march of the United States?

Fascinating Factoid: John Philip Sousa designed a special tuba, known as the sousaphone, for marching bands.

Word Play
A marching band consists of instruments belonging to the brass, woodwinds, and percussions categories. Unscramble each instrument. Then write it under the correct category.

TMUREPT   SEAB MURDS   COLCIPO   RANES RUDMS
UBAT   XAHOPSNEO   POHSOUSANE OMRTNBOE
NTCROE   CHERNF ONHR   TRILACEN   EULTF
MYALBSC

Brass	Woodwinds	Percussion
T _____	C_____	C _____
T _____	S _____	B_____
T _____	F _____	S_____
C _____	P _____	
F_____		
S_____		

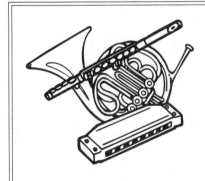

Activities
- Create a new musical instrument by combining two or more existing instruments. Use parts of the name of each to name your new instrument. Describe the sound of the instrument and illustrate it.
- Make a musical instrument from some things you can find in the classroom.

November 7
Paper Clip Machine Patented

• • • • • • • • • • • • • • • • • •

Other Events This Day
• Elephant became Republican Party symbol (1874)
• President Franklin Roosevelt elected to fourth term (1944)

The early methods of fastening papers together involved tying ribbons or strings through holes punched or cut in the papers. When straight pins were invented, they were used. These methods left a lot to be desired, as well as holes in the papers!

Along came a small, thin strip of wire shaped into a double oval shape, and the rest is history! Norwegian Johan Vaaler patented a device in Norway that was the first paper clip. He didn't follow up on his patent. Shortly afterward, Cornelius J. Brosnan patented the "Konaclip" in the United States. About that same time, the Gem Manufactoring Company patented a double-oval clip in England.

The standard paper clip was invented by Gem Manufactoring Ltd. However, it was William Middlebrook of Connecticut who, on November 7, 1899, patented the machine for making paper clips. With this machine, mass production was possible, and the ready availability and low price led to success for paper clips.

Response

The paper clip was called a Gem because of the name of its manufacturer. Can you think of another reason that Gem was a good name for the paper clip?

Fascinating Factoid: During the Nazi occupation of Norway in World War II, Norwegians wore a paper clip on their lapels as a symbol of national unity.

Word Play

It's fun to fasten paper clips together to make chains. Make a word chain by fastening some story words together. Use the ending letter of one word to begin the next word. Start with *clip*.

1. P __ __ __

2. S __ __ __ __ __

3. S __ __ __ __ __ __

4. T __ __ __ __ __ __ __

5. R __ __ __

6. T __

7. O __ __ __

8. L __ __ __

9. T __ __ __

10. S __ __ __ __

11. L __ __ __

12. T __ __ __

Activities

• Make paper clip jewelry from paper clips.

• Create a game to be played using paper clips. Write rules for your game.

November 8
First Storm Warning Issued

Other Events This Day
- Montana became 41st U.S. state (1889)
- HBO® premiered (1972)

● ● ● ● ● ● ● ● ● ● ● ● ● ● ● ● ● ●

Can you imagine living on the East Coast, not knowing that a hurricane is on the way, or living in Tornado Alley, not knowing a tornado is coming your way until you hear it roaring toward you? That's exactly what life was like until November 8, 1870, when the first storm warning was issued.

Dr. I. A. Lapham, assistant to the Chief Signal Officer of the Meteorological Division of the Signal Service, convinced Congressman Halbert Paine of the importance of storm warnings. Mr. Paine introduced a resolution requiring the Secretary of War to establish meteorological services to warn of approaching storms for the Great Lakes area. The resolution was passed by Congress and signed into law by President Ulysses S. Grant. Since that time, the National Weather Service has expanded into a nationwide organization that provides valuable information for our safety and convenience.

Many consider Cleveland Abbe to be the true father of the U.S. Weather Bureau since he was the meteorologist in charge of the organization from its establishment in 1870 until his death in 1916.

Response
What are the most common warnings for the National Weather Service to give in your area?

Fascinating Factoid: In 1743, Benjamin Franklin deduced the northeastward movement of a hurricane. This is the first recorded instance in which the progressive movement of a storm system as a whole is recognized.

Word Play
Find at least 10 little words in *tornado* and *weather*.

TORNADO

_____
_____
_____
_____
_____
_____
_____
_____
_____
_____

WEATHER

_____
_____
_____
_____
_____
_____
_____
_____
_____
_____

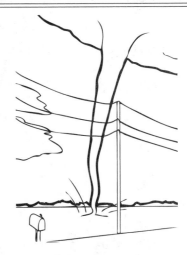

Activities
- Describe in your own words the difference between hurricanes and tornadoes.
- Write a poem about a tornado and copy it in a spiral design to resemble a tornado shape.

November 9
Carl Sagan's Birthday

Other Events This Day
- Holocaust began (1938)
- Berlin Wall torn down; East Germany opened border (1989)

Astronomer Carl Edward Sagan, who extolled and explored the mysteries of the universe, was born in New York City on November 9, 1934. His lifelong passion was searching for intelligent life in the universe. In the 1950s, he began researching the universe and he went on to play a leading role in every major U.S. space expedition. He served as a consultant/advisor to NASA. He briefed the Apollo astronauts before their historic flights to the moon. His experiments were conducted on the *Mariner, Viking, Voyager* and *Galileo* expeditions into space.

Mr. Sagan received many awards, which included two NASA Medals for Exceptional Scientific Achievement for Distinguished Public Service and the NASA Apollo Achievement Award. Asteroid 2709 Sagan was named for him.

In addition to his great scientific gifts, Mr. Sagan was a talented storyteller. His ability to communicate knowledge of the cosmos was demonstrated when he hosted a popular television series on PBS called *Cosmos*. His book, *Cosmos*, became the best-selling science book ever published in the English language.

Response

Carl Sagan was a gifted person. For what two gifts will he be remembered?

Fascinating Factoid: Carl Sagan received more than 20 honorary degrees for his contributions to science, literature, education, and preservation of the environment.

Word Play

In each group of words, circle the word that does not belong.

1. universe, cosmos, macrocosm, asteroid
2. expedition, experiment, excursion, voyage
3. Venus, Mars, Earth, Galaxy
4. mystery, research, puzzle, enigma
5. astronomy, space, astrology, meteorology
6. scientific, research, study, investigate
7. award, historic, prize, bonus
8. consultant, advisor, counselor, scientist
9. ability, inform, divulge, communicate
10. *Mariner, Voyager, Viking, Satellite*

Activities

- Look up the word *cosmos*. Write a definition. Then list as many different celestial words as you can, including heavenly bodies, man-made, or natural. Categorize the words in your list.

- Find at least one fascinating fact about 10 heavenly bodies. Use this information to create a board game. Be sure to include pitfalls such as black holes. Write the rules for your game.

November 10
Sesame Street®
Premiered

A children's educational television show named *Sesame Street*® took the country by storm when it premiered on November 10, 1969. Its purpose was to help prepare young children for kindergarten, as well as provide entertainment.

Children today love it every bit as much as the grownups who hold fond memories of watching it when they were kids. Although the setting is an urban city street, children of all backgrounds love the show. In addition to teaching letters, numbers, and social values, *Sesame Street* features a wide variety of people living together in harmony in the neighborhood.

Jim Henson's Muppets® were a key part of this program's success. Mr. Henson created such legends as Elmo, Big Bird, Oscar, Ernie, Bert, and Cookie Monster. Each muppet displays its own unique looks and distinctive personality. The programs are presented in fast-paced, interest-keeping segments. They teach skills suitable for young watchers, based on accepted learning ideas.

Response

What are some things that you may have learned from *Sesame Street*?

Fascinating Factoid: *Sesame Street* is viewed by over 120 million children in over 130 countries around the world.

Word Play

Connect adjacent letters with straight lines to name the *Sesame Street* characters shown in the box below. You may connect letters horizontally, vertically, and/or diagonally.

B	Y	B	E	C	E	M	O	N	O	E	R	Y
A	B	R	A	O	I	E	T	S	D	T	L	M
B	E	T	X	O	K	R	V	H	N	S	L	O
I	G	R	C	O	I	E	R	E	O	T	E	N
I	B	B	A	U	N	E	N	R	M	A	T	S
R	D	M	T	N	R	E	Y	R	Y	S	I	W
E	L	E	V	E	S	U	E	T	R	O	R	A
E	N	F	O	T	T	I	N	H	A	R	J	E
T	N	A	N	C	O	P	H	E	C	O	E	B
E	T	R	G	R	U	O	O	N	S	Z	P	A
U	L	S	R	E	Q	N	N	K	O	M	A	K
V	W	M	O	V	E	S	T	E	R	S	P	L

Baby Bear	Count von Count	The Honkers
Big Bird	Ernie	Oscar
Elefante	Cookie Monster	Zoe
Elmo	Ernestine	Rosita
Grover	Herry Monster	Papa Bear

Activities

• *Sesame Street* features people living in harmony in their neighborhood. If you were in charge of casting your own neighborhood for the show, which neighbor would you choose for the different *Sesame Street* characters such as Ernie, the Grouch, Cookie Monster, etc.?

Explain your choices.

November 11
Veterans Day Created

• •

Other Events This Day
• General George S. Patton's (Old Blood & Guts) birthday (1885)
• Washington State became 42nd U.S. state (1889)

In 1919, Congress passed a resolution calling for peaceful ceremonies on November 11 to honor the peace achieved with the signing of the armistice in 1918. In 1921, Congress directed the president to proclaim November 11 a federal holiday each year. Throughout the 1920s and 1930s, the president issued a proclamation each year.

On November 11, 1938, Congress passed a law making November 11 a legal federal holiday known as Armistice Day. Armistice Day became Veterans Day in 1954. In 1968, Congress passed the Monday Holiday Bill, and the fourth Monday in October became the new date to observe Veterans Day. People didn't like this date, so in 1975, Veterans Day was returned to November 11.

Both Memorial Day and Veterans Day honor those who served in the Armed Forces. The difference is that Memorial Day is a day for remembering and honoring those who died serving their country. On Veterans Day, we honor and thank those living who served in the military.

Response
Compare Memorial Day and Veterans Day.

Fascinating Factoid: There are over 25 million living veterans in the United States.

Word Play
Match each Armed Forces branch with words from its official song.

_____ 1. National Guard   a. "From the halls of Montezuma . . . ."

_____ 2. Coast Guard   b. "Off we go into the wild blue yonder . . . ."

_____ 3. Marines   c. "Over hill, over dale, as we hit the dusty trail . . . ."

_____ 4. Air Force   d. "Anchors aweigh, my boys, anchors aweigh . . . ."

_____ 5. Navy   e. "I guard America . . . ."

_____ 6. Army   f. "We're always ready for the call . . . ."

Activities
• What are some things you would like to ask a veteran? Make a list.

• Decorate your classroom door for Veterans Day. Use red, white, and blue paper and patriotic symbols.

• Plan a class Veterans Day Parade around the halls of your school. What songs could you sing or play on a CD? What will you and your classmates wear? What flags and banners will be carried? Submit your plan to your teacher.

November 12
First Professional Football Game

Other Events This Day
- First known photo of Loch Ness monster taken (1933)
- World War II battle of Guadalcanal begins (1942)

• • • • • • • • • • • • • • • • • •

On November 12, 1892, the Allegheny Athletic Association (AAA) football team defeated the Pittsburgh Athletic Club. It was not the football game itself that made this day an important one in the history of football but the fact that one of the AAA players, William (Pudge) Heffelfinger, was paid $500 to play for them. This marked the birth of professional football. Others may have been paid to play before this, but there is no record. There is, however, a record of the $500 game bonus payment to William (Pudge) Heffelfinger.

Most of the athletics clubs sponsored a football team during the 1880s. The clubs were not supposed to pay their players; however, some clubs obtained jobs for their stars. Others awarded expensive trophies, while some doubled the expense money to their players.

There was a lot of bickering when Pittsburgh alleged that Allegheny had paid Mr. Heffelfinger to play for them. The game was delayed so long that it had to be shortened in order to complete it before dark. Touchdowns were only worth four points at that time. In the game, Mr. Heffelfinger scored the only touchdown and Allegheny won 4-0.

Response
What makes a sports player a professional?

Fascinating Factoid: The greatest risk of injury to a professional football player is to the knee, which is involved in 58 percent of all major football injuries.

Word Play
Toss around the word *ball* and come up with compound words to fit the spaces below.

1. _F_ __ __ __ BALL
2. __ __ __ __ _E_ _T_ BALL
3. BALL _P_ _L_ __ __ __ __
4. __ __ _R_ _E_ BALL
5. BALL _P_ __ __ _K_
6. _C_ __ __ __ __ __ BALL
7. _T_ __ _T_ __ __ BALL
8. _B_ __ __ BALL
9. BALL _G_ __ __ __

10. BALL _P_ __ __ __ __
11. _E_ __ _E_ BALL
12. _V_ __ __ __ __ __ BALL
13. _H_ __ __ __ BALL
14. _O_ __ __ BALL
15. BALL _R_ __ __ __
16. _H_ __ _N_ __ BALL
17. _S_ __ __ __ BALL

Activities
- Think about all the numbers involved in a football game (e.g., scores, yards, downs). Create and solve at least five math story problems using football numbers.
- Think up some funny words using the word ball and write their definitions. (These don't have to be real words.)

November 13
Peanut Butter Invented

Peanuts go back over 1,000 years. The Incas used them to make a paste. Africans ground them into stews, and Civil War soldiers ate peanut porridge. Although records exist of a peanut paste in early ages, the refined peanut butter we know today originated in the United States just over 100 years ago on November 13, 1890. An unknown doctor experimented with making a paste for his undernourished patients. He convinced George Bayle to process and package it. It was first sold out of a barrel at six cents per pound (453.6 g).

About that same time, Dr. John Kellogg began experimenting with peanut paste. He and his brother began making and supplying it to local grocers. C. H. Sumner introduced peanut paste/butter to the world at the 1904 Exposition in St. Louis. His concession was quite successful and peanut butter was on its way to becoming an American favorite.

Krema Products of Columbus, Ohio, began selling peanut butter in 1908 and is still in operation. In 1922, Joseph Rosenfield began making a smoother peanut butter by churning it much like butter. At first, peanut butter could not be stored because the oil would separate from the nut paste and spoil. He received the first patent for peanut butter that had a shelf life. He licensed his product to Pond Company, makers of the Peter Pan® brand. In 1932, he began making his own brand called Skippy® and added chunks of peanuts to make crunchy peanut butter. In 1955, Proctor & Gamble started selling Jif® peanut butter.

Response
Describe one of the problems that had to be solved before peanut butter became successful.

Fascinating Factoid: Jif operates the world's largest peanut butter factory and it produces about 250,000 jars a day.

Word Play
Some foods go together like peanut butter and jelly. Complete each food pair.

1. chips and _____
2. peaches and _____
3. bacon and _____
4. sugar and _____
5. bread and _____
6. biscuits and _____
7. lettuce and _____
8. apple pie and _____
9. salt and _____
10. oil and _____
11. fish and _____
12. turkey and _____
13. cookies and _____
14. cheese and _____
15. coffee and _____
16. burgers and _____
17. hot dogs and _____
18. peas and _____
19. spaghetti and _____
20. ham and _____
21. pancakes and _____

Activities
- Write directions for making a peanut butter and jelly sandwich. Don't leave out a step.
- Baskin-Robbins® Ice Cream has 31 flavors of ice cream. Create your own gallery of peanut butter ice cream flavors. How many flavors of peanut butter ice cream can you have in your gallery by combining peanut butter with other flavors?

November 14
Nellie Bly Began Trip Around the World

On November 14, 1889, Nellie Bly, a daredevil reporter, left for a trip around the world. The trip was inspired by Jules Verne's book *Around the World in Eighty Days,* and it was her desire to show the world that a woman could do it in less than 80 days. She was successful in reaching her goal. She traveled by boat, train, and horse, returning home from the trip 72 days, 6 hours, 11 minutes, and 14 seconds after she departed.

Elizabeth Jane Bly was born May 5, 1864, to Judge Michael and Mary Jane Cochran in Apollo, Pennsylvania. After the death of Elizabeth's father, her mother remarried. Her abusive stepfather was probably the reason for Elizabeth's interest in women's rights.

When she was 18, Ms. Bly wrote an anonymous letter to the editor of the *Pittsburgh Dispatch.* The editor put an ad in his paper asking the author of this letter to come and introduce herself. This resulted in a reporting job for her. Nellie Bly became her pen name.

Women's rights were the focus of Ms. Bly's articles. She often went undercover to get material for her articles. When the newspaper proposed to send a man around the world in 80 days, Ms. Bly wanted that honor and convinced her bosses to let her do it.

Response

Why do you think Nellie Bly wanted to be the one to make this trip around the world?

Fascinating Factoid: Over one million people entered a contest to guess the time it would take Ms. Bly to circle the globe.

Word Play

Match each capital city to its country.

___ 1. Lisbon	___ 14. Ottawa	a. Germany	n. Russia
___ 2. Berlin	___ 15. Bogota	b. Spain	o. Kenya
___ 3. Madrid	___ 16. Santiago	c. Vietnam	p. Australia
___ 4. Bangkok	___ 17. Quito	d. Ireland	q. Italy
___ 5. Ankara	___ 18. Tegucigalpa	e. Nigeria	r. Norway
___ 6. London	___ 19. Dublin	f. Netherlands	s. Serbia
___ 7. Caracas	___ 20. Rome	g. Honduras	t. Belgium
___ 8. Hanoi	___ 21. Nairobi	h. Turkey	u. Canada
___ 9. Belgrade	___ 22. Bamako	i. Poland	v. Portugal
___ 10. Canberra	___ 23. Amsterdam	j. Mali	w. Colombia
___ 11. Moscow	___ 24. Abuja	k. Austria	x. Ecuador
___ 12. Vienna	___ 25. Oslo	l. Venezuela	y. Thailand
___ 13. Brussels	___ 26. Warsaw	m. Chile	z. England

Activities

- Write a newspaper article about a modern-day trip "Around the (moon, solar system, Mars, etc.) in Eighty Days."

- Make a list of all the different modes of transportation you could use if you were taking the same trip today as Nellie Bly did in 1889.

November 15
First America Recycles Day

• • • • • • • • • • • • • • • • •

Other Events This Day
• Articles of Confederation adopted by Continental Congress (1777)
• Explorer Zebulon Pike sighted Pikes Peak (1806)

On November 15, 1997, millions of people across America took part in the first national America Recycles Day. Many local events were sponsored to remind people of the extreme importance of preserving the bounty of this nation for future generations. Since that beginning in 1997, America Recycles Day is observed around the country each year. It unites environmental and community agencies, businesses, industries, and the general public in an effort to focus attention on the environment and recycling.

Recycling is just one of the ways to save resources and help create a better environment. Recycling has become one of the most successful environmental endeavors in history. Starting in 1990, Americans recycled 34 million tons (34,545,594.6 metric tons) of materials. In the years that followed, that number more than doubled to nearly 70 million tons (71,123,283 metric tons). The federal government is even doing its part by purchasing paper made from recycled products, retread tires, and many other recycled products. The nation continuously seeks ways to recycle waste.

At home and school, parents, children, and teachers can educate themselves about the benefits of recycling. They can support the effort by buying products made from recycled materials. Not only on America Recycles Day, but on every day of the year, we must do our part to preserve the environment.

Response
What are some ways in which you recycle?

Fascinating Factoid: Recycling and manufacturing provide one million jobs and $100 billion in revenue every year.

Word Play

A *prefix* is a "syllable added to the beginning of a word to change its meaning." The common prefix *re-* means "to do again." Can you put *re-* in front of a word that begins with each letter of the alphabet?

REA _____   REN _____
REB _____   REO _____
REC _____   REP _____
RED _____   REQ _____
REE_____   RER_____
REF_____   RES _____
REG _____   RET _____
REH _____   REU_____
REI _____   REV _____
REJ _____   REW _____
REK _____   REX_____
REL_____   REY _____
REM _____   REZ_____

Activities

• Find something that has been discarded and think of a clever way to recycle it. Display your creation with a short explanation of its rebirth.

• Write about why you think some people take recycling seriously while others do not.

November 16

First Family Moved into the White House

Other Events This Day

• Oklahoma became 46th U.S. state (1907)

• President Nixon signed bill authorizing construction of Trans-Alaskan Pipeline (1973)

• • • • • • • • • • • • • • • • •

The White House was first occupied on November 16, 1800. The White House is the most recognized house in America. It was called the *White House* because the sandstones from which it was built were coated with whitewash, and then later white paint, to keep the moisture out. President Theodore Roosevelt officially named it the White House in 1901.

In 1790, Congress established Washington DC as the permanent home for the president, Congress, and Supreme Court. George Washington picked the location for the president's house. Secretary of State Thomas Jefferson held a contest for the design. The winning designer would receive $500 or a medal of that value. James Hoban, an Irish builder working in America, won the contest. His first plans called for two stories and a raised basement, but some folks thought that was too large. So they agreed to two stories without the raised basement. The first cornerstone was laid in October 1792.

The building was still incomplete when President John Adams and his wife Abigail moved in. Many of the plastered walls were still wet, and some had not even been plastered at all. The grand staircase was a large hole. The East Room was a hull; Abigail used to hang the family laundry in it. Thomas Jefferson was the first president to spend an entire term in the White House. He added two long colonnades for offices and storage.

Response

Why is it important for the U.S. president to have such a large and grand house?

Fascinating Factoid: There are 132 rooms in the White House, including 32 bathrooms.

Word Play

By moving *day* from the front to the back of words, many compound words can be made. Make compound words using *day* in the following positions.

_____ DAY   DAY _____

DAY _____   _____ DAY

_____ DAY   DAY _____

DAY _____   _____ DAY

_____ DAY   DAY _____

DAY _____   _____ DAY

_____ DAY   DAY _____

DAY _____   _____ DAY

_____ DAY   DAY _____

On the back of this sheet, write more *day* words.

CAMP DAVID

Activity

• All presidents need a hideaway to get away from it all. For example, Camp David has been a favorite of many presidents. President George W. Bush likes to go to his ranch in Texas, as did President Lyndon Johnson. If you were president, where would you go for relaxation? Explain your choice.

November 17
U.S. Congress Moved to Washington DC

Other Events This Day

• Suez Canal opened in Egypt (1869)

• Panama Canal opened (1913)

On November 17, 1800, the Senate of the Sixth Congress met for the first time in the new Capitol Building in Washington DC, with only 15 senators present. President George Washington had laid the cornerstone for the building in 1793, and construction was slow. In 1796, it was decided to build only the Senate wing. The third floor of the Senate Wing was not completed, but the other two floors stood ready to welcome the Senate, the House, the Supreme Court, and Library of Congress.

During the War of 1812, the British burned the Capitol, along with the White House. Congress moved into temporary quarters in the Old Brick Capitol while repairs were made to the Capitol. The great rotunda was completed in 1824. Then in 1857, the House of Representatives moved into the completed south wing of the Capitol. Two years later, the Senate moved into its current home in the enlarged north wing.

During the Civil War, Union soldiers were housed in the Capitol. In 1863, the beautiful *Statue of Freedom,* created by Thomas Crawford, was placed atop the Capitol. The year of 1879 brought electric lighting. Through the years, there have been minor modifications to the building; but for the most part, it remains the same—a symbol of America crowning Capitol Hill.

Response

The Capitol Building is home to what important government agencies?

Fascinating Factoid: Dr. William Franklin was the original architect for the Capitol, but 13 different architects were involved before it was finished.

Word Play

Homonyms are words that sound alike but have different meanings. Write words from the story and a homonym for each.

Story Word	Homonym	Story Word	Homonym
_____	_____	_____	_____
_____	_____	_____	_____
_____	_____	_____	_____
_____	_____	_____	_____
_____	_____	_____	_____
_____	_____	_____	_____
_____	_____	_____	_____

Activities

• Make a list of your representatives and senators who work in the nation's capital.

• Flags are flown atop the Capitol in Washington DC. They are lowered and raised several times during the day, so they can be given to schools, deserving organizations, and citizens. Write your congress person about getting a flag for your school that has flown over the Capitol Building.

November 18
U.S. Time Zones Established

Long ago, timekeeping was a local concern. Each town set its clocks at noon when the sun was directly overhead. The official time for that town might be the clock on the church steeple or in the town square. This worked because people didn't travel great distances and there were no phone calls.

When railroads came into existence, people started traveling longer distances. That is when a big problem arose. People had to reset their timepieces constantly, and they missed their trains because of the time differences. The railroads began using time zones on November 18, 1883. (These time zones differ greatly from the ones used today.) The use of standard time gradually increased because of obvious advantages to communication and travel.

In 1878, Canadian Sir Sanford Fleming proposed the system of worldwide time zones used today. In 1884, a conference was held in Washington DC to standardize time and so select the Prime Meridian (zero degrees). Greenwich, England, was chosen, and 24 time zones were determined beginning at Greenwich. Not all countries switched immediately. Most of the United States began to use Pacific, Mountain, Central, and Eastern time zones in 1895. Time zones became mandatory in 1918.

Response
Name the time zones in the United States and identify the time zone in which you live.

Fascinating Factoid: The idea of Daylight Savings Time came from Benjamin Franklin.

Word Play
Complete the following timetable.

	seconds in a minute
	minutes in an hour
	hours in a day
	days in a week
	days in a year
	weeks in a year
	years in a decade
	years in a century
	years in a millennium
	centuries in a millennium

Activities
- Imagine that you are going to fly to your grandparents' home located in a city that is two time zones away from your home.
- Create a round-trip itinerary. Show departure and arrival times going in each direction.

November 19
"Battle Hymn of the Republic" Written

Other Events This Day

• U.S. President James Garfield's birthday (1831)
• President Lincoln gave the Gettysburg Address (1863)

One of our most stirring, favorite patriotic hymns is the "Battle Hymn of the Republic." Julia Ward Howe wrote it in 1861 during the Civil War after touring army camps where she heard troops singing "John Brown's Body." Her traveling companion Reverend Clark suggested that Ms. Howe write more acceptable lyrics for the song. She was so moved by the sight of the marching Union soldiers that in the wee small hours of November 19, 1861, she wrote what became the hymn that generations of Americans have sung for over a century.

Although the writing of the "Battle Hymn of the Republic" took place in November, it was not published until February 1862. It was published as a poem in the *Atlantic Monthly*. Editor James Fields is credited with giving it the name it is known by today.

Ms. Howe was a much-celebrated author of that time. She was the wife of a doctor and mother to five children. She was a supporter of the antislavery movement and she preached in a Unitarian Church. She worked for the advancement of women's causes, prison reform, world peace, and other reform movements.

Response

Why do you think Ms. Howe wrote the words to the "Battle Hymn of the Republic" in the "wee small hours."

Fascinating Factoid: It is said that Abraham Lincoln told people that he cried the first time he heard the "Battle Hymn of the Republic."

Word Play

Julia Ward Howe, who wrote the "Battle Hymn of the Republic," was honored by having her picture on a postage stamp in 1987. Many other famous American women have "left their stamp" on American history. Identify each American woman honored on a stamp.

1. M _ _ _ _ _ _ _   _ _ _ _ _ _ _ _ _ _ _
   (first first lady)

2. M _ _ _ _ _ _   _ _ _ _ _ _ _ _ _
   (carried water to soldiers during Revolutionary War)

3. J _ _ _ _ _ _ _ _ _ _   _ _ _ _ _
   (founded Girl Scouts of America)

4. E _ _ _ _ _ _ _ _ _ _   _ _ _ _ _ _ _ _ _ _
   (first woman doctor)

5. H _ _ _ _ _ _ _   _ _ _ _ _ _ _
   (leader of Underground Railroad)

6. R _ _ _ _ _ _ _   _ _ _ _ _ _ _
   (environmentalist)

7. G _ _ _ _ _ _ _ _   _ _ _ _ _ _ _
   (became famous painter late in life)

8. C _ _ _ _ _   _ _ _ _ _ _ _ _
   (founded American Red Cross)

9. P _ _ _ _ _ _ _ _ _ _
   (Powhatan princess who saved life of Captain John Smith)

10. S _ _ _ _ _ _ _ _ _
    (Shoshone guide to explorers Lewis and Clark)

Activities

• Research to find words to the song "John Brown's Body" and tell why you think the Union soldiers were singing it when they were observed by Julia Ward Howe.

• Research to determine which women, other than those cited in the Word Play, have been honored on a postage stamp. Make a list. Think of a woman you think is deserving of the same honor and write a letter on her behalf.

November 20
Traffic Light Patented

Other Events This Day
• Astronomer Edwin Hubble's birthday (1889)
• Passport photos first required (1914)

On November 20, 1923, Garrett Augustus Morgan patented a traffic signal. He was a businessman and inventor whose curiosity and intelligence led to the development of many useful products. He was the son of former slaves born in Paris, Kentucky, on March 4, 1877.

It is unknown why Mr. Morgan is known as the inventor of the traffic signal. He wasn't the first one to invent the traffic signal, and his wasn't the first patent for a traffic signal. The first traffic lights were installed in London in 1868. There were more than 60 traffic signals patented in the United States before Mr. Morgan's patent. The earliest U.S. traffic signal patent was issued to Ernest Sirrine in 1910.

Garret Morgan's invention came at a time when pedestrians, bicycles, horse-drawn carriages, and motor vehicles shared the same roadways. It was his experiences while driving the streets of Cleveland, Ohio, that led to the invention of his traffic signal. His design was a T-shaped pole unit that had three positions—stop, go, and an all-directional stop position to allow people to cross the streets. His device was used throughout America until the red, yellow, and green traffic light signals currently used replaced it. Mr. Morgan sold the rights to his signal to General Electric Corporation for $40,000—a lot of money in those days!

Response
Compare Mr. Morgan's traffic signal with those in use today.

Fascinating Factoid: The first traffic signal in London was illuminated by gas and was operated by a lever at its base. It was installed before automobiles were in use.

Word Play
A *synonym* is a word that has the same meaning as another word. Write each word under its corresponding synonym.

cease	depart	prudence	careful
start	quit	wariness	terminate
desist	stay	discontinue	watchful
begin	proceed	finish	conclude
close	initiate	vigilance	alertness
inaugurate	commence	leave	

Stop	Go	Caution
_____	_____	_____
_____	_____	_____
_____	_____	_____
_____	_____	_____
_____	_____	
_____	_____	
_____		

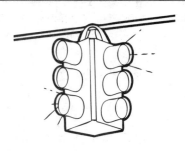

Activities
• Describe the playground game called Red Light, Green Light. Remember to write clear rules and directions.

• Choose one of the three colors of the signal light. Write a five senses poem about that color. Example: Yellow is…(words to explain what yellow tastes like), Yellow is…(words to explain what yellow feels like), etc.

November 21
First World Hello Day

A big hello to all of you fine students who are reading this page!

The first World Hello Day was held on this date in 1973. Since that time, nearly 200 countries around the world have observed World Hello Day.

World Hello Day began in 1973 in response to a conflict between the nations of Egypt and Israel. Brian and Michael McCormack worked together to promote this worldwide event.

The idea behind such a day was to encourage leaders of different countries to solve conflicts through communication, rather than war. By observance of this unique special day, it is an opportunity for people to express their concern for world peace. Organizers of the day encourage people to celebrate the day by simply saying hello to 10 people. It is hoped that this grass-roots level of communication will serve as an example to world leaders.

Find 10 people today who you do not normally greet and give them a great big hello, *bonjour*, or *hola*.

Response

How might World Hello Day contribute to world peace?

Fascinating Factoid: To say hello to the world, you would have to learn over 2,000 different languages.

Word Play

Shade in every letter that appears more than one time and then decode the secret message.

A	H	B	C	N	F	C	E	W	G
M	V	U	Q	N	Z	I	Y	P	N
J	P	O	A	F	B	C	X	E	V
B	T	A	F	E	P	G	K	R	N
T	G	M	U	L	C	T	U	J	M
P	T	G	S	Q	P	J	S	N	U
Q	Z	D	Z	B	F	N	X	P	V
B	E	F	X	Y	V	M	Z	J	T
C	E	G	S	K	J	K	X	Q	K
K	S	N	X	M	N	Z	M	Y	Z

Hello!   Caio!
Goddag!
Hola!   Salut!

Activities

- Research how to say *hello* in at least five different languages. Trace around your hand and write these greetings within the outline. Cut the hand out. Collect the hands and form a wreath to display on the door.

- Write a short account of your day's effort to say hello to 10 people whom you don't normally greet. Describe these 10 people and their reactions to your greeting. Did the conversations extend beyond the hello?

November 22
SOS (International Call for Help) Adopted

Other Events This Day
- Mount St. Helens in Washington State erupted (1842)
- U.S. President John F. Kennedy assassinated (1963)

The international distress signal in Morse code is three dots, three dashes, three dots. Translated, it means SOS. Many people believe that it stands for "Save our Ship," but that is not true. These letters were selected because of their simplicity so there could be no mistake in sending or receiving this signal.

England and other countries used the letters **CQD** while **SOS** was used by the Germans to transmit distress signals. The **CQ** was a general attention notice and when the **D** was added that meant distress. People thought it meant, "Come quick, distress." The CQD signal was adopted in 1904 as an international distress signal, but it didn't last long. It was replaced with SOS at the November 22, 1906, meeting of the second Berlin Radiotelegraphic Conference. Use of the CQD signal didn't stop immediately, especially with the British and Americans, but eventually SOS replaced it. Records show that the *Titanic* first used CQD to call for help. Then these calls were interspersed with SOS.

The first recorded American use of SOS was in 1909 when the SS *Arapahoe* radioed for help. Ironically, a few months later, the SS *Arapahoe* received an SOS distress call from the SS *Iroquois*. The SS *Arapahoe* had the distinction of being involved in the first two incidents where an SOS was involved at sea.

Response
Why did SOS become the international distress signal?

Fascinating Factoid: Guglielmo Marconi, inventor of the telegraph, suggested CQD as the international distress signal. Interestingly, he was waiting in New York to make the return trip to England on the *Titanic*, but it sank.

Word Play
Here is the international code. Find story words that can be made with the given number of dots and/or dashes.

A ._   B _...   C _._.   D _..   E .   F .._.

G __.   H ....   I ..   J .___   K _._

L ._..   M __   N _.   O ___   P .__.

Q __._   R ._.   S ...   T _   U .._

V ..._   W .__   X _.._   Y _.__   Z __..

_____ at _____ (3)   _____ (14)   _____ (9)

_____ (7)   _____ (12)   _____ (13)

_____ (11)   _____ (16)   _____ (17)

_____ (4)   _____ (5)   _____ (6)

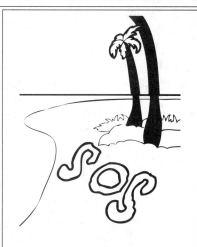

Activities
- Tell how you would create an SOS message on a remote mountain, desert, or beach that signals someone that you are stranded or lost.
- Send a secret message to a classmate or friend using the Morse code dots and dashes.

November 23
Campbell's® Soup Company Began

● ● ● ● ● ● ● ● ● ● ● ● ● ● ● ● ●

Campbell's® Soup Company started out as a canning company in New Jersey in 1869. An icebox maker, Abraham Anderson, and a fruit merchant, Joseph Campbell, founded it. Mr. Campbell bought out Mr. Anderson and expanded the business to bottling ketchup, salad dressing, mustard, and other sauces.

One of the company's investors, Arthur Dorrance, hired his nephew, Dr. John T. Dorrance, a chemist who had recently graduated from the Massachusetts Institute of Technology (MIT) and had a PhD from a German university. Dr. Dorrance quickly realized that soup was inexpensive to make but it was expensive to ship. He found that by taking the water out (condensing) of the soup, it was much easier to transport and could even be sold much cheaper—for 10 cents a can. The company became so successful from its soup business that on November 23, 1922, the Joseph Campbell Preserve Company changed its name to Campbell's Soup Company.

When advertising agents were looking for a way to attract a younger audience, they hired Grace W. Drayton to sketch the Campbell Kids. Along the way, they came up with the advertising jingle, "M'm! M'm! Good" that is still well known today. Another tradition of Campbell's Soup is the color of the cans. It is said that an executive attended a football game where one team was wearing red and white. He was so taken with the striking image, he convinced the company to adopt those colors.

Response

What was the big thing that brought about the success of canned soup?

Fascinating Factoid: Americans eat over 400 million cans of soup each year.

Word Play

Starting with the **C** above the **X** in the center of the grid, write out all the letters in a straight row. Insert vowels and identify 11 different flavors of Campbell's Soup.

Hint: the answers rotate in a clockwise pattern.

*	D	L	B	N	W	T	H	B
*	N	K	N	C	R	L	Y	C
S	N	C	L	T	M	T	N	N
R	K	H	T	C	H	V	D	C
T	C	C	N	**X**	L	G	L	R
S	H	F	L	F	B	T	C	M
D	C	M	R	C	L	B	H	F
N	C	R	D	N	N	K	C	M
N	K	C	H	C	M	R	H	S

Use the back of this paper to list the soups you identified.

Activities

- Create a new soup recipe and submit it with a letter to Campbell's Soup Company. Be sure your recipe includes all of the ingredients, their amounts, and step-by-step directions.

- Imagine that you are the new advertising executive for Campbell's Soup Company, and you think it is time for an update. Sketch a new Campbell's Kid, write a new slogan to replace "M'm! M'm! Good!" and design a new label.

November 24
First Use of Caterpillar Tracks

• • • • • • • • • • • • • • • • • •

Other Events This Day
- First U.S. presidential airplane christened (1954)
- Jack Ruby shot Lee Harvey Oswald, John F. Kennedy's accused assassin (1963)

"Caterpillar Tracks" is the trade name for an endless flexible belt of metal plates on which vehicles like tanks and bulldozers run. Caterpillar tracks take the place of ordinary wheels and improve performance on wet or uneven surfaces. The tracks actually protect the wheels from rough surfaces and allow a vehicle to drive over obstacles. Caterpillar tracks were used on November 24, 1904, by Benjamin Holt of Holt Manufacturing Company, which later became Caterpillar® Tractor Company.

With the invention of caterpillar tracks, war tanks changed forever. The tracks allowed the military tanks to operate better on all terrains because they distributed the weight evenly. Tanks could go in places they had not been able to go before. Over the past 100 years, the tracks have been improved greatly to allow for more mobility and more speed.

In early history, large rocks were probably moved using this same principle. Wooden rollers were placed under big rocks. When a big rock was pushed, it would move forward leaving the last roller free. That freed roller was then moved to the front of the rock for another push and roll.

Response

What do caterpillar tracks allow vehicles to do that regular wheels do not?

Fascinating Factoid: Caterpillar®, Inc. is an international company that markets its products in nearly every country in the world.

Word Play

Caterpillar is spelled with **ll**, as are many other words in our language. Find a word beginning with every letter of the alphabet that has double **"L"** in it?

1. ALL __ __ (permit)
2. B __ LL __ __ (yell)
3. C __ LL __ __ __ (gather)
4. D __ LL __ __ (money)
5. ELL __ __ __ __ (oval)
6. F __ LL __ __ __ (false idea)
7. G __ LL __ __ (ship kitchen)
8. H __ LL __ (greeting)
9. I __ __ __ __LL __ (perfectly)
10. J __ LL __ (peanut butter's companion)
11. K __ LL __ __ (slayer)
12. L __ LL __ __ __ __ __ (sucker)
13. M __ LL __ __ __ __ (1,000 years)

14. N __ __ __ __ __ LL __ (pertaining to nature)
15. O __ __ LL __ (by mouth)
16. P __ __ __ __ __ LL __ __ (antibiotic)
17. Q __ __ __LL (stiff feather)
18. R __ LL __ (meeting to arouse support)
19. S __ LL __ (humorous)
20. T __ LL __ (count)
21. U __ __ __ __ LL __ (ordinarily)
22. V __ LL __ __ __(depression between elevations)
23. W __ LL __ __ (tree)
24. X (no word for this letter)
25. Y __ LL __ __ (color)
26. Z __ LL __ __ __ (large number)

Activities

- Design a new type of transportation that uses the caterpillar tracks and then take it on an imaginary adventure. Write a short story about your creation and your adventure.

- Design an obstacle course for a remote-controlled toy caterpillar race. Some things to include might be hills, s-curves, rockslides, etc.

November 25
Woody Woodpecker Debuted

Woody Woodpecker, star of big screen and TV, made his debut on November 25, 1940, as a supporting actor in the movie, *Knock-Knock*. The movie starred two pandas, but Woody quickly stole the show.

In early days, Woody looked wild and naughty. His buggy eyes looked in different directions. He looked like a bully with a long, pointed beak. Even his famous laugh, "Heh, heh, heh, HEH, heh" was downright evil sounding. But in spite of being a crazy, ill-mannered character, the public loved him. After 1948, the voice of Woody was that of a woman, Grace Stafford, the wife of Walter Lantz, Woody's creator. About the same time Mrs. Stafford, took over as the voice of Woody, he underwent other changes: His personality became more endearing. His beak was blunted and his body was rounder and cuter. He even lost some of his naughty tendencies.

"The Woody Woodpecker Song" became very popular. Fan clubs sprung up. Woody's image could even be found on some military aircraft during World War II. In a place of honor in the National Museum of American History in Washington DC, a wooden statue of Woody stands to remind people of his importance in cartoon history.

Response
Express your opinion about which Woody makes the best cartoon character.

Fascinating Factoid: Woodpeckers actually store their long tongues inside their noses.

Word Play
Knock-Knock was Woody's first movie. Unscramble each "knock-knock" joke for a little "Heh, heh, heh, HEH, heh."

1. Knock, knock. Who's there? Wayne, Wayne Who?
   AYNEW, YAWNE, OG AYAW NAD MOCE GNIAA NTOHERA AYD.

   _____

   _____

2. Knock, Knock. Who's there? Jamaica. Jamaica who?
   MAJCIAA OGOD DAGRE NO ORUY ESTT?

   _____

3. Knock, knock. Who's there? Anita. Anita who?
   AITNA DRIE OT OSHCLO.

   _____

4. Knock, knock. Who's there? Juana. Juana who?
   UNJAA EOMC UTO NDA LAPY?

Activities
- Choose any bird and make it into a cartoon character. Give it a catchy name. Draw a picture. Describe its personality and mannerisms. Would your character be obnoxious like Woody Woodpecker or appear innocent like Tweety Bird?
- Write several "knock-knock" jokes.

November 26
First National Thanksgiving Proclamation

Other Events This Day

• First lion exhibited in America (1716)

• First meteor photograph (1885)

The Pilgrims in the Colonies first celebrated Thanksgiving in 1621, giving thanks for the abundant food supply and help from their new friends the Native Americans. Another Thanksgiving in 1777 celebrated victory over the British.

President George Washington issued a proclamation in 1789, calling for "Thursday, 26 November next, [to] be a day of public thanksgiving and prayer." He called upon everyone to give thanks for the successful end of the war; for the new government; for the tranquility, the union, and the plenty enjoyed by all. President Washington directed citizens to plead for continued blessings upon the country and its people.

This proclamation was apparently lost for over 100 years. It is believed that it was probably left behind when the government moved from New York to Washington DC, or that it was mixed in with some other papers and discarded. It was located at an auction sale in a New York art gallery and was bought for $300. It is now preserved and housed in the Library of Congress in Washington DC.

Response

In what way might this proclamation have influenced the date of our traditional Thanksgiving?

Fascinating Factoid: The magazine editor, Sarah Josepha Hale, was instrumental in getting President Lincoln to establish a national Thanksgiving holiday.

Word Play

Make an acrostic by placing letters in the blanks before and/or after the letters in *Thanksgiving*. The words you use should relate to Thanksgiving.

```
    T _ _ _ _ _ _
    _ H _ _ _ _ _
    _ _ A _ _ _ _ _
_ _ _ _ _ _ N _
    _ _ _ _ _ K _ _
    _ _ _ _ S
    G _ _ _ _ _ _ _ _
    _ _ _ _ _ _ I _ _
    _ _ _ _ V _ _
    _ _ _ _ _ _ I _ _
    _ _ _ _ N
    _ _ _ _ _ G
```

Activities

• Write about the things you are thankful for in your life, and write about the things you should be thankful for because you are an American.

• Write a menu for your ideal Thanksgiving dinner. Choose one item and explain how it is prepared.

November 27
Nobel Prizes Established

• • • • • • • • • • • • • • • • • • •

Other Events This Day
• Seminole Indian War began (1817)
• New York's Pennsylvania Station opened (1910)

Alfred Nobel, a Swedish chemist, invented dynamite. He thought the invention would put an end to all wars, but others thought it was an extremely bad invention. He was called the "Merchant of Death."

Mr. Nobel was born in 1833. He was tutored at home until he was 16. He loved reading literature and could speak five different languages fluently. He received a patent in 1862 for the Nobel lighter, which was a detonator. He opened a factory to manufacture nitroglycerine, a highly explosive substance. The factory blew up, but that did not stop him. He invented a newer and safer product called *dynamite*.

On November 27, 1895, Mr. Nobel wrote his final will, and it was locked away until he died on December 10, 1896. About 95 percent of his estate was left for the establishment of five prizes (physics, chemistry, physiology or medicine, literature, and peace). The prizes were to be awarded annually to people who contributed the greatest benefit to mankind the previous year. On the fifth anniversary of Alfred Nobel's death, December 10, 1901, the first set of Nobel Prizes were awarded.

Response
Explain why you think a man known as the "Merchant of Death" might be inclined to leave most of his wealth as a gift to benefit mankind?

Fascinating Factoid: If a person nominates himself or herself for a Nobel Prize, he or she is automatically disqualified.

Word Play
Unscramble each story word and write it on the longest lines in the puzzles. Use letters from these words to make new words that fit in the given spaces.

NADYITME

—
— —
— — —
— — — —
— — — — —
— — — — — — —
— — — — —
— — — —
— — —
—

ATONTORED

— —
— — —
— — — —
— — — — —
— — — — — —
— — — — — — — —
— — — — — —
— — — — —
— — — —
— — —
— —

Most Helpful

Activities
• Create a classroom prize patrol recognizing "noble" classmates. Determine categories such as most helpful, most organized, most responsible, etc. Select prizes or trophies to award. Establish rules as to how recipients will be chosen and when prizes will be awarded.

• Imagine that you are a newspaper writer in 1896. Write a story about the reading of Mr. Nobel's will. Be sure to include comments from a surviving relative.

November 28
First American Auto Race

• • • • • • • • • • • • • • • • •

Auto racing is a favorite pastime for many Americans. How exciting it is to see those sleek cars zoom around the tracks at mind-boggling speeds! What is seen today at the racetrack is a far cry from what spectators saw on November 28, 1895, when the first motocycle race took place. *Motocycle* was another name for the horseless carriage.

Other Events This Day

- Magellan passed through the Strait of Magellan to the Pacific Ocean (1520)
- U.S. spacecraft *Mariner 4* (the first successful mission to Mars) launched (1964)

The Chicago Times-Herald sponsored this event. Cars traveled round-trip from Jackson Park in Chicago to Evanston, Illinois, and back, which was about 54 miles (86.9 km). About 70 entries were received, but when November 28 rolled around, only six vehicles were ready for the race—four gasoline (one being a gasoline engine built by Americans Charles and Frank Duryea) and two electric cars powered by batteries.

There was a chilling excitement in the air when dawn arrived on race day. There was fresh snow on the ground. The cold and the poor road conditions caused four of the cars to drop out along the way. Averaging about 7.5 miles (12.1 km) per hour, the American-built gasoline motocycle driven by Frank Duryea won the race in about nine hours. With the prize money, the Duryea brothers established the first automobile manufacturing plant in America—the Duryea Motor Wagon Company.

Response

About how long would it take a car of today (going the legal speed limit) to make the trip from Chicago to Evanston, Illinois?

Fascinating Factoid: *The Chicago Times-Herald* awarded $2,000 to the winner of the first race and $500 to the fan who named the horseless carriages *motocycles*.

Word Play

Cars cost a lot of money. How much are some car names worth if each vowel is worth $5,000 and each consonant is worth $1,500? Write the price of each letter in the name of the car and then add them together to get the cost of the car name. You may use the back of this sheet for computing. Write the total cost on the blank beside the car name.

1. FORD _____
2. BUICK _____
3. HONDA _____
4. CHEVROLET _____
5. DODGE _____
6. MITSUBISHI _____
7. PONTIAC _____
8. JAGUAR _____
9. MERCEDES _____
10. ACURA _____
11. BMW _____
12. SAAB _____
13. JEEP _____
14. CADILLAC _____
15. LINCOLN _____
16. SATURN _____

Activity

- Write some metaphors about race cars such as "That car was faster than a speeding bullet." You can be creative and make them funny if you wish (*Metaphors* are figures of speech comparing two unlike things without using the words *like* or *as*).

November 29
Softball Invented

• •

Other Events This Day

• Thomas Edison demonstrated hand-cranked phonograph (1877)

• Author Madeleine L'Engle's birthday (1918)

How about a game of kitten ball? Or mush ball? diamond ball? indoor-outdoor ball? playground ball? If you said yes to any of these, then you'll be playing regular old softball.

Softball got its start in an unlikely way on November 29, 1887. A group of Harvard and Yale graduates were waiting to hear who won the Yale/Harvard football game that year. Upon hearing of the Yale victory, an excited Yale graduate, George Hancock, tossed a boxing glove at a Harvard student who tried to bat it back to him with a stick. With chalk, Mr. Hancock marked off the bases in a gym at the club and divided the men into two teams. That is how softball began. However, the name *softball* didn't surface until around 1926 when Walter Hukansen suggested it.

This new game caught on in Chicago and a little later was moved outside to be played on fields that were smaller than regular baseball fields. It was then called Indoor-Outdoor Ball. About the same time, Louis Rober, a Minneapolis fireman, laid out a field on a vacant lot next door to his fire station. He wanted to keep his firefighters in good shape and thought this game was a good way. Other firehouses started playing. At some point, Mr. Rober's team was named the Kittens. And that is how softball became known as "Kitten Ball" in Minneapolis.

Response

Softball began without a ball. Explain how you think it came to be named *softball*.

Fascinating Factoid: It is estimated that more than 25 million people enjoy playing softball in the United States.

Word Play

Use the chart below and the clues given to figure out which person plays which sport.

- *Jenny's* sport uses the smallest ball.
- *Tommy* used to play volleyball and softball but no longer likes these sports.
- Neither of the boys play soccer this year.

	Softball	Basketball	Volleyball	Soccer
George				
Jenny				
Tommy				
Mary				

Activities

- Imagine that you are a newspaper sports writer in 1887. Write an article covering that first impromptu game of softball.

- Create a new game using a softball. Write rules and directions for playing the game.

November 30
Samuel Clemens's (Mark Twain) Birthday

Samuel Clemens, also known as Mark Twain, is one of America's most beloved authors. He was born in Florida, Missouri, on November 30, 1835, and grew up in Hannibal, Missouri. He had one brother and one sister. Jenny, the family slave, was a huge influence on young Sam with her incredible storytelling ability.

Mr. Clemens apprenticed at a local print shop for a while and he became an avid reader. He eventually worked for his brother, Orion, who owned the newspaper in Hannibal and then later for a newspaper in Iowa. At one point in his life, Mr. Clemens planned to travel to South America and write about his travels. He abandoned that plan when traveling down the Mississippi River on a steamboat. He became so enthralled with the boat that he hired on as an apprentice and he spent three years traveling the Mississippi River. His pen name, Mark Twain, came from his experiences on the riverboat. When the depth of 12 feet (3.7 m) was detected, the lead man would always yell, "By the maaa-ark! twain!"

Mr. Clemens wrote novels, short stories, essays, articles, plays, and travel books under his pen name. He is best known for *The Adventures of Tom Sawyer* and *The Adventures of Huckleberry Finn*. One of his best-known short stories is entitled, "The Celebrated Jumping Frog of Calaveras County."

Response

How do you think Jenny, the family slave, influenced Mark Twain's writing career?

Fascinating Factoid: Mr. Clemens had predicted that since his birth coincided with the appearance of Halley's comet, his death would come when the comet returned. That prophecy was fulfilled when he died in 1910.

Word Play

Start with an **S** in the largest bordered box and write in words from the story. The next word must begin with the ending letter of the previous word. Dark boxes indicate word beginnings and endings. Follow the arrows.

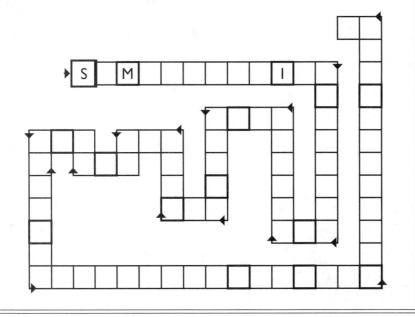

Activities

- Samuel Clemens's pen name was Mark Twain. Imagine that you are going to write a book and you want to use a pen name instead of your own. What name will you choose? Write about how you chose that name and why.

- Mark Twain had a dream that he would travel to South America and write about his travels. Write about a special dream you may have for your future. What is it you want to do? What will it involve? How long will it take?

December

Date	Event	Page
1	Scrabble® Copyrighted	163
2	Telescope Lens Cast	164
3	United Nations Adopted a Program of Action Concerning Disabled	165
4	America's First Thanksgiving	166
5	International Volunteer Day Established	167
6	*Encyclopedia Britannica* First Published	168
7	Pearl Harbor Bombed	169
8	Eli Whitney's Birthday	170
9	First Christmas Seals Sold	171
10	Puerto Rico Became Part of the United States	172
11	*Apollo 17* Landed on the Moon	173
12	Death of Joel Poinsett	174
13	Susan B. Anthony Dollar Released	175
14	George Washington's Death	176
15	Congress Enacted Bill of Rights Day	177
16	Beethoven's Birthday	178
17	First Flight at Kitty Hawk	179
18	Thirteenth Amendment Adopted	180
19	*A Christmas Carol* Published	181
20	Louisiana Territory Purchased	182
21	First Crossword Puzzle Printed	183
22	CC the Cat Was Cloned	184
23	Christmas Lights Invented	185
24	"Silent Night" Written	186
25	Christmas Celebrations	187
26	Kwanzaa Began	188
27	*Howdy Doody* Debuted	189
28	Chewing Gum Patented	190
29	First American YMCA Opened	191
30	Once in a Blue Moon	192
31	New Year's Eve	193

December 1
Scrabble® Copyrighted

• • • • • • • • • • • • • • • • • • • •

Other Events This Day

• First telephone installed in White House (1878)

• First drive-up gas station opened in Pittsburgh (1913)

Alfred Butts, an out-of-work architect, invented the world's best-selling word game in 1931. A copyright for Scrabble® was granted on December 1, 1948. Mr. Butts first called his game Lexico. It had letter tiles but no game board. He added a game board and values to the letter tiles. Then he changed the name of the game to It, New Anagrams, Alph, and Criss-Cross. Manufacturers still rejected it.

Finally, his friend James Brunot agreed to manufacture and market the game, but he made one major change—the name! He called it Scrabble. Rules were also simplified. Mr. Brunot and his wife manufactured the games in their home at first.

Even with the new name, it did not become a popular game until 1952 when a vacationing New Yorker, Jack Strauss, played the game and loved it. Mr. Strauss was chairman of Macy's Department Store in New York City and was instrumental in the game's success by stocking it in his store and promoting its sale. After that everyone who was anyone bought the game.

Response

Which name would you have selected for this game?

Fascinating Factoid: Over 100 million sets of Scrabble have been sold in 19 different languages.

Word Play

Find words from the story to fit the following point totals.

(vowels = 3 points, **X** = 8 points, other consonants = 1 point)

(3) _____
(4) _____
(5) _____
(6) _____
(7) _____
(8) _____
(9) _____
(10) _____
(11) _____
(12) _____
(13) _____
(14) _____
(15) _____
(16) _____
(18) _____
(19) _____
(20) _____

Activities

• In Scrabble, the letter tiles have different values, and tiles are put together to make words with a value. Give vowels a value of 8 points each and consonants **Q, K, Y, Z, J, V,** and **W** a value of 5 points each. All other consonants are worth 3 points each. Compute the value of your name. Next find the word with the largest value for each of these categories: noun, verb, adverb, adjective, and preposition. Then find a word with the largest value possible.

• Look in the dictionary and discover a new word for each letter of your name. Write its definition.

• Choose two vowels and five consonants. Write as many words with three letters or more, using only your chosen letters.

December 2
Telescope Lens Cast

Other Events This Day
- President Monroe announced his Monroe Doctrine (1823)
- First permanent artificial heart successfully implanted (1982)

On December 2, 1934, Corning Glass Company in Corning, New York, poured liquid glass into a 200-inch (5.1 m) mold heated to a temperature of 2700 degrees Fahrenheit (1482.2 degrees Celcius) to form a 17-foot (5.2 m) diameter mirror for a telescope. By cooling the glass down a few degrees a day, it took about 10 months to completely cool. It was necessary to cool it slowly so it would not crack. The mirror was shipped to California where it was ground and polished by hand. It became a part of the world's largest telescope—the Hale telescope at the Palomar Observatory on Mt. Palomar in California in 1949.

The telescope was named for George Ellery Hale, who built the largest telescope ever to use a conventional lens. At the beginning of the 20th century, when astronomers switched to focused mirrors for telescopes, he developed the largest mirror telescope at that time (one that was 5 feet [1. 5 m] in diameter).

Mr. Hale worked on the largest one ever up to that time—the 17-foot (5.2 m) diameter lens, but he died about 10 years before the telescope became operational. This telescope remained the premier telescope of the world until 1986 when Russia built a larger one.

Response

Approximately how many times your height is the lens of the Hubble telescope?

Fascinating Factoid: The Rockefellers gave $6,000,000 to develop the Hale Telescope.

Word Play

Telescopes are used to enlarge images. Enlarge each word by writing a larger word from the story.

1. CORN _ING_
2. _____ PA ____
3. __ OUR ____
4. _____ PER _____
5. _____ HE ____
6. _____ METER
7. _____ SCOPE
8. __ OLD

9. __ ON _____
10. _____ FOR _____
11. _____ VENT _____
12. _____ NO _____
13. BE _____
14. _____ AT _____
15. __ OR ____

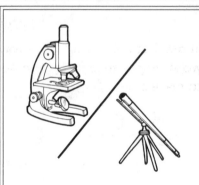

Activities

- Use a Venn diagram to compare and contrast a telescope and a microscope.
- Different scopes have various uses. On the back of this paper, list the use of each of these scopes: stereoscope, kaleidoscope, stethoscope, microscope, periscope, spectroscope, telescope, otoscope.

December 3

United Nations Adopted a Program of Action Concerning Disabled

On this day in 1982, the General Assembly of the United Nations adopted a World Program of Action Concerning Disabled Persons. Its purpose was to seek equality for the many disabled people of the world.

In 1992, the first International Day of Disabled Persons was proclaimed on the anniversary of the establishment of the World Program of Action. This special day promotes understanding of the issues faced by disabled persons and increases public awareness of the benefits of integrating disabled persons into all walks of political, social, economic, and cultural life. Disabled persons are capable citizens and can contribute greatly to society if they are not limited by the physical and/or social barriers put up by society.

Goya, a Spanish artist (1746–1828) became deaf at the age of 46, but he went on to create the most famous Spanish art of the 19th century. John Milton, an English author/poet (1608–1674) became blind when he was 43. He later wrote his most famous epic *Paradise Lost*. Helen Keller, who was blind and deaf, lived a productive life. Franklin D. Roosevelt was paralyzed by polio, but he was elected U.S. president four times. Walt Disney reportedly had learning disabilities.

Response

What does *disabled* mean to you?

Fascinating Factoid: More than half a billion persons are disabled as a result of mental, physical, or sensory impairment.

Word Play

In the first column, add one vowel to a story word to make a new word. In the second column, add one consonant to a story word to make a new word.

+ vowel	+ consonant
_____ _____	_____ _____
_____ _____	_____ _____
_____ _____	_____ _____
_____ _____	_____ _____
_____ _____	_____ _____

Activity

• Think what your life would be like if you had to go through a day without your sight or hearing. Write about it and explain how things would be the same and how they would be different.

December 4
America's First Thanksgiving

Other Events This Day
- French missionary Jacques Marquette erected mission on shores of Lake Michigan (1674)
- James Monroe of Virginia elected (by electors) 5th U.S. president (1816)

The American Thanksgiving celebration probably came from an English custom. The English always celebrated their harvest with special ceremonies, giving thanks to God for plentiful crops. It is a tradition that has continued in America since the English settlers came to this country.

We often think of the first Thanksgiving as a special celebration in early America, where the Pilgrims gathered to give thanks for surviving the harsh winter. This is probably the Thanksgiving from which our traditional, yummy Thanksgiving dinner comes. But, this was not really the first Thanksgiving in America.

The first Thanksgiving in America was held December 4, 1619 which was a little over a year before the Pilgrims landed in Massachusetts. It was entirely religious in nature and required by the charter of English settlers of Berkeley Plantation on the James River in Virginia. There was no special meal or feast. It was a time of religious ceremonies and prayer.

Response
What would your Thanksgiving Day be like without a big special meal?

Fascinating Factoid: Over 300 million turkeys are raised each year for Thanksgiving dinners in America.

Word Play
Match the word in the first column to a story word that is its synonym, antonym, or homonym. Indicate on the blank beside the word whether it is a **S**ynonym, **A**ntonym, or **H**omonym.

1. know _____ _____
2. habit _____ _____
3. last _____ _____
4. never _____ _____
5. scrumptious _____ _____
6. customary _____ _____
7. tradition _____ _____
8. taking _____ _____
9. their _____ _____
10. went _____ _____
11. abundant _____ _____

Activity
- It is not known for sure if turkey was served at early Thanksgiving feasts, but we do know that it has become a tradition in America. Think for a moment about those poor turkeys! Write a dialogue that might take place between two turkeys when they see Farmer Jones sharpening the ax.

December 5
International Volunteer Day Established

Other Events This Day
- Columbus discovered Hispaniola (Haiti) (1492)
- President Polk confirmed gold discovery (1848)

On December 17, 1985, the General Assembly of the United Nations established International Volunteer Day to be held on December 5 each year. International Volunteer Day is a day when the United Nations, governments from various nations, and other organizations join together to focus on improving the social and economic development of mankind.

Events such as rallies, parades, environmental projects, community projects, and free medical and dental care take place on this day every year. Volunteering is an important part of our society today. The history of volunteerism is hard to separate from the history of our country. President Kennedy established the Peace Corps in 1961, and President Clinton established the domestic volunteer program called AmeriCorps in 1993.

People are never too young to get involved. Some ways young people can volunteer are by picking up trash, visiting nursing homes, reading to someone who can't read, and even cleaning someone's yard. The opportunities are endless. Even the smallest act of volunteerism by an individual can strengthen an individual, a community, a nation, and the world!

Response

How do you think an individual act of volunteerism can strengthen an individual, community, nation, and the world?

Fascinating Factoid: The Volunteers of America Organization has more than 70,000 volunteers.

Word Play

The little word *up* is used in this story. There are many different ways in which *up* can be used in our language. See how "high up" your score will be in the following.

* If you can use the word up in 5 different ways, you score 80 points.

* If you can "think up" 10 different ways to use this little word, you score 90 points.

* If you can "turn up" 15 different ways to use up, then you are "way up there" with 100 points.

* Write a sentence illustrating the different ways in which up can be used. _____

_____

    Example: I <u>got up</u> from my chair.

        Mom <u>warmed up</u> the food.

(You may use the back of this sheet to write your answers.)

Activities

- Name some volunteers at your school. Don't forget those mothers who supply the party foods, etc. Plan a special day of recognition for them.

- Create your own volunteer project to benefit your school. Explain the purpose and how it will be carried out.

- Brainstorm and list ways in which you can volunteer (large or small).

December 6
Encyclopedia Britannica First Published

Other Events This Day

• Harriet Tubman escaped slavery in Maryland (1849)
• First sound recording made by Thomas Edison (1877)

Got a question? Look it up in that book that has information about everything—the encyclopedia. The *Encyclopedia Britannica* was published on this day in 1768 in Scotland. It was the brainchild of S. C. Macfarquhar and Andrew Bell. The editor of that first edition was 18-year-old William Snellie. The first edition was so successful that a more ambitious second edition followed with 10 volumes and over 8,000 pages.

Ownership of *Encyclopedia Britannica* changed several times over the years. It kept on growing and by the 11th edition, Sears, Roebuck and Company bought the trademark and publishing rights. Sears moved the organization to the United States.

In the 1980s, Microsoft® contacted *Encyclopedia Britannica* about working together on a CD-ROM. *Encyclopedia Britannica* turned down that idea. As a result, Microsoft partnered with Funk and Wagnalls to create an Internet encyclopedia known as *Encarta*. This caused a drop in sales of *Encyclopedia Britannica*. The owners did not quit. They jumped right into the electronics market by putting together their own CD-ROM. In 1994, they launched a complete online encyclopedia, which is available to people around the world for a subscription fee.

Now, *Encyclopedia Britannica* has a larger and more diverse line of products than ever before. They are still holding onto their basic dream to be the world's leader in reference education and learning.

Response

Which do you find more useful, a bound volume of an encyclopedia or the Internet version?

Fascinating Factoid: The first part of the first edition of *Encyclopedia Britannica* was priced at six pence ($4.78 in today's U.S. currency).

Word Play

Locate a word in the story for every letter of the alphabet but **x** and **z**. Write the words below.

A _____   B _____   C _____

D _____   E _____   F _____

G _____   H _____   I _____

J _____   K _____   L _____

M _____   N _____   O _____

P _____   Q _____   R _____

S _____   T _____   U _____

V _____   W _____   Y _____

Activity

• Encyclopedias include short biographies of famous people. Project your life into a successful future. Write an article about yourself for an encyclopedia. Read a few similar articles before you begin writing so that you will know what to include about yourself.

December 7

Pearl Harbor Bombed

On Sunday, December 7, 1941, the U.S. Pacific Fleet was attacked by Japanese forces at Pearl Harbor, Hawaii. When President Franklin Roosevelt addressed the American public in a radio broadcast, he said, "This is a day that will live in infamy." The United States suffered great losses to its Navy in that sneak attack.

Japanese Admiral Yamamoto, credited with masterminding the attack, had previously served in the Japanese Embassy in Washington DC. He knew of our industrial strength and temperament. He cautioned the Japanese about such an attack but was overruled. He is quoted as saying, "We have awakened a sleeping giant and have instilled in him a terrible resolve."

The surprise attack brought about an immediate show of unity from the American people. Young men volunteered to fight for their country. Women went to work in the factories. Those left at home planted victory gardens, bought U.S. War Bonds, and supported the war effort in other ways.

Response

Explain in your own words the meaning of Admiral Yamamoto's statement, "We have awakened a sleeping giant and have instilled in him a terrible resolve."

Fascinating Factoid: Over 1,100 crew members aboard the USS *Arizona* were killed when the ship was bombed at Pearl Harbor.

Word Play

Dive right into the middle of this activity by finding a story word to write in the blank between the two given words. Your word must make two different compound words when combined with the two words given.

1. to ___day___ light

2. home _____ shop

3. an _____ wise

4. fly _____ way

5. in _____ day

6. with _____ side

Activity

- Military people exhibit courage. What do you think *courage* means? List ways in which our Armed Forces show courage. List ways in which people who are not in the military show courage. Now list ways in which you show courage.

December 8
Eli Whitney's Birthday

• • • • • • • • • • • • • • • • •

American inventor and manufacturer, Eli Whitney, was born on this day in 1765 in Westborough, Massachusetts. He is best remembered as the inventor of the cotton gin in 1793; however, that was not the only important contribution that he made to society.

The cotton gin revolutionized the cotton industry, making Southern cotton crops a profitable endeavor for the first time in history. Prior to this piece of machinery, separating the seed from the fiber had been a tedious process done by hand. Mr. Whitney's cotton gin was a mechanical device that did the work faster and more efficiently. Although this invention had a major impact on the country, Mr. Whitney didn't profit from this invention.

Some believe that Eli Whitney's greatest contribution was the development and implementation of the manufacturer's assembly line, which he used to make rifles for the government in 1798. Until that time, every rifle was made by hand. Parts from each rifle were different and would not fit another. It was Mr. Whitney's idea to make the parts interchangeable. He did this by designing a rifle and then developing ways of cutting each part for a pattern. This process was called milling.

Through Mr. Whitney's genius, American society was changed dramatically. Cotton processing was revolutionized as well as the manufacturing process, which contributed greatly to the Industrial Revolution in the United States.

Response

What are some things in your life that are available because of the invention of the cotton gin?

Fascinating Factoid: It took 13 years for Eli Whitney's cotton gin patent to become validated. Meanwhile several imitations appeared.

Word Play

The word *cotton* is often misspelled as *cotten*. There are many words in our language that are frequently misspelled. Circle the misspelled word in each pair of words.

1. fiery   firey
2. jewelery   jewelry
3. restaurant   restuarant
4. supercede   supersede
5. calander   calendar
6. foreign   foriegn
7. usage   useage
8. twelfth   twelvth
9. potatos   potatoes
10. existence   existance
11. harass   harrass
12. grammer   grammar
13. preceed   precede
14. pidgeon   pigeon
15. library   libary
16. cemetery   cemetary
17. arctic   artic
18. occasion   ocassion

Activities

• Research to find the reason Eli Whitney did not profit from his invention of the cotton gin. Write a summary of your findings.

• Brainstorm and list things you would like to see invented. They can be frivolous or serious inventions.

December 9
First Christmas Seals Sold

Other Events This Day
- Tennyson's "Charge of the Light Brigade" published (1854)
- Famous clown Emmett Kelly's birthday (1898)

The first Christmas Seal went on sale on December 9, 1907, but the Christmas Seal story actually started in 1871 with a young doctor named Edward Trudeau. He had tuberculosis (TB), the most dreaded disease at that time. Because there was no known cure, he moved to a cottage in the woods to spend his remaining days. But he gradually got better. Because of his recovery, it was thought that rest, good nourishment, fresh air, and sunshine could cure TB. When he was well, he opened a small TB sanatorium. Others sprang up around the country, but there were so many cases of TB and not enough money to take care of all the sick people.

By 1907, a TB sanatorium doctor asked his cousin, Emily Bissell, a Red Cross worker, for help to raise money to keep his sanatorium open. She had read about a fundraiser in Denmark in which special Christmas seals for letters, in addition to the regular postage stamps were sold.

Ms. Bissell designed the first American Christmas Seal. She used the Red Cross in the center of a holly wreath above the words Merry Christmas. They were sold in the lobby of the post office in Wilmington, Delaware, for one penny. At the rate of sales, she saw that they would never raise enough money, so she contacted Leigh Hodges, a columnist with a newspaper in Philadelphia. With his help, over $3,000 was raised. Since that time, Christmas Seals have been raising money for the battle against TB.

Response

Give your own definition of *sanatorium;* then check it in the dictionary.

Fascinating Factoid: Each year about two million deaths are attributed to tuberculosis.

Word Play

Write one sentence showing two different meanings for each story word. Example: I <u>fell</u> while using an ax to <u>fell</u> the tree.

seal _____

well _____

cases _____

cross _____

post _____

rest _____

story _____

cure _____

stamp _____

Activities

- Many different kinds of seals are sold to help fund worthwhile causes. For example, Easter Seals are sold to help crippled children. National Wildlife Federation Seals raise funds to help protect animals. Choose a cause and design the kind of seal you think would help raise money for it.

- Learn more about the American Lung Association. What are their goals and purposes? Discover the most common lung problems they deal with today.

December 10
Puerto Rico Became Part of the United States

• • • • • • • • • • • • • • • • •

Puerto Rico is a Caribbean Island originally claimed by Christopher Columbus for Spain in 1493. He called it San Juan Bautista. At that time peaceful and gentle Taino Indians lived there. The Spanish enslaved them to mine the gold.

By 1508, the first Spanish Governor, Ponce de Leon had arrived. The island remained under Spanish control; but after the gold ran out, the Spanish neglected Puerto Rico. Military governors hindered the island's independence and kept the people poor. In 1897, the island was finally granted status as a Spanish dominion.

The United States defeated Spain in the Spanish-American War in 1898. As a result, Puerto Rico became the property of the United States. About 20 years after the war, it formally became a U.S. territory, and eventually, American citizenship was granted to Puerto Rico natives. Today, Puerto Rico is a self-governed territory, and its inhabitants have most of the benefits of American citizenship; however, they cannot vote for U.S. president.

Response

Why do you think the Spanish neglected Puerto Rico after the gold ran out?

Fascinating Factoid: Puerto Rico is an island that is only 100 miles (160.9 km) long and 35 miles (56.3 km) wide.

Word Play

Beside each letter in *Puerto Rico*, write the name of a city or town in Puerto Rico that starts with that letter.

P _____   R _____

U _____   I _____

E _____   C _____

R _____   O _____

T _____

O _____

Puerto Rico

Activities

• What if Puerto Rico became a state? That would mean 51 stars on the U.S. flag. Look carefully at the design of the stars in the flag now and when there were 48 states. Design the star field for 51 states.

• Most states have nicknames. For example, Missouri is the "Show Me State." Ohio is called "The Buckeye State" and Texas is "The Lone Star State." Research nicknames for other states. Read about Puerto Rico and then list several appropriate nicknames for Puerto Rico should it become a state. Put a star beside the name you like best.

December 11
Apollo 17 Landed on the Moon

Other Events This Day
- The *Mayflower* landed at Plymouth Rock (1620)
- First recorded display of Aurora Borealis in the United States (1719)

In 1961, the United States started sending unmanned spacecraft to the moon. The U.S. Apollo Space Program, involving manned missions, began explorations of the moon. There were 11 missions in all. *Apollo 11* was probably the most famous as that is the one that carried Neil Armstrong, Michael Collins, and "Buzz" Aldrin into space. It was from this mission that the words were heard, "Houston, Tranquility base here. The eagle has landed."

Apollo 17 was the finale and it was grand! It may have been the last manned flight to the moon, but it was probably the most successful of all. The other flights had paved the way. The crew of Eugene Cernan, Ronald Evans, and Harrison Schmitt launched December 7, 1972. Touchdown on the moon took place on December 11, 1972. Its mission was mainly to study the moon's surface. Mr. Schmitt was the first trained geologist to be on the moon.

Mr. Schmitt and Mr. Cernan set up six automatic research stations and brought back more rock samples and reels of film than any other mission. On the return journey to Earth, Mr. Evans completed a space walk, which was only the third ever completed. Now we know for sure—the moon is not made of cheese and, there was no sign of that "man in the moon" that we've heard about!

Response
Why do you think it was important for a geologist to be on a moon mission?

Fascinating Factoid: *Apollo 7*, launched in 1968, provided the first live TV broadcast from a manned spacecraft.

Word Play
Neil Armstrong sent a message back to Earth when he first stepped on the surface of the moon. To find out what that famous message was, rewrite the following sentence using clues for words to substitute for those shown.

This's single huge advance fore homosapien, won dwarf jump four humanity.

_____   _____   _____   _____
(antonym)   (synonym)   (antonym)   (synonym)

_____   _____ , _____   _____
(homonym)   (synonym)   (homonym)   (antonym)

_____   _____   _____ .
(synonym)   (homonym)   (synonym)

Activity
- Write a series of two-line stanzas for an "I Used to Think" poem about the moon. The first line of each stanza will start out with, "I used to think that… (*Example:* there was a man in the moon)".

  The second line of each stanza will start with "Now I know… (*Example:* it was only craters making the man's face)."

December 12
Death of Joel Poinsett

Other Events This Day
- George Grant patented the wooden golf tee (1899)
- Boys Town founded (1917)

Have you ever heard of Joel Robert Poinsett? And why is his death of interest? Mr. Poinsett introduced those beautiful flowers seen during the holidays to America. He was the first U.S. Ambassador to Mexico, appointed by President Andrew Jackson in 1820. He took cuttings of the poinsettia back to his home in South Carolina where he raised the plants and often gave them as gifts during the holiday season.

By an act of Congress, December 12 is known as Poinsettia Day. December 12 was chosen because Mr. Poinsett died on that day in 1851.

The Aztecs called the poinsettia *Cuetlaxochitle*. They used the sap from the plant to treat fevers. They made a red dye, from the plant. The poinsettia's botanical name is *Euphorbia pulcherrima*, which means "very beautiful." The showy colored parts of the plant that we think of as the flowers are actually called *brachts* (modified leaves). Ordinarily they are red, but they grow in many different colors. Poinsettias are not poisonous as previously thought; however, eating them could cause a stomachache. Poinsettias have become the best-selling potted plant in America even though most are sold within a six-week period around Christmas.

Response
Why do you think poinsettias are given as gifts during the holiday season but at no other time of the year?

Fascinating Factoid: Two hundred twenty million dollars worth of poinsettias are sold during the holiday season each year.

Word Play
Many words in our language have double letters. Find each story word with double letters that matches the clue given.

1. _____ (named officially)

2. _____ (an authorized representative)

3. _____ (part of a plant that will grow into a new plant)

4. _____ (named)

5. _____ (giving up something for money)

6. _____ (flower planted in a container)

7. _____ (seized something)

8. _____ (deserved)

Activities
- Poinsettias are associated with Christmas holidays. Lilies are associated with Easter. List other major holidays. What flower do you think would be good to represent these holidays?

- Each month has a flower designated as its official flower. For example, the chrysanthemum is November's flower. Research and determine what flower is associated with each month and make a chart or poster with pictures of the flowers.

December 13
Susan B. Anthony Dollar Released

Other Events This Day

• Sir Francis Drake set sail from England for an around-the-world trip (1577)

• First music store in America opened in Philadelphia (1759)

The Susan B. Anthony one-dollar coin was first issued on December 13, 1978. The coin pictured Susan B. Anthony on the front side and an eagle landing on the moon on the reverse side. It is made of copper and nickel. Ms. Anthony is the first woman ever to have been pictured on any U.S. coin. To date, only one other woman, Sacajawea, has been honored in that manner.

In October 1978, President Jimmy Carter signed the bill that created the Susan B. Anthony dollar coin. These coins were often called Suzy Bucks or Carter's Quarters. The coin didn't really catch on with the public—probably because it looked and felt very much like a quarter. It was easy to mistake the two. In 1999, the government announced the replacement of the Susan B. Anthony dollar with a gold colored coin featuring Sacajawea.

Ms. Anthony was instrumental in the passage of the Fourteenth Amendment and securing the rights for women to vote but was not until 14 years after her death that over 8 million American women voted for the first time in history on November 2, 1920.

Response

Why do you think the Susan B. Anthony dollar is a collectible item?

Fascinating Factoid: As of October 1997, there were 126,800,000 million Susan B. Anthony coins in circulation.

Word Play

Many different coin combinations total $1.00. Using the names of the coins instead of the amounts, write at least one coin combination by the given number of coins to total $1.00.

Number of Coins	Combination	Number of Coins	Combination
(2)	_____	(9)	_____
(3)	_____	(10)	_____
(4)	_____	(11)	_____
(5)	_____	(12)	_____
(6)	_____	(13)	_____
(7)	_____	(14)	_____
(8)	_____		

Activities

• Sacajawea and Susan B. Anthony have both been honored on a U.S. coin. What other woman would you nominate for such an honor? Justify your choice.

• The United States has a five-dollar bill, but no five-dollar coin. Who will be the first person honored on a five-dollar coin? What should be shown on the tail's side. Make a drawing (both sides) to show what this coin might look like. Specify the size and content so that it is not easily mistaken for other coins.

December 14
George Washington's Death

Other Events This Day

• Alabama became 22nd U.S. state (1819)
• South Pole first reached by Roald Amundsen (1911)

At 10:00 P.M. on December 14, 1799, George Washington passed away at his beloved Mount Vernon. He was 67 years old. He became ill after working on his farm in rain and sleet. By the time he went inside and changed his clothes, he was beginning to suffer with chills and nausea. However, he continued his indoor work. As nightfall came on, he joined the family for dinner and then went into the library to complete some paperwork before going to bed for the night.

He had a long feverish night but he didn't awaken anyone. The following morning, he consented to allow a "bleeding." This was believed to be a cure in those days. However, his condition didn't improve. Doctors were called in, but their medicines did not help.

As night approached again, Washington knew that his time had come. He reportedly told an old friend that he was dying, but he was not afraid. There were no sighs, groans, or struggles to indicate to the bystanders that he had passed away. It took a few moments for them to realize that he was gone and not sleeping. Henry Lee best eulogized George Washington with this statement, "First in war, first in peace, and first in the hearts of his countrymen."

Response

What was meant by Henry Lee's eulogy of George Washington?

Fascinating Factoid: Arlington National Cemetery is located on land that was once owned by George Washington Parke Custis, President George Washington's adopted grandson.

Word Play

George Washington was the first man to become a U.S. president.

Match each *man*-word to its definition.

_____ 1. manatee	a. midget
_____ 2. mane	b. insect
_____ 3 manger	c. trough
_____ 4. manager	d. estate house
_____ 5. maniac	e. nail care
_____ 6. manicure	f. handbook
_____ 7. manor	g. one who guides a team
_____ 8. mantis	h. hair
_____ 9. manual	i. lunatic
_____ 10. manikin	j. handle
_____ 11. manganese	k. require
_____ 12. mandate	l. metallic element
_____ 13. manipulate	m. sea mammal

Activities

• Henry Lee praised Washington upon his death by stating, "First in war, first in peace, and first in the hearts of his countrymen." Write a short speech in honor of George Washington's life and accomplishments.

• Use maps, encyclopedias, or the Internet to find and list as many towns or cities named for Washington that you can find. Be sure to tell the state in which each is found.

December 15
Congress Enacted Bill of Rights Day

● ● ● ● ● ● ● ● ● ● ● ● ● ● ● ● ● ●

Bill of Rights Day was established and signed into effect on December 15, 1941, by Franklin D. Roosevelt. It was 150 years after the actual signing of the Bill of Rights (the first 10 amendments of our Constitution) in 1791.

In 1787, a convention was held to deal with the new nation's government. After electing George Washington the president of the Convention, our plan of government (the U.S. Constitution) was written. It was finished and signed in 1787. Some states approved it only on the condition that a Bill of Rights would be added. They wanted the Bill of Rights to protect them from a strong national government similar to the one from which they had so recently won their freedom.

The First Amendment guarantees freedom of religion, speech, press, and the rights of peaceful assembly and petition. Other amendments guarantee the rights of the people to form a well-regulated militia, to keep and bear arms, the right to private property, fair treatment for accused criminals, protection from unreasonable search and seizure, freedom from self-incrimination, a speedy and impartial jury trial, and representation by counsel.

Response
Choose one of the freedoms guaranteed in the First Amendment and explain why it is important.

> **Fascinating Factoid:** The Constitution was the plan for the government—what would actually be done—and was different from the Declaration of Independence, which stated goals.

Word Play

Bill of Rights Day is December 15. There are many other special days. Using a word from the Word Box, write the name of the special day on the blank beside the date on which it is celebrated.

1. June 14 _____
2. November 11 _____
3. December 7 _____
4. April 18 _____
5. July 4 _____
6. January 15 _____
7. September 17 _____
8. February 22 _____
9. 2nd Sunday in May _____
10. 3rd Sunday in June _____

Word Box

Martin Luther King Jr.'s Birthday (actual)	George Washington's Birthday (actual)
Flag Day	Independence Day
Paul Revere Day	Mother's Day
Pearl Harbor Day	Citizenship Day
Veterans Day	Father's Day

Activities

- A bill of rights guarantees certain privileges and freedoms. Create a bill of rights for students in your classroom.

- Choose one of the rights guaranteed by the Amendments to the Constitution and write about what life in the United States would be like without that right.

December 16
Beethoven's Birthday

• •

Other Events This Day
• Boston Tea Party (1773)
• First White House press conference held (1953)

Ludwig van Beethoven was a musical genius. He was born into a family of musicians on December 16, 1770, in Bonn, Germany. By the time he was 12, he had published several musical compositions. Although Beethoven is thought of most often as the creative genius of piano sonatas, he composed music for orchestras, stringed instruments, and even vocal presentations.

Beethoven moved to Vienna to study. His early years brought a lot of hard work but earned him praise. He was an accomplished pianist who displayed brilliance, turbulence, fantasy, and a depth of feeling in his music. His music reflected his powerful and troubled personality; however, it was not all stormy and powerful. Much of his music reflects a gentle and lyrical mode. His most popular works are probably his nine symphonies.

The first symptoms of an untreatable deafness showed up when he was 29. He was very depressed; however, he came out of this period of despair and continued to compose and his music took on a new style. He would take inspiration for his music from his nature walks. Despite his handicap, he went on to create some of his greatest works.

Response

How do you think Beethoven could continue writing music when he could no longer hear it?

Fascinating Factoid: About 10,000 people attended Beethoven's funeral in 1827.

Word Play

Complete the word puzzle below by making words using the letters in *accomplishments*. All of the words above *accomplishments* must contain an **i**. All the words below must contain an **a**.

—
— —
— — —
— — — —
— — — — —
— — — — — —
— — — — — — —

ACCOMPLISHMENTS

— — — — — — — —
— — — — — — —
— — — — — —
— — — — —
— — — —
— — —
— —
—

Activities

• Different types of music create different types of feelings within individuals. For example, slow, soft music might make you want to take a nap or relax. Fast music might make you want to walk quickly or run. Think of songs that might create the following feelings: happy, sad, relaxed, energetic, patriotic, hungry.

• Beethoven took inspiration for his music from nature walks. Think of and describe the type of music that might be inspired by walking at the mall, in the mountains, by the ocean, in the ballpark, in your backyard, in your neighborhood, and on your school grounds.

December 17
First Flight at Kitty Hawk

Other Events This Day
- France recognized independence of American Colonies (1777)
- U.S. Army ended Japanese Internment Camps in United States (1944)

The first successful airplane flight took place on this date in 1903. The Wright Flyer was invented, designed, created, and flown by brothers Orville and Wilbur Wright. The plane was a fabric-covered biplane with a wooden frame. The power to the two-propeller plane came from a 12-horsepower engine.

Orville and Wilbur Wright worked for many years trying to build a flying machine before they finally succeeded. They first built a glider, but it failed on its first test in 1900. By 1901, they had worked out some of the problems and the machine fared better on the next test. They chose Kitty Hawk, North Carolina, to test their glider because of the steady winds and sand dunes that would make a safer landing. Their first really successful glider flight was in 1902.

Meanwhile, back at the bicycle shop in Ohio, the Wright Brothers were working on an engine to power a two-prop plane. On the first test, the engine stalled. After three days of repair, the plane flew—not very long and not very far—but it flew! The first flight with Orville at the controls lasted for 12 whole seconds and flew 120 feet (36.6 m). On the fourth test, Wilbur flew the plane 852 feet (259.7 m) and stayed airborne for 59 seconds! The Wright Flyer is housed permanently at the National Air and Space Museum in Washington DC.

Response
How do you think building a glider first helped the Wright Brothers build their biplane?

> **Fascinating Factoid:** Winds averaged 17 miles (27.4 km) per hour at the time of the first successful flight of the Wright Flyer.

Word Play
The Wright Flyer was a biplane. *Bi-* is a prefix (word part added to the front of a root word to change the word's meaning). Some prefixes stand for numbers. Add each of the following prefixes to a root word to make a new word and then tell what number the prefix represents.

a. centi _____

b. bi _____

c. octo _____

d. uni _____

e. hepta _____

f. tri _____

g. quad _____

h. penta _____

i. hex _____

j. deca _____

Activity
- Create a business card for the Wright Brothers. A business card includes the name, address, phone number, slogan and/or logo, and e-mail address. Be creative in selecting information for your card. The information on your card does not have to be real—it can be silly or whimsical.

December 18
Thirteenth Amendment Adopted

• • • • • • • • • • • • • • • • • •

Other Events This Day

• Japan admitted to the United Nations (1956)

• Dr. Suess's *How the Grinch Stole Christmas* aired for the first time on TV (1966)

The U.S. Secretary of State William H. Seward proclaimed on December 18, 1865, the passage of the Thirteenth Amendment which states: "Section 1—Neither slavery nor involuntary servitude, except as punishment for crimes where of the party shall have been duly convicted shall exist in the United States, or any place subject to their jurisdiction. Section 2—Congress shall have power to enforce this article by appropriate legislation."

Although slavery had been officially stopped by the Thirteenth Amendment, the freed slaves did not have an easy time. In many instances, the newly freed slaves worked under the same conditions they had when they were slaves. African-Americans were jailed for not having a job, and then they were hired to do slave labor. In some areas, African-American children were forced to work in local factories. African-Americans were kept from buying land. They were not paid fair wages for their work. They were denied the right to vote.

The slave era of the U.S. history is not one for which we can be proud. It does not present a pretty picture.

Response

Rewrite the Thirteenth Amendment in your own words.

Fascinating Factoid: The Titles of Nobility Amendment would have been the Thirteenth Amendment had it been ratified before 1865.

Word Play

An *acronym* is made up of the beginning letters of words. For example, *US* is the acronym for the *United States*. An *abbreviation*, on the other hand, is a shortened version of a word. For example, *mo.* is the abbreviation for *month*. Select the acronym from each pair below and write the words for which it stands.

1. SWAK—ATTN   _____

2. MO—HQ   _____

3. AVE—SWAT   _____

4. VIP—LT   _____

5. TLC—REV   _____

6. APT—ASAP   _____

7. DJ—ST   _____

8. UFO—GOV   _____

9. CIR—COD   _____

Activity

• In 1776, the Declaration of Independence stated that all men are created equal. In 1865, the Thirteenth Amendment was passed, banning slavery. Why do you think it took almost 100 years to right this wrong? Explain.

December 19
A Christmas Carol Published

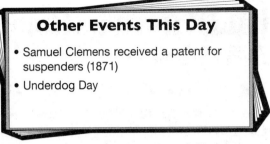
On December 19, 1843, *A Christmas Carol* by Charles Dickens was published. The main character, Ebenezer Scrooge, a miserly, cold-hearted man, was stingy, greedy, and mean-spirited. He thought of Christmas as "Humbug!" On Christmas Eve, three ghosts visited Scrooge in a dream: the Ghost of Christmas Past, the Ghost of Christmas Present, and the Ghost of Christmas Yet to Come. They showed Scrooge the error of his ways in placing more value on money rather than people. The bleak picture of his life frightened Scrooge. The three ghosts helped him understand that unless he changed his ways, he was headed for big trouble. Scrooge woke up a changed man!

The author, Charles Dickens, was born in Portsmouth, England, on February 7, 1812, the second of eight children. When he was 12, Mr. Dickens's father was jailed for a bad debt and he had to go to work in a blacking warehouse, a factory which manufactured shoe polish. He was not treated well there.

Mr. Dickens had little formal schooling, but he taught himself how to write. He landed a job as a reporter for a newspaper. He also contributed essays and stories to magazines. He went on to become one of literature's greatest writers. He died in 1870 and is buried in Poet's Corner of Westminster Abbey in London.

Response

What character traits must Dickens have possessed that helped him become one of the world's greatest writers?

Fascinating Factoid: The life of Bob Cratchit in *A Christmas Carol* reflects Mr. Dickens's own life.

Word Play

Action words have different tenses that show action in the past, present, and future. Beside each action word from the story, write the other two tenses of that word.

	Past	Present	Future
1.	was	_____	_____
2.	visited	_____	_____
3.	changed	_____	_____
4.	treated	_____	_____
5.	died	_____	_____
6.	buried	_____	_____
7.	taught	_____	_____
8.	thought	_____	_____
9.	showed	_____	_____
10.	_____	work	_____

On the back of this paper, make a chart of several action words showing past, present, and future tenses.

Activities

- Draw three pictures—a vision of your own Christmas Past, one of your own Christmas Present, and one of your own Christmas Yet to Come.
- Create your own modern-day Scrooge story, patterned after *A Christmas Carol.*

December 20
Louisiana Territory Purchased

• • • • • • • • • • • • • • • • • • • •

Other Events This Day

- Sacagawea, interpreter for Lewis and Clark, died (1812)
- Missouri imposed $1 bachelor tax (1820)

What was the big deal about the Louisiana Purchase? It is considered one of the greatest real estate deals ever! In 1762, France ceded this area to Spain, but regained it in 1800. Napoleon, the Emperor of France, didn't really need the territory and he didn't have troops or funds to support it. He offered to sell it to the United States.

President Thomas Jefferson had already sent men to Paris to negotiate the purchase of the lower Mississippi River area. However, the French offered to sell the entire area from the Mississippi River to the Rocky Mountains and from the Gulf of Mexico to the Canadian border. That would double the size of the United States, making it one of the largest nations in the world at that time. For $15 million, the United States bought more than 800,000 square miles (2,071,990 sq. km) of land. In a ceremony on December 20, 1803, the French turned the Louisiana Territory over to the United States.

All or part of 15 states have been carved from the Louisiana Territory. The states involved in the original Louisiana Territory are Montana, New Mexico, Kansas, South Dakota, Missouri, Wyoming, Texas, Nebraska, Minnesota, Arkansas, Colorado, Oklahoma, North Dakota, Iowa, and Louisiana.

Response

What was the significance of the Louisiana Purchase?

Fascinating Factoid: The United States directly paid $11,250,000 for the land in the Louisiana Purchase. The United States assumed French debts to American citizens for the rest of the $15 million.

Word Play

Find and write an unusual city or town name in each of the Louisiana Purchase states.

Arkansas _____

Colorado _____

Iowa _____

Kansas _____

Louisiana _____

Minnesota _____

Missouri _____

Montana _____

Nebraska _____

New Mexico _____

North Dakota _____

Oklahoma _____

South Dakota _____

Texas _____

Wyoming _____

Activity

- To decrease our national debt, imagine that the president and Congress have decided to auction off one of our states. Which state should be put on the auction block to bring in the most money? List the reasons for your choice.

December 21

First Crossword Puzzle Printed

• • • • • • • • • • • • • • • • •

A crossword puzzle is a game of words in which you are given a hint and the number of letters for a word. You must fill in the boxes by finding the right words to fit the meaning and given spaces.

Arthur Wynne, an immigrant to the United States from England, created the first known published crossword. It first appeared December 21, 1913, in *The New York World* Sunday newspaper. It was called *word-cross*. That name changed to *cross-word* and then eventually to *crossword*. Mr. Wynne's puzzle was diamond shaped and had no empty spaces.

Crossword puzzles caught on like wildfire. Within a few years, almost every newspaper was printing crosswords. In 1924, Simon and Schuster Publishers even printed a book of crossword puzzles.

Response

Why do you think crossword puzzles are as popular today as they were almost 100 years ago?

Fascinating Factoid: *The New York Times* was one of the last newspaper holdouts to the crossword craze by not publishing a crossword until 1942.

Word Play

This puzzle is similar to the first crossword puzzle.

Clues

2–3 a fighter	7–23 food consumer	17–24 conflict
4–5 stitch	20–21 big mouse	M–5 cut grass
6–7 one of ten	22–23 average	21–26 a flap
8–9 pea container	24–25 speed detector	1–28 container
10–11 shade of brown	26–27 forbid	29–30 father
12–13 pen point	11–19 mesh	M–6 congregated
14–15 first 2-digit number	8–16 sharp fastener	22–27 cooking vessel
16–17 original	4–20 sedate, subdued	3–10 go bad
18–19 wager	2–9 place to sleep	18–25 to prevent

Activity

• Create your own crossword puzzle with a solution key. Choose any theme or subject area. You may use a square or rectangular shape or the diamond shape like the first crossword puzzle.

December 22
CC the Cat Was Cloned

Other Events This Day

• Abigail Adams's birthday (1844)

• Thomas Edison patents a magneto-electric machine (1879)

CC was born on December 22, 2001. CC stands for "copycat" or "carbon copy." CC is a white cat with gray stripes. The thing that is so special about the birth of CC is that she is the first cloned pet.

CC's clone mother is Rainbow, a calico shorthair cat. CC doesn't look at all like her mother. She was only one of nearly 90 cloned embryos to survive in this experiment conducted at Texas A&M University at College Station, Texas. While cloning creates a genetic copy of an animal, it does not guarantee an identical personality or appearance.

The experiment at Texas A&M was funded by John Sperling who wanted his dog Missy cloned. He funded the research with over three million dollars. Operation CC was an experiment in the larger project called Missyplicity to clone Mr. Sperling's Dog. Researchers say the commercial aspects of being able to clone a pet cat are one thing. More important is that cats have a feline strain of AIDS and provide a good model for researching and looking for a cure for human AIDS.

CC is now living in the home of one of the researchers and is a healthy, energetic cat. She is curious and playful. CC is probably the one and only cloned cat for Texas A&M researchers because the funding is now depleted. The university researchers have successfully cloned a pig, a bull, and a goat—but no dog as of yet.

Response

Why do you think researchers named the cloned cat CC?

Fascinating Factoid: A cat has 32 muscles in each ear.

Word Play

Carbon Copy Cat is alliterative. It has the same letter at the beginning of each word. Write an alliteration for each of the following animals.

_____	aardvark	_____	macaw
_____	baboon	_____	nuthatch
_____	camel	_____	octopus
_____	dingo	_____	panther
_____	elephant	_____	quetzal
_____	falcon	_____	raccoon
_____	goat	_____	salamander
_____	hyena	_____	toucan
_____	iguana	_____	unicorn
_____	jackal	_____	walrus
_____	kangaroo	_____	yak
_____	leopard	_____	zebra

Use the back of this sheet for your answers.

Activities

• Research to determine what other animals have been cloned. Make a list of the animals, their names, and their birthdates.

• Explain the significance of the Texas A&M cloning project being named Missyplicity.

December 23
Christmas Lights Invented

Other Events This Day

- Lincoln Tunnel in New York opened to traffic (1937)
- "Chipmunk Song" hit number one on the charts (1958)

Christmas lights were introduced to the public on this day in 1882. Thomas Edison invented the first Christmas lights three years after the lightbulb was invented. They were first used in the home of Mr. Edison's friend, Edward Johnson. The lights were red, white, and blue. They flashed while the tree rotated.

In the beginning, Christmas lights were too expensive for most families to own. Some just rented the lights. They were dangerous because they got so hot. Outdoor Christmas lights didn't come along until 1927. Many of the first Christmas lights were blown in molds used to make glass ornaments and then painted by toy makers.

General Electric was the first company to offer prewired Christmas tree lights. Before that, they had to be hand wired onto the tree. Their lights were not patented, so it wasn't long until the market was flooded with Christmas lights. Carl Otis is credited with inventing the bubble light that became so popular. Today, Christmas lights are available in just about any size, shape, or color imaginable.

Response

Predict the next fad in Christmas lighting. In the past, bubble lights were a fad, and not long ago icicle lights became a fad.

Fascinating Factoid: The bell-shaped lights were first designed in 1932 for use in model train stations.

Word Play

Many people decorate lavishly for the holidays. Can you determine which "decoration" word belongs with each clue?

1. l i g h t s (icicle type are pretty)
2. _ _ _ _ _ _ (twinkle, twinkle)
3. _ _ _ _ _ _ _ (bright and shiny)
4. _ _ _ _ _ _ _ _ (can't burn them at both ends)
5. _ _ _ _ _ _ _ _ _ _ (come give me a kiss)
6. _ _ _ _ _ _ (a girl's name)
7. _ _ _ _ _ _ _ _ _ _ (pretty flower)
8. _ _ _ _ _ _ _ _ _ (fill me up, Santa)
9. _ _ _ _ _ _ _ _ (pretty rope)
10. _ _ _ _ _ _ _ _ (door hangers)
11. _ _ _ _ _ _ (ring-a-lings)

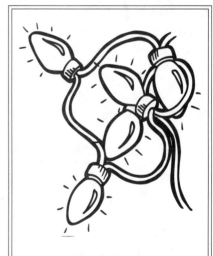

Activities

- List several major holidays and design appropriate lights to use for decorations on these holidays.
- Design a winning entry for a holiday decoration contest for your front yard. Draw and explain your design.

December 24
"Silent Night" Written

Other Events This Day
- Fire devastates Library of Congress in Washington DC, destroying 35,000 volumes (1851)
- Walt Disney's *The Aristocats* released (1970)

There are varying stories about the origin of the Christmas carol "Silent Night." A manuscript discovered in 1995 authenticated that it was written by Reverend Joseph Mohr in 1816 and that Franz Gruber composed the music in 1818.

One popular version of the story is that in the winter of 1818 in Obendorf, Austria, at St. Nicholas Church, the organ was broken: there was no way that it could be repaired and operational for the special Christmas service. Mr. Mohr was forced to improvise and came up with the last-minute idea of setting a poem to music that he had written two years before. On December 24, he asked Franz Gruber, the church organist, to compose music for a guitar accompaniment for his poem "Silent Night." Although it was a last-minute creation, the resulting music was wonderful. Mr. Mohr and Mr. Gruber sang the new song on December 25, 1818, at St. Nicholas Church.

The song's popularity did not spread until after 1825 when the organ was being rebuilt. The repairman found the handwritten sheet music and took it home with him. It soon became a favorite of traveling singers. Some accounts of the story suggest that mice ate the bellows of the organ, while others say Mr. Gruber broke the organ, and still others say that the organ rusted because of flooding. An entirely different version says that Mr. Mohr simply wanted a new carol to be sung with guitar accompaniment because he liked guitar music.

Response

Which account of the broken organ do you believe? Explain.

Fascinating Factoid: An off-screen choir at the end of the 1951 film *A Christmas Carol* sang "Silent Night."

Word Play

"Silent Night" is one of the most beautiful Christmas carols, although many others have been written. Supply the name for each serious Christmas carol with a "not-so-serious" description.

1. _
(small lad percussionist)

2. _ _ _ _ _ _ _ _ _ _ _ _ _ _ _ _ _ _
(stored in a hay bin)

3. _ _ , _ _ _ _ _ _ _ _ _ _ _ _ _ _ _ _
_ _ _ _ _ _ _ _ _ _ _
(small place in Israel)

4. _ _ _ _ _ _ _ _ _ _ _ _ _ _ _ _ _ _   (the original Christmas)

5. _ _ _ _ _ _ _ _ _ _ _ _ _ _
(Sir Walter Raleigh with laryngitis)

6. _ _ _ _ _ _ _ _ _ _ _ _ _ _ _ _
(Martin Luther, Nat Cole, Lear)

7. _ _ _ _ _ _ _ _ _ _ _ _ _ _ _ _
_ _ _ _ _ _ _ _ _ _ _ _ _ _ _ _
(12:00 P.M. on a starlit night)

8. _ _ _ _ _ , _ _ _ _ _ _ _ _ _
_ _ _ _ _ _ _ _ _ _ _
(listen, divine messengers are making musical noise)

Activity

- Research your favorite holiday song and the story surrounding its creation. If you can't locate the history of your song, improvise and write one of your own.

December 25
Christmas Celebrations
• • • • • • • • • • • • • • • • • • •

Other Events This Day
- George Washington crossed the Delaware River and surprised the Hessians (1776)
- President Andrew Johnson granted unconditional pardon to all involved in the Southern rebellion that resulted in the Civil War (1868)

Christians celebrate December 25 as the birthday of Jesus Christ of Nazareth. It is time of worship, family gatherings, tree decorating, gift giving, scrumptious dinners, and caroling.

In 1870, Christmas was declared a national holiday in America. Celebrations and traditions come from traditions around the world, in addition to some innovations of our own. *A Christmas Carol,* written by Charles Dickens, was published in 1843. It was a story about the importance of charity and goodwill toward mankind.

Fireplace traditions probably came from Norway and their Yule log. The custom of decorating evergreen trees has always been a part of the German winter tradition. The beautiful poinsettias seen at Christmas originally came from Mexico. The idea of Christmas greeting cards, eating plum pudding, and caroling are English holiday customs that we embrace. Celtic people have long used mistletoe.

While many countries have a figure similar to our Santa Claus, it was from the poem by Clement Moore, "A Visit from St. Nicholas," that we get our modern image of Santa Claus as a jolly, round man in a red suit who leaves gifts for good little boys and girls.

Response

How does something become a tradition?

Fascinating Factoid: The idea of a celebration on December 25 originated in the 4th century CE.

Word Play

Complete the pyramid using words associated with the Christmas holiday. When you have completed this pyramid, make one of your own on the back of this sheet using another category of words (e.g., other holidays).

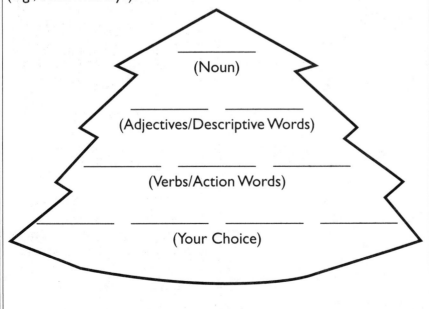

_____
(Noun)

_____ _____
(Adjectives/Descriptive Words)

_____ _____ _____
(Verbs/Action Words)

_____ _____ _____
(Your Choice)

Activities

- Design and make holiday greeting cards for family and friends.
- Write a recipe for a Very Happy Holiday. Put in all of the ingredients and amounts of each, as well as the directions for mixing. Include such things as family, gifts, decorations, etc.

December 26
Kwanzaa Began

Ron Karenga, also known as Ron Everett, created Kwanzaa. The first Kwanzaa took place from December 26, 1966, through January 1, 1967. Kwanzaa is a unique celebration that is neither political nor religious in nature. It is not intended as a substitute for Christmas. It is simply a time of reaffirming African-American people, their ancestors, and culture. Kwanzaa comes from a phrase in Swahili that means "first fruits."

During Kwanzaa, homes are decorated in red, green, and black with a Kinara and other symbols of Kwanzaa prominently displayed. The Kinara holds seven candles that reflect seven principles that are the foundation of Kwanzaa. Gifts can be given at any time during the weeklong event, but traditionally are presented on January 1. A feast (Karamu), usually a cooperative event, is traditionally held on December 31.

It is believed that in 2004 around 28 million joined in Kwanzaa celebrations. Families may celebrate Kwanzaa in their own way, but celebrations often include songs and dances, African drums, storytelling, poetry reading, and a large traditional meal. On each of the seven nights, in a family gathering, one of the candles on the Kinara is lit. The first night the black candle in the center is lit and the principle (unity) it represents is discussed. The next candle is lit the following night with the appropriate principle being discussed. Each night another candle is lit and another principle discussed.

Response
What holiday tradition does your family have?

Fascinating Factoid: In 1997, the U.S. Postal Service released its first Kwanzaa stamp.

Word Play
Match each African word with its meaning. Hint: Each one is a principle of Kwanzaa.

_____ 1. Umoja   a. collective work and responsibility

_____ 2. Imani   b. unity

_____ 3. Ujamaa   c. purpose

_____ 4. Kujichagulia   d. self-determination

_____ 5. Kuumba   e. cooperative economics

_____ 6. Nia   f. creativity

_____ 7. Ujima   g. faith

Activities

- Make an *mkeka* (em-kay-kah), a special placemat. Weave strips of red, green, and black paper or ribbon together. Research to learn the significance of this item to Kwanzaa.

- Create your own new holiday. Give details of what the holiday will celebrate, symbols involved, traditions to become a part of it, who will celebrate it, etc.

December 27
Howdy Doody Debuted

Other Events This Day
- Radio City Music Hall opened (1932)
- World Bank was created (1945)

Howdy Doody was one of the first children's TV shows. The show made its debut on this date in 1947 and ran through 1960 on NBC. It not only entertained children, but it was a major force in selling TV sets.

Howdy Doody took place in a fictional circus town called Doodyville. Howdy Doody was a freckle-faced boy puppet that wore blue jeans, a plaid shirt, and cowboy boots. His sister was Heidi Doody. The show included other puppets named Mr. Bluster, Dilly Dally, Princess Summerfall Winterspring, and Flub-a-Dub. Bob Smith, who wore western clothes, hosted the show. Other human characters were Clarabell the clown, Chief Thunderthud, and later, Princess Summerfall Winterspring. About 40 children were seated on bleachers on stage during the program. This marked one of the first audience-interaction programs on air.

Howdy Doody reflected America's fascination with technology with a machine that read minds and a machine that translated goose honks into the English language. Television innovations such as split screens, cross-country connections, and daily color were also associated with the program, which aired five days a week.

For those who were youngsters in the 1950s—perhaps your grandparents—*Howdy Doody* holds a special place in their memories.

Response

Consider the names of Howdy Doody and his sister Heidi Doody. What names do you think might have been chosen for the mother and father if they had been characters on the program?

Fascinating Factoid: Actor William Shatner, Captain Kirk of *Star Trek* fame, played Ranger Bill on the show in 1954.

Word Play

Howdy Doody was a forerunner to many TV shows produced for a young audience. Can you remember some of these shows from your early TV viewing days?

1. Miss Piggy's domain _____

2. family from the Stone Age _____

3. neighborhood of fuzzy puppets _____

4. characters with an antenna on their heads _____

5. a huge dog _____

6. an aardvark with glasses_____

7. a big purple friend _____

8. magical dragon land _____

9. an Australian band _____

10. a big, blue airplane _____

Activity

- Design a puppet that you think would appeal to kindergarteners. Write a script for your puppet play that kindergarteners would enjoy and understand.

December 28
Chewing Gum Patented
• • • • • • • • • • • • • • • • • • • •

Other Events This Day

• Osceola led Seminole warriors in Florida into the Second Seminole War (1835)

• First U.S. patent for commercial dishwasher (1886)

On December 28, 1869, William Finley Semple became the first person to patent chewing gum, although people had chewed gum since the days of Ancient Greece. Mr. Semple's chewing gum was made of a combination of rubber and other ingredients. It was never commercially produced.

Ancient Greeks chewed *mastiche*, a type of chewing gum made from the resin of a mastic tree. Ancient Mayans chewed chicle, which is sap from sapodilla trees. North American natives chewed sap from spruce trees. Early American settlers made a chewing gum by adding beeswax to spruce sap.

The chewing gum story continues into the 1800s when John Curtis made and sold the first commercial chewing gum in 1848. In 1871, Thomas Adams patented a machine to manufacture gum. In 1880, John Colgan invented a way to make the good taste last longer. New gum products, such as Dentyne®, appeared. In the early 1900s, Blibber-Blubber—the first bubble gum—was a big hit with gum chewers.

Now, many brands and flavors of gum are sold. The U.S. military is researching a chewing gum formula with antibacterial agents in an effort to improve hygiene on the battlefield.

Response
What is your favorite kind and flavor of chewing gum?

Fascinating Factoid: Wrigley's chewing gum is enjoyed in more than 150 countries worldwide.

Word Play
The inventors of chewing gum probably never dreamed of all the different flavors of gums today and the colors associated with the flavors. Match each flavor to its color.

_____ 1. sour apple   a. red

_____ 2. cinnamon   b. yellow

_____ 3. grape   c. orange

_____ 4. raspberry   d. white

_____ 5. orange   e. pink

_____ 6. spearmint   f. purple

_____ 7. strawberry   g. light green

_____ 8. banana   h. blue

Activities
• Survey classmates to determine their favorite flavor of chewing gum. Show your results in a pictograph.

• Design and conduct an experiment to determine which gum flavor lasts longest. Start with a hypothesis and show supporting data you collected during your experiment. Write your conclusions either supporting your hypothesis or disproving it.

December 29

First American YMCA Opened

• • • • • • • • • • • • • • • • •

Other Events This Day

• Texas became 28th U.S. state (1845)

• Last major battle of the Indian Wars took place at Wounded Knee Creek (1890)

The first Young Men's Christian Association (YMCA) in America opened on December 29, 1851, in Boston, Massachusetts. Thomas Valentine Sullivan, inspired by the success of the YMCA that had been established in London, formed the Boston YMCA. George Williams, appalled by the lack of healthful activities for young men in cities, established the YMCA movement in London in 1844.

The YMCA is a community service organization that offers programs based on Christian values. In America, the YMCA is most often thought of as a place of sports, but the YMCA offers much more. One can also find services such as childcare, fitness centers, educational activities, and conference centers.

The YMCA is organized as a federation of local associations. It was originally established to help young men acquire spiritual and moral tools to help them succeed in life. The Y has become an organization that is dedicated to helping men and women; it now operates in 122 countries.

Response

What do you believe is the most useful service provided by a YMCA?

Fascinating Factoid: About one in every three Americans reports being a member of the YMCA at some time in his or her life.

Word Play

Many organizations are commonly known by the beginning letters of the words in their name. For example, YMCA is an acronym for Young Men's Christian Association. Supply the full name for each acronym. Hint: Each one is an American organization.

1. YWCA _____

2. NASA _____

3. AARP _____

4. BBB _____

5. AAA _____

6. MADD _____

7. OSHA _____

8. IOC _____

9. FAA _____

Activities

• Research to determine the services offered by the YMCA in your area. Explain which service interests you most.

• What about a YKA (Young Kids Association)? Do you think it would be a good idea for someone to establish one? What services would it offer? How would it be financed? What ages would be served?

December 30
Once in a Blue Moon

Other Events This Day
- Dinner party held inside a life-sized model of an Iguanodon (dinosaur) in London (1853)
- First color TV sets go on sale for about $1,175 each (1953)

On the night of December 30, 1982, a blue moon lit the sky. Well, the moon didn't actually turn blue! Nonetheless, there was a blue moon on that date.

Before 1943, a *blue moon* was described as the "third full moon in a season that has four full moons." Now the term *blue moon* has come to refer to a second full moon in a calendar month. Such an event doesn't happen often, thus giving rise to the expression, "once in a blue moon." The time span between two full moons is 29.5 days. In order for a blue moon to occur, the first full moon must appear at the beginning of the month so the second full moon (the blue moon) will fall in the same month. A single blue moon occurs once every two and three-fourths years.

Even more rare than a blue moon are two blue moons in a year. This happens about once every 19 years. The next year in which two blue moons occur will be 2018. Normally, a blue moon doesn't look any different from any full moon; however, when a high concentration of dust particles is in the atmosphere (after a volcanic eruption), the moon may appear to look blue. While the December 30, 1982, blue moon was no different than other blue moons, it offers the opportunity to focus our attention on this interesting astronomical phenomenon.

Response

People used to say the moon was made of cheese. Do you think they said the blue moons were made of blue cheese? Where do you think people got the idea that the moon was made of cheese?

Fascinating Factoid: There are no blue moons in 2006, 2011, 2014, or 2017.

Word Play

Past cultures have given the moon special names. Write the name of the month for each cultural name.

1. Moon after Yule __ __ __ __ __ __ __ __
2. Hay Moon __ __ __ __
3. Moon before Yule __ __ __ __ __ __ __ __
4. Ice Moon __ __ __ __ __ __ __ __
5. Hunting Moon __ __ __ __ __ __ __
6. Budding Moon __ __ __ __ __
7. Falling Leaf Moon __ __ __ __ __ __ __ __ __
8. Leaf Moon __ __ __ __ __
9. Harvest Moon __ __ __ __ __ __ __ __ __
10. Blossom Moon __ __ __ __
11. Blackberry Moon __ __ __ __ __ __
12. Honey Moon __ __ __ __

Activities

- Research superstitions associated with a full moon. Write a short report summarizing your findings.
- Illustrate a chart showing the different cycles of the moon.

December 31
New Year's Eve

Other Events This Day
- Henri Matisse's birthday (1869)
- General Motors becomes first U.S. corporation to make over $1 billion in a year (1955)

The day before the beginning of a new year is known as New Year's Eve. It has become a holiday almost as important as the first day of the new year. It is a huge social event in America. People gather with friends and party until the moment the old year transitions into the new year. At the stroke of midnight, it is customary for sweethearts to kiss and sing "Auld Lang Syne." Fireworks are also a part of many celebrations.

Probably the best-known celebration in America takes place in Times Square in New York City. The Times Square celebration started in 1904. Since 1907, a ball has been lowered from atop Times Square. The original ball was made of iron and wood. It weighed 700 pounds (317.5 km) and was 5 feet (1.5 m) in diameter. It was lit with 100 25-watt lightbulbs.

Now the ball that is lowered is not any old ball, but a Waterford Crystal ball that weighs 1,070 pounds (485.3 kg) and is 6 feet (1.8 m) in diameter. The lowering of the ball begins at 23:59:00 and reaches the bottom of the tower at the stroke of midnight and the event is televised. This lowering of the crystal ball has become a worldwide symbol of the turn of the new year and is seen via satellite by more than a billion people every year.

Response

Does your family have any special New Year's Eve traditions. List some ways to celebrate New Year's Eve.

Fascinating Factoid: About 750,000 people gather in Times Square each year to celebrate New Year's Eve.

Word Play

New Year's Eve is a good time to party. How many ways can you say *party*?

If you can list five synonyms for *party*, then you are doing fine.

1. _____
2. _____
3. _____
4. _____
5. _____

If you can list 10 synonyms for *party*, you are definitely thinking *party*.

6. _____
7. _____
8. _____
9. _____
10. _____

Activities

- Today is a good day to make a list of New Year's resolutions. Think carefully before you compose your list.
- Research and compare New Year's Eve customs and traditions around the world.

Word Play Answer Key

July Answers

Page 5
1. b
2. p
3. d
4. g
5. f
6. o
7. i
8. m
9. k
10. j
11. r
12. l
13. q
14. h
15. n
16. e
17. a
18. c

Page 6
James—hot dog
Jenny—fried chicken
Joanie—cheeseburger
Jerry—sandwich

Page 7
1. j
2. a
3. b
4. c
5. e
6. k
7. g
8. h
9. f
10. i
11. d

Page 8
1. U.S. Capitol
2. White House
3. American flag
4. bald eagle
5. Liberty Bell
6. Uncle Sam
7. Lincoln Memorial
8. Arlington National Cemetery
9. great seal
10. Statue of Liberty

Page 9
1. "Hound Dog"
2. "Blue Christmas"
3. "Love Me Tender"
4. "Return to Sender"
5. "Heartbreak Hotel"
6. "Jailhouse Rock"
7. "All Shook Up"
8. "It's Now or Never"
9. "Are You Lonesome Tonight?"
10. "Don't Be Cruel"
11. "Good Luck Charm"
12. "Viva Las Vegas"
13. "Suspicious Minds"

Page 10
1. Martha
2. Eve
3. Juliet
4. Wilma
5. Minnie
6. Daisy
7. Betty
8. Cleopatra
9. Lois Lane
10. Pocahontas
11. Maid Marion

Page 11
Amy—Amazing Bar
James—Big Bar
Michael—Mammoth Bar
Robyn—Baby Bar

Page 12
1. little
2. tiny
3. microscopic
4. miniscule
5. petite
6. slight
7. slender
8. minute
9. huge
10. giant
11. gigantic
12. tremendous
13. immense
14. voluminous
15. bulky
16. enormous

Page 13
1. linesman
2. fault
3. singles
4. advantage
5. point
6. deuce
7. love
8. ball
9. sideline
10. baseline
11. doubles
12. umpire
13. match
14. racket
15. net
16. serve

Page 14
a. 1 wheel on a unicycle
b. 2 halves in a whole
c. 2 nickels in a dime
d. 3 blind mice
e. 4 quarts in a gallon
f. 5 fingers on a hand
g. 5 pennies in a nickel
h. 6 sides on a hexagon
i. 7 colors in a rainbow
j. 8 legs on a spider

Page 15
Answers will vary.

Word Play Answer Key *(cont.)*

July Answers *(cont.)*

Page 16
1. attributed
2. horizontal
3. vertical
4. stylus
5. miniature
6. anniversary

Page 17
1. cornerkick
2. kickoff
3. match
4. shinguard
5. score
6. soccer
7. sport
8. goal
9. football
10. midfielder
11. goalie
12. ball
13. penalty
14. stadium
15. offside
16. pitch
17. header
18. referee
19. obstruction
20. red card

Page 18
1. a
2. e
3. g
4. i
5. h
6. f
7. d
8. c
9. b

Page 19
Answers will vary.

Page 20
1. altimeter
2. anemometer
3. barometer
4. odometer
5. ohmmeter
6. pedometer
7. spectrometer
8. speedometer
9. blood pressure
10. radiation hazards
11. acceleration
12. color

Page 21
Answers will vary.

Page 22
1. apricot
2. aquamarine
3. bittersweet
4. thistle
5. magenta
6. maize
7. goldenrod
8. melon
9. flesh
10. periwinkle
11. orchid
12. lavender
13. mulberry
14. salmon
15. sepia
16. cornflower

Page 23
1. miles
2. feet
3. yards
4. miles
5. inches
6. inches
7. feet
8. feet

Page 24
1. Cherokee
2. Choctaw
3. Chickasaw
4. Creek
5. Seminole
6. Apache
7. Apache
8. Nez Perce
9. Comanche
10. Lakota

Page 25
1. comedienne
2. nurse
3. doctor
4. journalist
5. writer
6. artist
7. aviatrix
8. astronaut
9. Native American chief
10. sharpshooter
11. tennis player
12. opera singer
13. talk show hostess
14. ballerina

Page 26
1. waitress
2. actor
3. usher
4. comedienne
5. sculptress
6. poetess
7. duchess
8. hero
9. steward
10. landlady
11. authoress
12. executrix

Page 27
Answers will vary.

Word Play Answer Key (cont.)

July Answers (cont.)

Page 28

Answers will vary.

Page 29

  a. unicycle

  b. tricycle

  c. quadricycle

  1. unicorn

  2. quadruplets

  3. bilingual

  4. biannual

  5. trilogy

  6. quadruped

  7. quartet

Page 30

  1. compound words

  2. can be singular or plural

  3. adjectives

  4. synonyms

  5. proper nouns

  6. prepositions

  7. conjunctions

  8. words with a prefix

  9. words with a suffix

  10. adverbs

  11. onomatopoeia

Page 31

  1. I'm going to get that crazy rabbit if it's the last thing I ever do.

  2. That rascally rabbit has bothered me for the last time.

  3. Bugs Bunny is a fictional cartoon rabbit that appears in *Looney Tunes* and *Merry Melodies* and is one of the most recognizable characters, real or imaginary, in the world.

  4. No one really knows who actually created Bugs Bunny. There are many people who helped create him, but no one knows who the one person was.

Page 32

  1. beetle

  2. rodent

  3. lizard

  4. caterpillar

  5. legume

  6. meteorite

  7. herb

  8. marsupial

  9. graphite

  10. feathered

Page 33

  1. weird

  4. relevant

  5. leisure

  6. consensus

  7. existence

  8. fiery

  11. collectible

  14. inoculate

  15. indispensable

Page 34

  1. waffles

  2. coffee

  3. pancakes

  4. grapefruit

  5. muffins

  6. eggs

  7. omelet

  8. doughnuts

  9. oatmeal

  10. French toast

     corn flakes

Page 35

  1. muggles

  2. Hogwarts

  3. wizard

  4. goblet

  5. Hermione

  6. spells

  7. mystery

  8. witch

  9. casting

  10. adventure

August Answers

Page 37

  1. Alcatraz Island

  2. Lombard Street

  3. Golden Gate Bridge

  4. Angel Island

  5. Chinatown

  6. Fisherman's Wharf

  7. cable cars

Page 38

  1. earned

  2. time

  3. obstacle

  4. principles

  5. people

  6. money

  7. goodbye

  8. evil

  9. fool

  10. money

Page 39

  1. c

  2. h

  3. c

  4. c

  5. h

  6. h

  7. h

  8. h

  9. c

  10. h

  11. h

Word Play Answer Key *(cont.)*

August Answers *(cont.)*

12. h
13. c
14. c
15. h
16. c
17. h

Page 40

1. b
2. a
3. e
4. k
5. f
6. i
7. h
8. j
9. c
10. d
11. g

Page 41

1. c
2. a
3. f
4. h
5. j
6. m
7. k
8. l
9. i
10. g
11. e
12. d
13. b

Page 42

1. makeup
2. ugly
3. tall
4. big
5. hungry
6. tired

Page 43

1. Medal of Honor
2. Distinguished Cross
3. The Silver Star
4. Distinguished Flying Cross

Page 44

1. Thomas Jefferson
2. Lyndon Baines Johnson
3. John Adams
4. Abraham Lincoln
5. James Buchanan
6. John F. Kennedy
7. Jimmy Carter
8. Bill Clinton
9. Theodore Roosevelt

Page 45

1. The Three Bears
2. Winnie the Pooh
3. Baloo
4. The Berenstein Bears
5. Care Bears™
6. Yogi Bear
7. Cubs
8. Gummy Bears

Page 46

1. sore throat
2. baby teething
3. toothache
4. headache
5. stomachache
6. cold
7. rheumatism

Page 47

1. glass cup
2. plate saucer
3. bowl platter
4. oven refrigerator
5. blender toaster
6. knife fork
7. skillet pot
8. tongs spatula

9. kettle pitcher
10. spoon blade

Page 48

1. kick—dropkick, kickstand, kickoff
2. space—spaceman, backspace, spacecraft
3. proof—childproof, proofread, waterproof
4. bread—cornbread, sweetbread, breadwinner
5. stop—stopwatch, backstop, shortstop

Page 49

Answers will vary.

Page 50

VJ Day was the end of a war that started when Japan bombed Pearl Harbor on December 7, 1941.

Page 51

1. tornado—f
2. hurricane—g
3. tsunami—d
4. blizzard—e
5. gustnado—a
6. typhoon—c
7. nor'easter—b

Page 52

1. golf—c
2. basketball—f
3. tennis—b
4. hockey—h
5. baseball—e
6. cycling—a
7. track & field—g
8. football—d
9. boxing—i

Word Play Answer Key *(cont.)*

August Answers *(cont.)*

Page 53

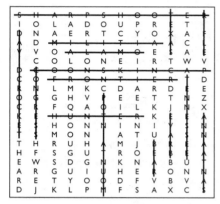

Page 54

```
          A
        A N
      A N D
    L A N D
  P L A N T
I S L A N D
```

Page 55

Answers will vary.

Page 56

This radio station was first to broadcast election results on August 31, 1920.

Page 57

1. luau
2. pineapple
3. Honolulu
4. macadamia
5. Iolani Palace
6. volcano
7. surfing
8. lei
9. grass skirt
10. hula

Page 58

1. aft
2. ahoy
3. berth
4. bow
5. bridge
6. deck
7. galley
8. mast
9. port
10. schooner
11. stern
12. zephyr

Page 59

1. bright
2. pass
3. rain, night
4. weather, clear
5. soon
6. warning, delight
7. cloak
8. snows
9. showers
10. late

Page 60

```
S T E S  F R U B M S  N I U N
E O R I G I N A L A Y S T O
L L S I R T L R M L N G O S
G D A H A B O B U T A R R O
N F L T D O W E R A C F U U
I A T X D D F C U F E D D R
R S A U E O A U F D V E L C
P H N L H U T E F V P E L E
C I D R C A N D L I N N S A
O O N I O N B J E N O O C R
H N H I V L M O S E V N C M
C E G R O O V Y C G Z A F D
R D F B A K E D L A N B V C
L D O S A L T A N R B O M
```

Page 61

1. ask for the moon
2. over the moon
3. many moons ago
4. once in a blue moon
5. promise the moon
6. reach for the moon
7. shoot for the moon

Page 62

1. vote
2. right
3. women
4. equality
5. amendment
6. constitution

Page 63

1. argue
2. study
3. trite
4. agree
5. murky

Page 64

Answers will vary.

Page 65

meat

celery

onions

bean sprouts

water chestnuts

mushrooms

bamboo shoots

Page 66

```
ATTORNEY            MARYLAND
HISTORY             AMERICAN
SUPREME    LANDMARK
RIGHTS              SENATE
SEGREGATION         HOWARD
COURT               BALTIMORE
NOMINATED           LAWYER
APPOINTED           LINCOLN
```

Page 67

1. cart
2. tart
3. taut
4. cats
5. pats
6. pits

Word Play Answer Key *(cont.)*

September Answers

Page 69
1. unbeatable
2. uncleanable
3. unemployable
4. unacceptable
5. unallowable
6. unalienable
7. unapproachable

Definitions will vary.

Page 70
Monday
Tuesday
Wednesday
Thursday
Friday
Saturday
Sunday

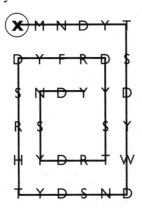

Page 71
Answers will vary.

Page 72
1. old—young
2. last—first
3. night—day
4. poor—wealthy
5. sister—brother
6. sold—bought
7. ugly—beautiful
8. red—blue
9. big—little
10. accepted—rejected

Page 73
1. celebrated
2. afterward

Other answers will vary.

Page 74
1. on
2. life
3. over
4. crew
5. long
6. to
7. land
8. water
9. down
10. clothes
11. cheese

Other answers will vary.

Page 75
Across
Atlantic City
gown
talent
swimsuit

Down
idea
bloomers
Miss America
contest
pageant

Page 76
Salute the flag by standing at attention, facing the flag, with hand over heart.

Page 77
Answers will vary.

Page 78
1. d
2. e
3. c
4. b
5. a
6. f
7. g

Page 79
1. Babe
2. tune
3. been
4. begin
5. bead
6. toast
7. butter
8. ugly
9. teeth
10. true
11. brush or shrub
12. stir
13. bunt
14. tie

Page 80

				A	L	A	B	A	M	A	
				S	P	A	C	E			
		S	E	P	T	E	M	B	E	R	
D	E	C	A	T	U	R					
E	N	D	E	A	V	O	R				
				N	A	S	A				
		W	O	M	A	N					
		L	A	U	N	C	H				
		S	T	A	N	F	O	R	D		

Page 81

America	earliest
army	Thomas
yankee	symbols
era	supplied
Abraham	drew
many	wear
you	red
uncle	doodle

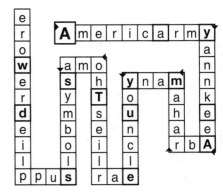

Word Play Answer Key *(cont.)*

September Answers *(cont.)*

Page 82

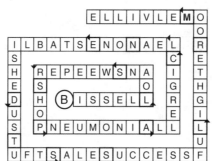

Page 83
1. first–last
2. different–alike
3. long–short
4. lot–few
5. give–take
6. success–failure
7. day–night
8. over–under
9. maximum–minimum
10. add–subtract

Page 84
Compound Story Words

airship   1. race
however   2. glass
nightmare   3. which
without   4. light
walkway   5. crew
inside   6. with
atop   7. day
into   8. walk

Other answers will vary.

Page 85
Answers will vary.

Page 86
1. calf
2. palm
3. chalk
4. talk
5. Lincoln
6. salmon
7. calm
8. walk
9. balk
10. half

Page 87
Bissell
loans
sweepers
shop
pneumonia
allergic
clean
none
established
dust
tufts
sales
successful
lighter
room
Melville

Page 88
This big voyage by Magellan provided the first proof that the world was round!

Page 89
1. redder
2. dear
3. reading
4. ears
5. eater
6. dream
7. dreary
8. deadly
9. dreading
10. dragon

Page 90
1. vanilla
2. strawberry
3. Swiss almond
4. chocolate marshmallow
5. peanut butter and chocolate
6. cappuccino
7. chocolate toffee
8. eggnog
9. cookies and cream
10. chocolate amaretto
11. cherry
12. tutti frutti
13. vanilla fudge
14. coffee
15. fudge ripple
16. butter pecan
17. blueberry cheesecake
18. nutty coconut
19. peppermint

Page 91
Answers will vary.

Page 92
1. Miss Piggy
2. Kermit
3. Animal
4. Beaker
5. Fozzie Bear
6. Gonzo
7. Rizzo
8. Swedish Chef
9. Scooter
10. Rowlf

Page 93
newspaper
bookstore
coffeehouse
howe ver
because
because
businessman
Other answers will vary.